# *Tomato*

# TOMATO

## *A Fresh-from-the-Vine Cookbook*

**LAWRENCE DAVIS-HOLLANDER**

*Foreword by* **DEBORAH MADISON** ✳ *Photography by* **SABRA KROCK**

Storey Publishing

*The mission of Storey Publishing is to serve our customers by
publishing practical information that encourages
personal independence in harmony with the environment.*

Edited by Margaret Sutherland, Dianne M. Cutillo, Andrea Chesman, and Siobhan Dunn
Art direction and book design by Alethea Morrison, based on a first edition design by Wendy Palitz
Text production by Liseann Karandisecky

Photography by © Sabra Krock
Food and photo styling by Sabra Krock
Engravings from antique seed catalogs courtesy of the author, except for those on pages ix, 3, 6, 16, 53, 105,
    and 228 from The LuEster T. Mertz Library of the New York Botanical Garden, Bronx, New York

Indexed by Christine R. Lindemer, Boston Road Communications

**Storey Publishing**
210 MASS MoCA Way
North Adams, MA 01247
*www.storey.com*

Printed in the United States by R.R. Donnelley
10  9  8  7  6  5  4  3  2  1

LIBRARY OF CONGRESS CATALOGING-IN-PUBLICATION DATA

Davis-Hollander, Lawrence.
  Tomato : a fresh-from-the-vine cookbook / by Lawrence Davis-Hollander.
    p. cm.
  Rev. ed of: The tomato festival cookbook, 2004.
  Includes index.
  ISBN 978-1-60342-478-3 (pbk. : alk. paper)
  1. Cookery (Tomatoes) 2. Tomatoes.
  I. Davis-Hollander, Lawrence. Tomato festival cookbook. II. Title.
TX803.T6D38 2010
641.6'5642—dc22
                          2009045295

To Margo, Forest, and Gabriel.
And to those people who labor in fields
maintaining our food plant heritage
out of love and necessity.

# Contents

# Credits & Acknowledgments

My special thanks to Claire Hopley, who worked on the recipes and tested most of them. To all the seed savers out there, including Carolyn Male for her great tomato knowledge, Alan Kapuler for his longtime dedication, Will Weaver for all of his research, Kent Whealy, Neil Lockhart, Bill Minkey, Joe Cavanaugh, Jeremiath Gettle, and many, many others. For the chefs too numerous to mention but including Peter Hoffmann, Greg Higgins, Michel Nischan, William Webber, Peter Platt, Dan Smith, Jody Adams, Melissa Kelly, Josie Le Balch, Diana Kennedy, Alice Waters, and Deborah Madison for recipes and a great introduction. Andy Smith for his tireless research on the tomato and conversation, Amy Albert, Joel Patraker, Michael Batterberry, Patrick Martins, and more. To all the folks at Storey Publishing who helped make it possible. To my agent, Annie Brody, for making things happen and many consultations. And lastly to everyone else who I haven't mentioned — your help was greatly appreciated.

Rick Bayless's Essential Quick-Cooked Tomato and Chipotle Sauce on page 31 and Tomato-Rice Casserole with Poblanos, Beef, and Melted Cheese on page 188 are reprinted with the permission of Scribner, an imprint of Simon & Schuster Adult Publishing Group, from *Mexican Kitchen: Capturing the Vibrant Flavors of a World-Class Cuisine*, by Rick Bayless, © 1996 by Richard Lane Bayless.

Deborah Madison's Chilled Sun-Gold Tomato Soup on page 78 is reprinted here with the permission of the publisher. From *Local Flavors: Cooking and Eating from America's Farmers' Markets*, by Deborah Madison, © 2002 by Deborah Madison. Used by permission of Broadway books, a division of Random House, Inc.

Daniel Boulud's Heirloom Tomato and Goat Cheese Salad on page 96 is reprinted with the permission of Scribner, an imprint of Simon & Schuster Adult Publishing Group, from *Daniel Boulud's Café Cookbook: French-American Recipes for the Home Cook*, by Daniel Boulud and Dorie Greenspan, © 1999 by Daniel Boulud and Dorie Greenspan.

Lois Ellen Franks's Lamb-Stuffed Green Chiles with Fresh Tomato Purée on page 192 is reprinted with permission from *Foods of the Southwest Indian Nations*, by Lois Ellen Frank, © 2002 by Lois Ellen Frank, Ten Speed Press, Berkeley, California. 800-841-2665, www.tenspeed.com.

Diana Kennedy's Zucchini and Tomatoes with Cream on page 213 is reprinted here with the permission of the publisher. From *The Essential Cuisines of Mexico*, by Diana Kennedy, © 2000 by Diana Kennedy. Used by permission of Clarkson Potter, a division of Random House, Inc.

Carol Costenbader's Ratatouille on page 206 is reprinted from *The Big Book of Preserving the Harvest: 150 Recipes for Freezing, Canning, Drying, and Pickling Fruits and Vegetables*, by Carol W. Costenbader, revised by Joanne Lamb Hayes. Published by Storey Publishing, © 1997, 2002 by Carol W. Costenbader.

Janet Ballantyne's Dilled Green Cherries on page 249 and Green Tomato Chocolate Cake on page 226 are reprinted from *Garden Way's Red and Green Tomato Cookbook*, by Janet Ballantyne, © 1982, Storey Publishing.

Maggie Oster's Cooked Tomato Salsa on page 252 is reprinted from *Herbal Vinegar*, by Maggie Oster, Storey Publishing, © 1994 by Maggie Oster.

# Foreword

Like so many, many others, I love tomatoes. I mean, of course, real tomatoes, the kind that take the center stage of this book.

I've had some experiences with the other kind — those hybrid tomatoes that are born and bred to travel, picked when green, unable to fulfill in any way any promise of sensuous pleasure. My first summer job was working in the laboratory of a Hunt's plant, not a job that left me with a passion for tomatoes. But later I learned that taste has a way of prevailing, and that no matter how you pronounce it, a tomato is never just a tomato, at least not in the world of real tomatoes. Here is a vegetable/fruit that dwells in a multiplicity of forms and colors, a plant that has journeyed far from its origins to travel the continents and the oceans of the world, only to return home to take its place as our all-time favorite vegetable. Let's face it. We don't wax rhapsodic over carrots or eggplants, as good or as gorgeous as they might be, the way we do over tomatoes. And while the potato may outsell the tomato, it's mostly consumed as fries and chips — fast food and junk food — so I don't think it really counts. Tomatoes don't play such lowly roles. They play roles that are much more splendid and varied, as this book so enticingly points out.

We've come close to losing this treasure, this reserve of juice with its sweetness and acidity, this powerhouse of antioxidants, these varied orbs and ovals of brilliant color. We've gone, as we have with so many of our foods, from the specific world of particulars that comes with true diversity, to the broad, dumb strokes that paint the picture of the monotonous, mass-market hybrid. But the tomatoes that are the basis of the recipes in this book are those treasured fruits picked a day or two ahead of eating and set in flats, not thrown into a box. Hands, not machines, rustle the fragrant leaves and blossoms as they grope for a hefty Mortgage Lifter, or pluck an entire spray of tiny Currant tomatoes. They return to the plant over and over again until a hard frost puts an end to all the fun. These are tomatoes whose walls might be irregular; whose sizes vary and therefore resist standardization; whose pretty starlike sepals stay attached to the fruit. These are delicious tomatoes that might be pink instead of red, or orange, or green, or black-red. They have names that conjure an image and start a story: Ponderosa, Indian Moon, Aunt Ruby's German Green. Not all are heirlooms — there are some pretty-good-tasting hybrids in this collection — but they all have names, characters, and histories. They represent not just great taste and exciting variety, but, in the end, our true heritage.

Without the efforts of seed savers, without people with taste memories, without people with the passion to reclaim our wonderfully rich legacy, such a book as *Tomato* could not have been written. And because *Tomato* doesn't represent the passion of only one lone aficionado but that of many cooks and farmers, it is a sure sign that the true tomato has come home.

— DEBORAH MADISON
Author, *Local Flavors: Cooking and Eating from America's Farmers' Markets*

# Introduction

The United States is a country of tomato eaters. From its humble beginnings as a wild plant in South America, the tomato has traveled around the planet and back again. In ancient times, tomatoes played an important role in the development of Mexican foods. Today, many of the world's cuisines use tomatoes. From England, France, and Italy to Africa, India, and China to South America and the Caribbean, the tomato has found its way into kitchens and stomachs. In America, with our great mélange of food customs brought by immigrants, the tomato neatly weaves its way into cocktail lounges, neighborhood pizzerias, fast-food joints, family kitchens, diners, and fine dining rooms.

I think it is safe to say that the tomato is a universally loved food, certainly one of the most loved vegetables. Its versatility in cooking is phenomenal. From soup to bread, from entrée to dessert, the tomato has been incorporated into every phase of the meal at one time or another. In the United States, only potatoes rank higher among vegetables in terms of per-capita consumption.

This book brings together a mere 150 tomato recipes to represent the enormous world of tomato cookery. Generally, these are home-style recipes requiring relatively uncomplicated cooking techniques and are easy to follow. They come from around the globe, though a majority reflect European and Mexican influences. Fantastic chefs across the United States have contributed to this effort. Many of the recipes are interpretations of classic tomato-based dishes, and some are historic recipes updated to modern tastes and ingredients.

Heirloom tomato varieties are emphasized in this book because these are the best "in-season" eating and cooking tomatoes available today. Many of these great varieties were on the brink of extinction, and some are still very rare. Names such as Livingston's Golden Queen, Aunt Ruby's German Green, Indian Moon, and Mortgage Lifter stimulate the imagination into a world of culinary history and taste. Without the seed-conservation movement, the practice of saving rare seeds for future generations, many varieties would surely have disappeared.

Fresh tomatoes available in supermarkets are usually pretty disappointing. In many cases their only affiliation with tomatoes is that they look like them. While some improvements have been made, they still lack real tomato flavor. Bought out of season, they are often dreadful.

In testing one of the recipes for this book, the Fresh Rainbow Salsa, I had to use commercial tomatoes purchased in January. Normally I would never purchase a tomato in the winter, but in this case it was the only choice. On their own, the tomatoes were terrible. Poor texture, poor taste. After 30 minutes or so of soaking in their own juices, with salt, onions, and cilantro, they improved considerably. Still, it was nothing like the same recipe made in summer with good garden-ripe tomatoes.

The best solution to this taste problem is to start eating more of our food seasonally and locally. All of us have gotten used to the easy convenience of going into our supermarket and getting "fresh" foods all year long. Now it's not only oranges we can buy in the winter but star fruit and passion fruit, raspberries, strawberries, chayote, tomatoes, peppers, and more. Certainly a wonderful thing — if you have a hankering for fresh salsa and chips in the dead of winter. But that is part of the problem. First of all, those out-of-season items really don't taste very good, not compared with the real things grown in your backyard or on a small farm nearby. We are losing touch with what tastes good.

We are also losing touch with how things are grown, where they come from, and what time of year they are ripe. The result is a homogenization of sense and taste. We are out of touch with the very environment that sustains us, with food that keeps us healthy, and with farming practices that can help our children.

It is our own misaligned consumer habits, willingness to compromise, and nature deficit disorder that allow us to readily accept poor and often out-of-season substitutes for the real thing. Eating seasonally means voting with our food dollars to support our local farmers and to preserve a way of life, a culture, and our landscape.

Or we can vote for corporate food produced with no consideration for our health, the health of farm workers, and the health of the planet.

Presumably, if you are reading this book, you do cook, and that is a good thing. It is a legacy that needs to be passed down to our children and reinforced at home. The hearth was and is the gathering place for family and friends. Eating is one of our most basic and pleasurable experiences as human beings.

I am not suggesting we give up all our modern eating experiences. Certainly they are here to stay. But I am strongly suggesting that we not give up traditions practiced for centuries. They are integral to being human. It is natural to take care of ourselves as best we can, with the highest quality food, to maintain our connection with the earth — lest we find that we have given the best in our lives to corporations whose responsibility is to a very small number of shareholders and not to our children and grandchildren.

Eating well is one of the best things we can do for ourselves to maintain good health at relatively little additional cost and with great benefits to our families and our regions. It can be accomplished in many ways — by buying at the farmers' market, joining a community-supported agriculture (CSA) farm, buying organic or local foods at our health food stores or supermarkets, and, best of all, growing some of our own.

We can still sing the praises of the voluptuous tomato in all its many emanations, because of generations of people who gardened, cooked, ate, selected various strains, and kept them going. The tomato should never be just a number in a plant breeder's notebook; it should be a living entity full of grace, character, and life, something we can love for what it is — one of the fruits of God's creation with a little help from humankind.

Since the first edition of this book was published a mere six years ago, another turn in the upward spiral in the evolution of food and agriculture has taken place. Ten years ago the phrase "heirloom tomato" invariably brought quizzical looks from people. Today I routinely see heirloom tomatoes in supermarkets, occupying a small section of the produce bins alongside the still-dominant offerings of dull, uniform, and tasteless tomatoes. Our food consciousness has deepened and crept — sometimes slowly and sometimes more rapidly — toward a closer reconnection with fresh food.

As the economy began to look more uncertain in spring 2008, something remarkable began to happen. Many people, some who had not grown their own food for years and others who had never grown it, decided to plant vegetable gardens. In 2009, with a very uncertain economy, many more people decided it was time they increased their food security by growing their own vegetables. Lots of little "mom and pop" vegetable stands sprouted up in the countryside to sell excess produce.

So what does all this have to do with a cookbook? Cooking is an antidote to the fast life and the instant gratification of fast foods. When we cook, we savor. When we savor, we enjoy. What we eat and how we cook are other evolving pieces of our relationship with food. Consciously raised and local food boosts the quality of our cooking.

Eating well is now equated with healthful living, and more healthful food is available to a wider range of the population. We just need to take advantage of what's out there.

Reviewing the recipes collected here reminded me how good this cookbook really is and how well tomatoes combine with so many different foods. Inevitably, as I read each recipe, I found myself becoming hungrier. My stomach began to have that empty, gnawing feeling, begging to be satisfied through a delicious experience in which thousands of taste buds joyously announce to the brain that the glory of man and God have joined forces again and another great dish is on the way. Then, when I looked at Sabra Krock's wonderful photographs, I got even hungrier. You are not supposed to say how good your own book is, but after six years, I have gained a little objectivity. There are a lot of good recipes here. And if you don't believe me, try them yourself.

— LAWRENCE DAVIS-HOLLANDER
*December 2009,* looking west at snow-embraced Mount Race and Mount Everett

CHAPTER ONE

*Cooking with*

# HEIRLOOM TOMATOES

When you cook with fresh sun-ripened tomatoes from your garden, you are cooking with one of the finest ingredients in the world. If it is an heirloom variety, it's even better. The flavors of the heirlooms vary from variety to variety and change with different growing conditions. No two varieties taste exactly alike. And that sets up a wonderful lifetime experience of limitless experimentation in the kitchen. There is always something to learn and another variety to try.

If endless experimentation doesn't thrill you, then try out some different varieties until you figure out what you like. If you grow your own tomatoes, one or two slicing varieties plus one early variety are sufficient for fresh eating and culinary needs. Add to that one or two paste types for processing, plus one or more cherry types for garnish or salads, and you are set. If you want to grow tomatoes but don't have a lot of outdoor space, consider a container or two. (See "Growing Tomatoes in Containers," page 7.) If you are browsing farmers' markets and farmstands, continue to buy the varieties you know you like, but experiment as different shapes and names and colors catch your eye.

I grow at least several red-hued varieties, a yellow, an orange, a black, a green, a bicolor, and a couple of cherries and pastes. Right there you see I am up to a dozen varieties. They really make the tomato season a visual and gastronomic treat. Yet such variety is not required to eat good tomatoes.

# GROWING TOMATOES IN CONTAINERS

If you do not have a garden site, you can raise tomatoes in containers on decks, balconies, and rooftops. The containers can vary, but they should not have ever held any toxic materials. Half wooden barrels, flower pots — plastic or clay — constructed containers, or buckets can all be utilized. For each full-size tomato plant, allow a minimum of five gallons of container space and more if feasible. You can grow plants in smaller containers, but less than two gallons is impractical. Plants in larger and deeper pots generally do better. Some specially developed "patio" varieties grow in smaller pots, as many of these varieties are quite dwarfed. They produce less-than-exciting tomatoes. Small-fruited tomatoes such as cherries or early-maturing varieties such as Stupice are good. You can also use any determinate or indeterminate variety, assuming they have enough container space for their roots and headroom. Indeterminate plants such as the heirlooms, in less-than-adequate-size containers, will produce dwarfed fruit, but it will be just as tasty as full-size fruit.

For a soil mix, use one of the commercial soilless mixes or a compost mix. Small amounts of garden soil, not more than one-third of its volume, can be added. A compost mix will require less watering, making the plant less subject to stress. Weight can become a consideration, particularly if you want to move your containers around or if you are growing on certain rooftops. Soil and compost will greatly add to the weight of the container, and clay pots are much heavier than plastic to start with. You can add some water-absorbing plant gel granules to either mix, reducing the watering requirements. With either type, you should add some organic granular fertilizer to the mix. Or you can add one of the slow-release chemical fertilizers. If you are using the soilless mix on its own, you must be sure to fertilize weekly with liquid feed.

At the bottom of the container, place some sharp stones, gravel, or pieces of broken clay pots. If you want to reduce the weight of the container, you can use perlite at the bottom of the container to make one-tenth to one-third of the total volume. Make sure your container has adequate drainage holes. Fill it with soil to within two or three inches of the top. If you are using five-gallon containers, one plant per pot is good. A bigger barrel or a constructed container can hold several plants, but they should be planted two feet apart and pruned. Plants should be staked, trellised, or attached to twine that's firmly secured to a wall, roof, or railing.

## Choose the Best Tomatoes and Store Them Properly

Some of the recipes in this book have suggestions for specific tomato varieties. Only in rare cases will those varieties be available to you unless you grow them yourself and plan during the previous winter what you are going to cook — an unlikely scenario. In a few cases where a recipe calls for a specific type of tomato — a cherry tomato, for example — substituting a large slicing tomato will produce a much different outcome. In most instances, just use the best tomatoes available to you.

One of the most important things to know about tomatoes is never to refrigerate them. Yes, refrigeration keeps them longer, but what's the point if their flavor and texture are compromised? A tomato picked ripe with no cracks or rot spots should keep for about a week.

Tomatoes can be kept cool, at 50°F plus, but no colder. Most of us do not have the ability to keep them at that temperature in summer. If your tomatoes are about to spoil, eat them — don't refrigerate them. Or cook them up for sauce and put them into the freezer.

While not every heirloom has great flavor, it is safe to say that every heirloom tomato I have ever cooked down into a sauce has made a tasty sauce, far better than any commercial sauce I have ever bought. The depth and complexity of tastes are extraordinary and usually a revelation for the uninitiated. The flavors concentrate tremendously. When using heirloom tomatoes for cooking, almost any type will do, although some are better suited for particular purposes.

## Reduce the Water Content in Cooked Tomato Recipes

Some of the best flavors to be found in heirloom tomatoes come from the larger slicing types. These are usually rather juicy and contain a fair to large number of seeds. They require very long cooking times to reduce their water content to a thickened sauce or purée, and their volume shrinks considerably from start to finish. From an energy standpoint, they are very inefficient to cook with because of the long cooking time involved. But they do make very good sauce.

One effective means of evaporating some of the moisture and developing a caramelized

flavor is to roast the tomatoes in a hot oven before cooking them on the stove. To roast the tomatoes, cut them in half horizontally, arrange them cut side up in a single layer in a roasting pan, and roast at 450°F for about one hour, or until the tomatoes are somewhat collapsed and wrinkled. Or you can add a couple of tablespoons of canned tomato paste to a watery sauce, which will absorb the extra water content and thicken the sauce without affecting the taste.

Either before or after the sauce has thickened, I put one-half to two-thirds of the sauce through a food mill to get rid of a portion of the seeds and skin. Leaving some unprocessed sauce creates more texture, and I don't mind eating some skin in my sauce. If the recipe calls for a smooth sauce or purée, you can process the whole batch.

## PEELING TOMATOES

To peel tomatoes, drop them into a pot of boiling water for 5 to 10 seconds. Use a slotted spoon to transfer them to a bowl of ice water and let cool for about 1 minute. Then remove the skin with a paring knife.

### The Best Tomato for the Recipe

The following recommendations for using heirloom tomatoes are based on my cooking experience using varieties that I have come to know and love. Do not be intimidated by specific variety names; work with varieties to which you have good access, whether heirloom or hybrid.

Meatier tomatoes, such as Brandywine, Purple Brandy, Lambert's General Grant (Dr. Neal), Winsall, Pruden's Purple, and Oxheart, require less cooking time than many of the classic heirlooms, such as the Livingston varieties Paragon or Magnus, or others such as Cardinal, Eva Purple Ball, or Trucker's Favorite. In my opinion, the best tomato flavors tend to come from the less meaty, slightly seedier red-hued heirloom types. These tend to have distinctive sweet-acid balance that intensifies when cooked down. Other people prefer the flavor of Brandywine or the milder bicolor, orange, and yellow group. Early tomatoes typically don't have as well-developed flavors as the later varieties and consequently are not as desirable for cooking purposes. But if you are using a flavorful early variety, such as Stupice, you will get good results.

All of the red-hued tomatoes make excellent sauces for a wide range of uses — they work well in any classic Italian tomato-based pasta or polenta dish, and they're excellent for pizza toppings and chicken dishes, with mussels and most other types of seafood, to roast or grill, and in Mexican cuisine. Thinly sliced, they are excellent baked on top of toast or grilled bread. They also make great soup and tomato juice.

Yellow and orange tomatoes have a milder taste. The orange Indian Moon or Earl of Edgecombe make great soup, especially when paired with shellfish or a smoky ingredient such as bacon. Yellow sauces derived from Manyel, Limmony,

Azoycha, or Livingston's Golden Queen develop very good flavor; all require long cooking times. Lillian's Yellow Heirloom and Yellow Brandywine are meatier and will cook faster. Yellow sauce works great with pasta, especially when combined with seafood, because the milder tomatoes will not compete with more delicate flavors of seafood. Yellow tomatoes make very good jams and chutney.

Bicolors, such as German Stripe or Big Rainbow, are better for sauces than for fresh eating, in my opinion. They make a sauce similar to that from the yellow/orange group, but it is sweeter and a bit milder in flavor. These tomatoes also go nicely with seafood or fish and a white, slightly fruity wine.

Black tomatoes, such as Black Krim or Black from Tula, cook down to various-hued purplish or deep red colors with excellent, slightly salty flavors. For a unique sauce, try using Purple Calabash. These varieties work very well with pasta or red meat and make great barbecue sauce and ketchup. White tomatoes, such as White Queen, make a mild, pleasant sauce but fail to really have that tomato taste. Food writer William Woys Weaver suggests that they make "a delicate white tomato sauce for fish."

Mixing tomatoes of different colors is fine for cooking, but to retain color, keep the orange-yellow separate from the red to pink types and the black types. When cooked for short time periods or when canned using a water bath, the various-colored tomatoes retain much of their color. The major exception is green tomatoes, which when cooked for a while develop a brownish green color

that is not terribly attractive, though they retain good flavor. Using a yellow and a red sauce (or any other contrasting color combination) makes a visually striking two-toned pasta dish, pizza, soup, lasagne, or drink.

Slicing tomatoes also make wonderful dried tomatoes. Most of the seeds and gel will fall away from them when you slice the fresh tomato for drying. When drying is complete the slices will weigh a fraction of their fresh weight. It will take 15 to 20 pounds of these tomatoes to make a pound of dried fruit. But drying is well worth the effort.

## SEEDING TOMATOES

To seed a tomato, cut it in half horizontally. Then gently squeeze each half to release the seeds. Don't worry if a few seeds remain.

Druzba, Brandywine, and Trucker's Favorite are particularly memorable as dried tomatoes, but any slicing tomato will work. For contrast, use some orange or yellow varieties. Salt the tomatoes lightly before drying.

For fresh salsas and salads, there is nothing better than having a variety of colors and shapes to choose from. Fresh tomatoes are delicious with nothing more than a little salt. Try one of the hand-harvested coarse ("gourmet") sea salts, which can really enhance the tomatoes. Or just serve with a little oil, vinegar, and salt. My grandmother used only vegetable oil and white distilled vinegar,

# A FEW KEY TOMATO TERMS

**Bush-type tomato:** A type of determinate tomato that stays fairly short, requiring no staking. Semi-bush tomatoes may be a bit taller and require some support but remain relatively short.

**Currant tomato:** A different species of tomato (*Lycopersicon pimpinellifolium*); yields very small, dime-size fruit, often in great profusion, with intense sweet flavor.

**Determinate:** Plants that when mature grow to only a few feet in height and then stop growing.

**Grape tomato:** Now an industry-generated term referring to various prolific hybrid cherry tomatoes, generally with mediocre flavor. Formerly used as the name of some types of small tomatoes.

**Heirloom:** An old variety that has been handed down in a family for two or more generations and/or is at least 50 years of age and is open-pollinated.

**Hybrid:** A variety that has been crossbred from two or more distinctly different parents, resulting in an offspring whose characteristics are different from those of either parent, and therefore does not "breed true."

**Indeterminate:** A plant that continues to grow in height throughout the growing season, reaching 5, 6, or even 10 feet or more, depending on the variety and growing conditions.

**Open-pollinated:** A variety that "breeds true"; that is, the offspring will be the same as the parent, and therefore seeds can be saved.

**Paste tomato:** A type of tomato that typically has a lower water content and higher "solids" content, making it ideal for sauce. While shapes vary, often paste tomatoes are pear-shaped or long and pointed.

**Saladette tomato:** An industry term referring to a tomato that is larger than a cherry but smaller than a beefsteak or slicing tomato. It may be round in shape, so small slices or chunks can be obtained from it.

**Slicing tomato:** A larger tomato, ranging from six ounces or so up to a pound or more, typically rounded in shape or somewhat flattened (oblate). The meatier versions are referred to as beefsteaks.

which is admittedly quite sharp. For a slightly sweeter approach, try extra-virgin olive oil and balsamic vinegar. Or try a dash of lemon. Real mayonnaise goes very well with sliced tomatoes, and the combination with the resultant tomato juice is divine. Thin slices of red or sweet onion complement the tomatoes nicely, as do additions of herbs, such as basil.

The bicolors served fresh are put to their best use visually. Commingled with slices of other colors, such as Aunt Ruby's German Green, Black from Tula, Brandywine, Indian Moon, Livingston's Beauty, or Winsall, garnished with a few white and red currant tomatoes, these tomatoes create a stunning display. Or take these same varieties and chop them up for salsa. If the Mexican form of salsa is not your style, try sliced or chopped tomatoes marinated in their own juices with salt.

Underutilized in cooking are the small cherry tomatoes. Lightly cooked in extra-virgin olive oil and garlic in a hot skillet, they work wonders with pasta. Or put them into a soup or pasta sauce a couple of minutes before serving, or use as fresh or cooked garnishes on pizza. They also make good pickled tomatoes and look great in clear vinegars. Sauces and jam from these types are quite interesting, but you should get rid of a good portion of the seeds and skin by passing the cooked tomatoes through a food mill.

Almost any kind of tomato can be stuffed provided it is of sufficient size and preferably slightly flattened on the bottom. Large cherries make interesting fresh canapés stuffed with crab or lobster salad, or baked with various breadcrumb-based mixtures. There are a few varieties of true stuffing tomatoes. Two of the best known are Red and Yellow Stuffer, both of which greatly resemble bell peppers. These

## PREPARING TOMATOES FOR COOKING

For most recipes, washing, coring, then slicing or cutting the tomatoes into chunks is all the preparation required. Peeling isn't necessary if you are going to use the tomatoes raw in salads or salsas. In cooked dishes, if the tomatoes are finely chopped, you won't notice the skins. If the tomatoes go into the pot in big chunks, the skins will shrivel and toughen, sometimes adding an unpleasant texture. You can peel the tomatoes before cooking, or you can run the cooked tomatoes through a food mill to get rid of the skins.

varieties yield quite well and are fairly dry in texture, much like a pepper but with milder flavor. They make an excellent substitute for peppers without the strong pepper flavor.

When making sauce or dried tomatoes, the most obvious choices are the plum or paste tomatoes. These tomatoes have a greater solids content and a lower moisture and seed content, meaning they turn into sauce or purée faster and with greater yields than the round slicing types. The long red carrot types, such as Opalka, or other long types, such as Amish Paste or Howard German, or pear types such as Red Pear, King Humbert, or Purple Pear, all make great sauce. Sometimes these have such low moisture content that if you are not careful when cooking them, they can scorch.

Among my favorite sauce tomatoes are Black Plum and Black Pear. Both make dark, flavorful rich sauces and full-flavored jams. You can simply slice the small black plums in half, put them into a heavy pan, and 25 minutes later have sauce for dinner.

Orange Banana, Roughwood Golden Plum, and Peace Yellow Paste all make excellent yellow-orange sauces. While small, Yellow Plum and Yellow Pear also make a nice sauce, as well as being useful for garnishes, salads, pickling, and making into jams.

All of the tomatoes in the paste group make great dried tomatoes. Best for drying are those that can be cut in half lengthwise with the skin intact to yield two small to medium-size pieces capable of drying within 24 hours, depending on your drying technique and climate. There are some very large tomatoes, some of the meaty oxheart types, for example, that need to be cut in three or four pieces to dry in a day — these are not as well suited for drying as the other types. Dried tomatoes can be lightly marinated in extra-virgin olive oil or other combinations with balsamic vinegar, salt, garlic, and other herbs for additional flavor.

All of the above-mentioned varieties (and many others) are good to use for drying. Black Plums become very dark and tasty, while Yellow Pears and Yellow Plums retain their color and unique mellow characteristics. Opalka and related types, Orange Banana, Purple Pear, Black Pear, Red Pear, and King Humbert are all excellent for drying. While not exactly a plum tomato, Plum Lemon makes excellent dried tomatoes. Any of these tomatoes lightly smoked either during or after drying produce a very tasty treat.

Drying the smaller cherries also produces excellent raisinlike results. They need to be pricked with a knifepoint or needle to dry properly. Try any of the currants such as Ciudad Victoria or white, red, and yellow, or cherry varieties, such as Hawaiian, Matt's Wild Cherry, Blondkopfchen, and many others. Or use any of the larger sizes such as Green Grape, Reisentraube, Pink Ping Pong, or Sarah Goldstar Cherry, cut in half. Hybrids such as Sweet 100s (or try its open-pollinated equivalent, Peacevine Cherry) or Sun Gold make a good dried cherry, too.

If heirlooms are not available to you, there are certainly equivalents in some of the categories of commercial hybrids. Round slicing tomatoes, and often at least one other color type, pastes such as Roma, and a couple of types of small cherry or grape tomatoes are available at most larger markets.

# CHEFS COLLABORATIVE

The Chefs Collaborative is a national network of more than one thousand members of the food community who promote sustainable cuisine. The collaborative is dedicated to supporting artisanal producers, many of whom are preserving valuable traditions; local growers, who enrich our communities by providing restaurants and farmers' markets with distinctive and delicious produce; and individuals who work in the sustainable-agriculture, aquaculture, and animal husbandry fields. The collaborative is especially concerned with conservation practices that lessen our impact on the environment. Members understand that the sources of their ingredients — the way they have been grown, raised, or caught — have a significant effect on the flavor and quality of their meals. They believe that choosing sustainable food products helps support the environment, the heritage, and the economy of entire communities.

According to Rick Bayless, restaurant owner and cookbook author, it is the practices of the collaborative members that really make a difference.

"It's not what I say but what I do. I believe that Chefs Collaborative and its participant chefs are leaders in promoting important foods such as heirloom tomatoes. For instance, financially assisting a farmer in increasing his cropping ability for tomatoes allows me to have a steady supply for our restaurants, benefits the farmer and his other clients, and keeps heirloom-tomato production going."

Chefs Collaborative believes that chefs are in a unique position to educate the dining public through their menu choices. If chefs' habits change, consumer habits will change, too, making a sustainable food system more understandable and accessible. According to Michel Nischan, "Our role as chefs goes well beyond making good food — we can educate our clients, help our farmers, and help our environment all at the same time. For example, chefs have been instrumental in promoting the use and revival of heirloom tomatoes, thus bringing a great product to the table but also helping with their preservation through generating economic activity."

# CHAPTER TWO

# SAUCES & SALSAS

# Fast Tomato Sauce

SERVES 4

The flavor of the tomatoes, basil, and garlic in this quickly made sauce remains fresh and lively because the cooking time is so brief. The recipe comes from Massimo Capra, owner-chef of Mistura restaurant in Toronto. Serve it with gnocchi or other pasta, or use it to top crostini.

½ cup extra-virgin olive oil

3 garlic cloves, peeled and finely sliced

2 pounds (10–12 large) Roma or other plum tomatoes peeled, seeded, and sliced

6 basil leaves (or more to taste), torn

¼–½ teaspoon crushed red pepper flakes (optional)

salt and freshly ground black pepper

1. Warm the oil in a large skillet over medium heat. Add the garlic and let it soften without browning for a minute.

2. Stir the tomatoes into the oil and garlic. Add the basil and red pepper flakes, if desired. Season with salt and pepper. Increase the heat and cook briskly for 2 to 4 minutes, until the tomatoes collapse into a chunky sauce. Serve immediately.

# Italian-Style Fresh Tomato Sauce

For topping pasta, there are dozens of variations on this Italian *sugo di pomodoro*, and all of them aim to capture the fresh flavor of tomatoes, enhancing it with garlic and herbs. As with any basic, unadorned recipe, the results will be as good as the tomatoes that go into it. For the best results, use any heirloom paste tomato, especially Opalka, King Humbert, or Amish Paste. If your harvest is bountiful, double or triple the recipe and freeze the extra.

¼ cup extra-virgin olive oil

4 garlic cloves, peeled and thinly sliced

1 medium onion, finely chopped

3 pounds (15–18 large) red plum tomatoes, washed, seeded, and coarsely chopped

salt

6 basil leaves, torn

1 teaspoon chopped fresh oregano, or to taste

**1.** Warm the oil in a large skillet over medium heat and stir in the garlic. Cook gently for 1 to 2 minutes without browning, and then stir in the onion and cook for 2 minutes longer, until the onion has softened.

**2.** Add the tomatoes and sprinkle with salt. Stir in the basil and raise the heat so the mixture bubbles. Cook for 4 to 6 minutes, or until the tomatoes are tender but not mushy. Stir in the oregano and cook for a minute longer. Taste and add salt if needed.

**3.** Serve immediately or, if you prefer a smooth sauce, process it in a food processor or blender, then reheat it before serving.

# The First Tomato Sauce

**MAKES ABOUT 3 CUPS**

Antonio Latini's book *Lo Scalco alla Moderna*, published in Naples in 1692, contains the first two printed recipes for tomatoes. One of them is this sauce, which he called "Tomato Sauce Spanish Style" and which doesn't differ much from many that we make today. Interestingly, it contains chiles, which, like tomatoes, are New World natives taken to Europe by the Spanish conquistadors of South America. Here is my adaptation.

2 pounds (about 12 large) plum tomatoes

⅔ cup chopped onion

1 serrano chile, seeded and cut into strips

1 teaspoon fresh thyme or ½ teaspoon dried

salt and freshly ground black pepper

1–2 tablespoons extra-virgin olive oil

1 teaspoon cider vinegar or white wine vinegar

1. Preheat the oven to 450°F. Cut a cross in the stalk end of the tomatoes and place them on a metal pan, such as a pie plate. Roast them for 15 to 20 minutes, or until the skins have split and the tomatoes are soft.

2. Let the tomatoes cool, then peel off the skins and discard the core and seeds. Combine the tomatoes in a food processor with the onion, chile, and thyme. Process until well blended.

3. Season to taste with salt and pepper, then stir in 1 tablespoon of the oil and the vinegar. Taste and add more oil or salt if necessary. Serve immediately with meats, or simmer to thicken for 5 minutes and serve with pasta or keep for later use.

## THE 1692 VERSION

*Take half a dozen tomatoes that are ripe, and put them to roast in the embers, and when they are scorched, remove the skin diligently, and mince them finely with a knife. Add onions, minced finely, to discretion; hot chili peppers (peparolo, Neapolitan dialect), also minced finely; and thyme (serpolo o piperna) in a small amount. After mixing everything together, adjust it with a little salt, oil, and vinegar. It is a very tasty sauce, both for boiled dishes or anything else.*

As translated by Rudolf Grewe in his article "The Arrival of the Tomato in Spain and Italy: Early Recipes" (*Journal of Gastronomy 3*, summer 1987).

# Marinara Sauce

MAKES ABOUT 4 CUPS

Here is the classic Italian American marinara sauce. Use it to sauce pasta or boil it down more and spread it on pizza. This version includes anchovies. They disappear into the sauce during cooking, adding a backbone flavor that complements the sweetness and acidity. The anchovies do not give the sauce a fishy taste, but if you want a vegetarian sauce, omit them.

10 pounds (about 2 dozen large) very ripe tomatoes, quartered, or 3 quarts home-canned tomatoes

4 large onions, peeled and coarsely chopped

8 garlic cloves, peeled and smashed

3 tablespoons extra-virgin olive oil

8 anchovy fillets, packed in oil, rinsed and dried (optional)

4 stems basil, each with about 8 large leaves

1 tablespoon chopped fresh oregano or 2 teaspoons dried

1 teaspoon salt

freshly ground black pepper

1–3 teaspoons sugar

1. Cook the tomatoes in a large saucepan over very low heat for 4 to 5 minutes, stirring occasionally, until their juice is running. Stir in the onions and garlic. Raise the heat a little and simmer the tomato mixture, covered, for 15 minutes, or until the onions are tender.

2. Pass the tomato mixture through a food mill and into a large bowl, removing seeds, skins, and other coarse bits.

3. Wipe out the saucepan, add the oil, and warm over low heat. Coarsely chop each anchovy into 3 or 4 pieces and stir them into the oil. Pour in the strained tomato mixture and the basil stems and oregano. Season with the salt, pepper to taste, and 1 teaspoon of the sugar. Simmer for 45 to 60 minutes, until the sauce has reduced and thickened to a consistency suitable for coating pasta. (If you want the sauce for topping pizza, simmer it for 20 to 30 minutes longer, until it has thickened to the consistency you like.)

4. Remove and discard the basil stems. Taste the sauce and add more salt and pepper if needed and 1 to 2 additional teaspoons of the sugar if necessary to pull the flavors together. Pour into jars and store in the refrigerator. Use within one week. Alternatively, pour into plastic freezer containers and freeze.

# Roasted Heirloom Tomato Sauce

MAKES ABOUT 5 CUPS

Practice makes perfect, and that's how chef Kevin Schmitz of the Marketplace Kitchen in Great Barrington, Massachusetts, created this outstanding recipe. After he developed the recipe, I held tastings, and everyone agreed that this was the best tomato sauce ever. For a yellow tomato sauce, follow the recipe, substituting Indian Moon or Earl of Edgecombe and either German Striped or any other large bicolor tomato, such as Regina's Yellow. If you don't happen to grow any of these varieties, substitute your own homegrown tomatoes. You won't re-create Kevin's recipe, but you will have a tasty sauce for pasta. Roasting tomatoes creates a wonderful caramelized flavor great with chicken or any pasta, including ravioli, lasagna, and gnocchi.

5 pounds heirloom tomatoes (a mix of Brandywine, Eva Purple Ball, Rose de Berne, and Livingston's Favorite is recommended)

12 garlic cloves

leaves from 12 sprigs fresh thyme

1 cup extra-virgin olive oil

2 cups chopped Spanish onions

2 cups dry white wine

4 stems fresh basil, each with about 8 large leaves

salt and freshly ground black pepper

1. Preheat the oven to 350°F.

2. Wash the tomatoes, cut out the tough stem ends, then cut the tomatoes in half. With a teaspoon, scoop the seeds into a bowl and set the bowl aside. Place the halved tomatoes, cut side up, in a roasting pan or other baking dish that will hold them in a single layer.

3. Peel and chop 6 cloves of the garlic and scatter it evenly over the tomatoes. Sprinkle on the thyme leaves, and then drizzle ½ cup of the oil on top. Roast the tomatoes for 30 to 40 minutes, or until they are very soft.

4. Let the tomatoes cool to lukewarm. Pass them through a food mill, using the small holes, or rub them through a sieve to remove the skins and any remaining seeds.

5. Warm the remaining ½ cup oil in a large nonreactive pan over medium heat. Stir in the onions. Peel and chop the remaining 6 garlic cloves and stir into the onions. Let the mixture sweat gently for 8 to 10 minutes, or until the onions are translucent.

**6.** Add the wine, then raise the heat and simmer for 15 minutes, or until the liquid has reduced by half. Add the strained tomato pulp. Place a sieve over the pan and pour the bowl of seeds into it so the juice runs into the tomato mixture.

**7.** Stir in the basil and 1 teaspoon of salt. Bring to a boil and simmer for 15 to 25 minutes, stirring often to prevent sticking. When the sauce is thick, taste and add salt and pepper as desired. Remove and discard the basil. Serve hot.

## A SHAPELY TOMATO

Early-American tomatoes were ribbed, but cherry and paste types existed. Other colors and shapes made their appearance in the 1820s and '30s, including larger and less ribbed forms, and the availability of many varieties became widespread by the 1860s. These appeared through some chance mutation, accidental or intentional cross-breeding, or repeated selection.

The larger, round, and distinctly smooth tomatoes that resemble modern varieties were at first an exclusively American breeding phenomenon and did not appear until around 1870. After that, breeding efforts by many individuals and seed companies made relatively uniform tomatoes commonplace.

# Tomato-Porcini Sauce

**SERVES 4–6**

**M**ushrooms add a hearty flavor to a meatless tomato sauce, especially when you use porcini. Their name means "little pig" in Italian. Black tomatoes, in particular, have a robust flavor that complements the mushrooms. Try Black Plum or Black Pear, or a black slicer, such as Black from Tula. Serve this sauce with polenta, pasta, or steak.

⅓ cup dried porcini pieces

1 cup warm water

3 tablespoons extra-virgin olive oil

2 garlic cloves, peeled and finely chopped

1 small onion, chopped

3 cups fresh or canned skinned, seeded, and chopped tomatoes

2 teaspoons chopped fresh thyme or 1 teaspoon dried

1½ teaspoons chopped fresh oregano or ½ teaspoon dried

1 bay leaf

salt and freshly ground black pepper

1½ cups sliced cremini or white button mushrooms

**1.** Rinse the porcini pieces. Put them into a small bowl, cover with the water, and soak for 60 to 90 minutes, or until they have become somewhat tender.

**2.** Strain the mushrooms and set them aside. Simmer the strained soaking water in a small saucepan for 5 to 7 minutes, or until it has reduced to 3 to 4 tablespoons. Chop the strained porcini into pea-size pieces (leaving behind any sediment), and stir them into them into the reduced liquid; set aside.

**3.** Warm 2 tablespoons of the oil in a medium saucepan over medium heat. Add the garlic and onion and cook for 3 to 4 minutes, until slightly softened. Add the tomatoes and stir in half of the thyme, the oregano, the bay leaf, and salt and pepper to taste. Simmer for 5 to 10 minutes, or until the onions and tomatoes are soft. Add the porcini mixture to the tomatoes. Cover the pan and simmer for 5 minutes longer.

**4.** Heat the remaining tablespoon of oil in a large skillet over high heat. Stir in the cremini slices and the remaining half of the thyme. Salt lightly. Sauté, stirring constantly, for 3 to 4 minutes, or until the edges of the mushroom slices are golden.

**5.** Just before serving, add two-thirds of the sautéed cremini to the tomato sauce and reheat it. Use the remaining cremini as garnish.

Fresh Rainbow Salsa, *p. 37*

Crostini with Tomatoes, Avocado, and Preserved Lemons, *p. 51*

Scallops with Asian Noodle Salad and Tomato-Ginger Jam, *p. 70*

Chilled Sun-Gold Tomato Soup, *p. 78*

# Tomato and Meat Sauce for Pasta

**S**ausage zings the flavor of this rich tomato sauce, a standby for family suppers. The recipe can be doubled or tripled and the extra sauce frozen. One batch is enough to sauce one pound of pasta.

2 tablespoons extra-virgin olive oil

1 large onion, chopped

2 garlic cloves, peeled and finely chopped

1 medium carrot, peeled and grated

¾ pound lean ground beef

½ pound sweet Italian sausage

¼ pound hot Italian sausage or an additional ¼ pound sweet Italian sausage

1 teaspoon fresh oregano, or more to taste

salt and freshly ground black pepper

1 bay leaf

3 cups peeled, seeded, and chopped fresh or canned tomatoes (about 5 large fresh tomatoes)

2–3 tablespoons tomato paste

1–2 teaspoons sugar (optional)

**1.** Warm the oil in a large skillet over medium heat. Stir in the onion and garlic. Cover the pan and cook gently for 4 to 5 minutes, until the onion has softened. Stir in the carrot and cook for 1 minute. Add the ground beef, breaking it up with a wooden spoon as you cook, for 3 to 4 minutes, or until it has browned.

**2.** If the sausage has casings, remove them. Cut the sweet sausage into 1-inch chunks and add them to the pan. Crumble the hot sausage and add it, too. Cook over medium heat, stirring occasionally, until the sausage has browned, 4 to 5 minutes.

**3.** Sprinkle the oregano over the meat mixture. Season with salt and pepper to taste and add the bay leaf and tomatoes. Cover the pan and let the mixture simmer over medium heat until the tomatoes are tender, 5 to 7 minutes, depending on their ripeness.

**4.** Stir in 2 tablespoons of the tomato paste and continue cooking over medium-high heat to evaporate the liquid. If the tomatoes are exceptionally juicy or if you want to intensify the tomato flavor, add the additional tablespoon tomato paste. When the sauce has thickened, reduce the heat to medium-low.

**5.** Taste and add 1 to 2 teaspoons of sugar if desired. Season with pepper and additional salt to taste. Serve hot.

# Ragù di Salsicce

SERVES 4

Sausage forms the backbone of a richly flavored sauce from Massimo Capra, owner-chef of Mistura restaurant in Toronto. Serve it with his polenta recipe on page 181. He also recommends serving it with pasta, adding it to risotto, or simply eating it with crusty bread.

¼ cup extra-virgin olive oil

1 tablespoon butter

4 garlic cloves, smashed and peeled

1 medium onion, chopped

4 sweet Italian sausages, preferably with fennel seeds, removed from the casings, at room temperature

½ cup white wine

6 plum tomatoes, peeled and seeded

¾ cup tomato juice (page 235)

salt and freshly ground black pepper

½ teaspoon fennel seeds (optional)

**1.** Heat a large skillet over medium heat; add the oil and butter. When the butter has melted, stir in the garlic and sauté for just a few seconds. Stir in the onion and sauté for 3 to 4 minutes, until translucent.

**2.** Add the sausage to the onion mixture, stirring and breaking it up, until the sausage bits have browned, 2 to 3 minutes. Add the wine, raise the heat to high, and let the wine bubble for 4 to 5 minutes, until it has almost all evaporated.

**3.** Stir in the tomatoes and tomato juice. Season to taste with salt, pepper, and fennel seeds, if desired. (Little seasoning may be needed at this point, because the sausage is already seasoned.) Simmer for 10 minutes, or until the mixture is a thick, chunky sauce. Adjust seasoning to taste. Serve immediately.

# Massimo Capra
## MISTURA, *Toronto, Ontario*

Capra grew up in the beautiful northern Italian city of Cremona in an extended farm-based family. As is the tradition in Italy, his mother cooked and she "cooked very, very well." Being the youngest in the family, he spent considerable time in the kitchen with his mother. When he was seven years old he began helping her with their Saturday-night pastime — making fresh pasta for the week.

In 1974, when he was 14, he had to decide what direction his career would go in. He chose to go to Salsomaggiore Terme, the national cooking school in Parma, where he learned French technique and continental cuisine. He worked in various grand hotels where kitchen staffs of 35 cooked for 150 guests. But when economic conditions in Italy declined, so did the quality of ingredients. Frozen meats from Argentina and canned soup bases became too much for Massimo.

In 1982, he immigrated to Canada, cooking "French with a splash of Italian." In the late 1980s, Massimo helped turn Prego della Piazza into the finest Italian restaurant in Toronto. It was a vibrant combination of pizzeria, trattoria, high-end cuisine, and catering, and even included a French room. In 1997, he opened Mistura with his partner, Paolo Paolini. He characterizes his food as "contemporary Italian . . . simple presentation, simple flavors, and the best ingredients."

Massimo believes it is important to cook with the seasons as much as possible and is a great advocate of buying local foods when possible. In the summer he preserves some of the local food, canning and freezing roasted red peppers and other vegetables. In winter he serves lots of rapini, fennel, Swiss chard, and cabbage. He likes to serve local lake fish such as pickerel or whitefish.

As a chef, Massimo feels it is important to have developed a palate from the ground up, literally. "I am from farmer stock. I am conscious of seasonal flavors, what do and do not complement each other on the plate. Nature intended certain flavors to be present with others at certain times of the year. And that is what I try to bring to my food."

# Tomato, Tofu, and Garlic Sauce

**MAKES ABOUT 4 CUPS**

I developed this recipe when I wanted a meatlike substitute from the most commonly available vegetable-based protein source — tofu. Those who find tofu too bland should try this. I think it will be a revelation. Savory herbs, along with lots of fresh garlic, help make a delicious sauce. If you can get fresh garlic from a local farmer instead of supermarket garlic, the sauce will be even better. The sauce is great with spaghetti or any other pasta.

½ pound (½ package) extra-firm tofu

¼ cup extra-virgin olive oil

5 large garlic cloves, peeled and chopped

1 medium onion, coarsely chopped

3 cups fresh or canned tomatoes, peeled, seeded, and coarsely hopped

10 basil leaves, torn

2–3 fresh sage leaves, coarsely chopped (optional)

2 bay leaves

1 (1-inch) sprig of rosemary

pinch of fennel seed

1 tablespoon sugar, or more to taste

salt and freshly ground black pepper

1. Pat the tofu dry with paper towels. Crumble it into irregular-shaped pieces with your hands.

2. Heat 3 tablespoons of the oil in a small skillet over medium heat. Stir in the tofu and garlic and cook for about 7 minutes, until the tofu is golden, turning and stirring occasionally. Set aside.

3. Heat the remaining tablespoon oil in a medium saucepan over medium heat. Stir in the onion and cook for 4 to 5 minutes, until softened. Stir in the tomatoes, followed by the basil, sage, if desired, bay leaves, rosemary, fennel seed, sugar, and a light seasoning of salt and pepper. Simmer over low heat, stirring from time to time, until a thick sauce has formed, 20 to 30 minutes.

4. Gently fold the tofu mixture into the tomato sauce and cook for 2 to 3 minutes longer. Taste for seasoning and add more salt, pepper, or sugar if necessary. Serve hot.

HOLT'S MAMMOTH SAGE

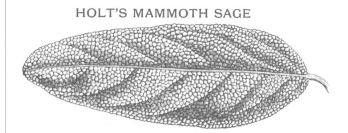

# Rick Bayless's Essential Quick-Cooked Tomato-Chipotle Sauce

## MAKES ABOUT 1¼ CUPS

In his book *Rick Bayless's Mexican Kitchen: Capturing the Vibrant Flavors of a World-Class Cuisine,* Chicago-based author and restaurateur Rick Bayless calls this sauce "earthy hued . . . gently balanced between smokiness and natural sweetness." The sauce combines particularly well with meats. It is great for Mexican dishes such as pork or chicken tacos, enchiladas, tamales, and grilled or smoked game birds. Try it with bits of chèvre and salmon in a tortilla. I like this sauce so much that I've enjoyed it just spread on French bread.

4 garlic cloves, unpeeled

4–5 (about 1½ pounds) medium-size ripe tomatoes

4 canned chipotle chiles in adobo sauce

1 tablespoon rich-tasting lard or vegetable oil

about ½ teaspoon salt

1. Place a small heavy skillet over medium heat and add the garlic cloves. Let them toast, turning them over once or twice, until the skins are charred. Remove and let cool. Slip off the skins and coarsely chop the garlic.

2. Turn your broiler as high as it will go. Lay the tomatoes on a baking sheet and place about 4 inches below the broiler. When they blister, blacken, and soften on one side, in about 6 minutes, turn them over and roast on the other side. Cool, then peel, collecting all the juices with the tomatoes.

3. Scrape the tomatoes and their juices into a food processor or blender and add the chiles and garlic. Pulse the machine until the mixture is nearly a purée — it should have a little more texture than canned tomato sauce.

4. Heat the lard in a heavy medium-size saucepan over medium-high heat. When hot enough to make a drop of the purée sizzle sharply, add it all at once and stir for about 5 minutes as it sears and concentrates to an earthy, red, thick sauce — about the consistency of medium-thick spaghetti sauce. Taste and season with salt.

5. Serve hot. The sauce will keep for several days, covered, in the refrigerator. It freezes well; after defrosting, boil it briefly to restore its great texture.

# Pesto Rosso

MAKES ABOUT 1 CUP

I take tremendous pride in my oven-dried tomatoes. Packed in extra-extra-virgin olive oil and infused with herbs, these dried heirloom plum tomatoes are exquisite on their own or combined with other ingredients. Here I make a dressing for pasta that takes its inspiration from basil pesto. The recipe makes enough to sauce two to three pounds of pasta. It can also be used as a topping for bruschetta or as a sandwich spread.

¼ cup pine nuts

18 Oven-Dried Tomatoes in Herbed Olive Oil (page 250), or commercial sun-dried tomatoes packed in extra-virgin olive oil, drained and reserved

⅓ cup extra-virgin olive oil, or more as needed, preferably from the jar of tomatoes

6–8 tender basil leaves, torn

2 garlic cloves, peeled and minced

¼ cup freshly grated Parmesan cheese

sea salt

½ teaspoon sugar (optional)

1. Preheat the oven to 250°F.

2. Spread the pine nuts in a single layer on a baking sheet and toast until they are golden, about 5 minutes. (Watch them toward the end, as they scorch easily.)

3. Put the tomatoes in a food processor or blender. Add the oil and basil and process until roughly blended. Add the garlic and process again. Finally, add the Parmesan and about ½ teaspoon salt and continue processing until you have a thick sauce. You may need additional oil to get the right almost-smooth consistency; if so, use more oil from the jar of tomatoes or any other flavorful oil.

4. Taste for seasoning. Add more salt if necessary. Also consider whether a little sugar would help pull the flavors together, and if so, add it.

5. Serve at room temperature, thinned with a little pasta cooking water if you are using it to dress pasta. You can keep leftover Pesto Rosso in a jar in the refrigerator for 2 weeks — a useful standby.

# Yellow Tomato and Ginger Sauce

**G**inger and lemon team with mild yellow tomatoes to make this sunny sauce. It is especially good with seafood, which is easily overwhelmed by red tomato sauces. Try it also with pork chops or slices of pork loin. Limmony and Manyel are excellent yellow tomatoes for this sauce.

3 tablespoons extra-virgin olive oil

2 tablespoons finely chopped or grated fresh ginger

2 tablespoons finely chopped onion

2 garlic cloves, peeled and finely chopped

2 pounds (2½–3 cups) yellow tomatoes, peeled, seeded, and chopped

1 teaspoon grated lemon zest

1 teaspoon lemon juice, or more to taste

½ teaspoon ground coriander

salt

½ teaspoon Worcestershire sauce

**1.** Heat 2 tablespoons of the oil in a skillet over low heat. Stir in the ginger, onion, and garlic, and cook gently for 4 to 5 minutes, until they are fragrant and softened.

**2.** Stir in the tomatoes, lemon zest, lemon juice, and coriander. Add salt to taste. Cook over medium-high heat until most of the juice has evaporated and the tomatoes are soft, 10 to 15 minutes, depending on the ripeness of the tomatoes. Add the Worcestershire. Taste and add lemon juice if desired, and more salt if necessary.

**3.** Pour the tomato mixture into a food processor, blender, or food mill. Add the remaining tablespoon oil and purée the mixture into a smooth sauce.

**4.** Serve warm or at room temperature. Store in the refrigerator for up to 3 days.

# BRADLEY COUNTY PINK TOMATO FESTIVAL
## WARREN, ARKANSAS

Bradley County is a very rural part of Arkansas characterized by pristine natural areas and small farms. Commercial tomato crops were first planted there in the 1920s, and the type of tomato raised was exclusively pink. Bradley became synonymous with pink tomatoes, and it was dubbed the Pink Tomato Capital of the World.

The first varieties grown in the area are now heirlooms, such as Gulf State Market and Pink Shipper. In the early 1960s, the Bradley tomato was developed exclusively for the Bradley County growers by the University of Arkansas, using heirloom stock. The Arkansas Traveler was bred from the Bradley.

Bradley County had one of the longest-running tomato auctions in the country. Three auction sites existed, one each in Warren, Hermitage, and Monticello. Farmers would bring truckloads of tomatoes up to the main shed, and the winning buyer would have them delivered to his own adjacent shed. The transaction was immediate — the farmer got paid right away. Today tomatoes are taken to a broker and the farmer never knows what price his produce will bring nor precisely when he will get paid. As the old-timers died out, so did the auction. The last

tomato auction in the country was held in Warren in 2001.

Because of Warren's celebrated pink tomatoes, the chamber of commerce and the Lions Club decided to initiate a tomato festival in 1955 in order to further promote their cherished tomatoes. The festival occurs on the second full weekend in June. In 1956 they instituted the "all-tomato lunch," a traditional part of the festival that continues today.

The festival starts on Thursday night; Friday night festivities continue with a street carnival, talent shows, various foods, and more. A tomato-cutting contest includes both dignitaries and the public. It is the longest continuously running festival in Arkansas, and the governors have regularly participated, including former President and Arkansas Governor Bill Clinton, who was known "to chomp down quite a few tomatoes in five minutes."

The festival also includes a tomato-packing contest, Warren being one of the only places left in the country where every tomato is individually wrapped in tissue paper in a two-layer 20-pound box. It's hoped that some things will never change in Bradley County.

# Tomatoes à la Indienne

**SERVES 4**

This recipe is based on a recipe in a chapter titled "One Hundred Ways to Cook Tomatoes" in Olive Green's book *How to Cook Vegetables*, published in 1909. Coconut milk gives the sauce a luxurious velvetiness. The sauce goes well served on top of white or brown basmati rice topped with sautéed tofu. This also makes a good side dish in an Indian meal along with dal and raita.

2 cups canned or fresh peeled, seeded, and chopped tomatoes

1 green bell pepper, seeded and cut into ½-inch strips

¼ cup chopped onion

1 garlic clove, peeled and finely chopped

2 teaspoons ground ginger

¼ cup water, if needed

½ tablespoon butter

2 teaspoons curry powder

1 tablespoon all-purpose flour

½ cup coconut milk

salt and freshly ground black pepper

**1.** Mix the tomatoes, bell pepper, onion, garlic, and ginger in a large saucepan. If using fresh tomatoes, add the water; if using canned, include the juice in the can. Simmer, covered, over low heat for 20 minutes, or until the pepper and onion are soft. During the last 10 minutes of cooking, remove the lid from the pan so most of the liquid can evaporate.

**2.** While the tomatoes are cooking, melt the butter in a small pan over low heat. Remove the pan from the heat and stir in the curry powder and then the flour. Stir in about ¼ cup of the coconut milk to make a smooth mixture. Return the pan to low heat and stir in the remaining coconut milk. Continue cooking, stirring often, until the mixture simmers and thickens.

**3.** Add the coconut milk mixture to the tomatoes and stir the sauce over low heat until combined. Serve hot.

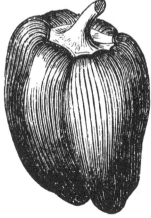

**Sweet Mountain**

# Salsa

A basic, easy-to-make salsa, this one can be characterized as medium hot. Vary ingredient proportions according to taste — you can always add an extra tomato if the salsa gets too spicy. Using two tomato colors such as orange and red makes a more dynamic presentation. I prefer to roast the peppers, as it mellows the "green" pepper taste. Serve with tortilla chips, tacos, or burritos, or as an accompaniment to chicken.

⅔ cup chopped onion

2 tablespoons lemon juice

1½ teaspoons sea salt

1 poblano or green bell pepper

5 medium (about 1½ pounds) tomatoes, chopped

⅓ bunch fresh cilantro, chopped

2 garlic cloves, peeled and minced

1 teaspoon minced medium-hot fresh chile, such as jalapeño or serrano

½ teaspoon ground cumin

**1.** Preheat the oven to 350°F.

**2.** Combine the onion, lemon juice, and salt in a medium bowl and let sit while you prepare the other ingredients.

**3.** Roast the pepper on a baking sheet for 25 minutes, until the skin is blistered and slightly blackened. Let cool and then slip off the skin. Remove the stem with the majority of the seeds (some seeds can remain). Coarsely chop the pepper and add it to the onion mixture.

**4.** Add the tomatoes, cilantro, garlic, chile, and cumin, and mix well. Taste and adjust the seasonings. Allow the salsa to stand for at least 15 minutes before serving.

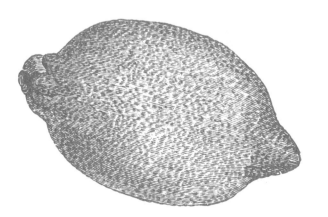

# Fresh Rainbow Salsa

**MAKES ABOUT 4 CUPS**

A rainbow array of height-of-the-season tomatoes makes an incomparably beautiful salsa. The precise amounts of tomatoes, tomatillos, and hot peppers can vary. Other produce can be added, such as cooked sweet corn or scallions. Try a combination of Aunt Ruby's German Green, Indian Moon, Limmony, Black Aisberg, and any of the red tomatoes, such as the Ponderosa and the Livingston varieties. Use the salsa as a dip or as a topping for tortillas or omelets.

½ cup diced onion

salt

½ pound (about 6) ripe tomatillos

2–2½ pounds fresh tomatoes, including cherry tomatoes, preferably heirloom varieties of various colors: red, pink, green, black, orange, and yellow

1 medium-hot chile, such as serrano or jalapeño, or ½ teaspoon crushed red pepper flakes

2 tablespoons chopped fresh cilantro

1 garlic clove, peeled and minced

1. Mix the onion with 1 teaspoon salt in a small bowl and let sit while you prepare the other ingredients.

2. If the tomatillos are truly ripe and yellow-green, they can be used raw. Simply remove their papery covering, and then chop them into small pieces. Typically, however, they are sold green and unripe. In that case, preheat the oven to 350°F. Place the peeled tomatillos on a baking sheet and bake for 15 minutes. Let them cool and then chop them into pieces.

3. Dice all the larger tomatoes. Cut small cherry tomatoes in half and large ones into 4 to 8 pieces. Leave very small tomatoes whole. Combine all the tomatoes and the diced tomatillos in a mixing bowl. If you do not want a hot salsa, carefully remove the seeds and the membranes from the chile pepper, and then mince the flesh. (If you like hot spices, leave in some of the seeds, use hotter peppers, or add an additional one.) Gently stir in the cilantro, garlic, and salted onion. Add more salt to taste.

4. Let sit for 20 minutes before serving. The salsa is best on the day it is made, but it will keep refrigerated for about one week.

# Tomato and Corn Salsa

**MAKES 4–5 CUPS**

Two great seasonal vegetables, sweet corn and tomatoes, both of Mesoamerican origin, are combined in this salsa. If you can find an old type of sweet corn, such as Golden Bantam, try it for added corn flavor. Then use some meaty heirloom tomatoes, such as Brandywine or Ponderosa. The olives make a delightful contrast to the tartness of the tomatoes and lime, while the corn adds splashes of sweetness and texture. Serve with chips, on tacos, or on tortillas — it won't hang around the kitchen long before being consumed.

kernels from 2 ears of corn

12 kalamata or other black olives, pitted

2 pounds (about 5 medium-large) tomatoes, peeled, seeded, and diced

1 medium green bell pepper, cored and diced

1 jalapeño pepper, stemmed, seeded, and finely diced

1 small red onion, cut into ¼-inch dice

grated zest of 1 small lime

2 tablespoons chopped fresh cilantro, plus a few sprigs for garnish

1 teaspoon chopped fresh thyme

salt and freshly ground black pepper

**1.** Bring a large pot of water to a boil. Drop in the corn and cook for 2 to 4 minutes, until the kernels are tender when you pierce them with a knifepoint. Remove the corn from the water with tongs and drop into a bowl of cold water to stop the cooking process. When the ears are cool enough to handle, scrape off the kernels into a medium serving bowl.

**2.** Coarsely chop half of the olives and add them to the corn. Add the tomatoes, bell pepper, jalapeño, onion, lime zest, cilantro, and thyme. Season with salt and pepper to taste. Gently but thoroughly toss to combine.

**3.** Let the salsa stand in a cool place (but not the refrigerator) for at least 30 minutes so the flavors can blend.

**4.** To serve, gently toss again. Garnish with the remaining whole olives and the cilantro sprigs.

# Pipirrana

MAKES 3–4 CUPS

Pipirrana, a fresh tomato salsa, comes from Spain. It includes either hard-cooked eggs or avocados, as in this version. In Mediterranean countries a chunky dip such as this is often referred to as a salad, though it is essentially a fresh tomato salsa. Pipirrana is a perfect accompaniment for cold cooked seafood or fish. Or you can simply treat it like familiar Southwestern salsas and scoop it up with tortilla chips.

2 large tomatoes, seeded and chopped

3 scallions, white and tender green parts, chopped

1 small green bell pepper, cored and cut into ½-inch dice

1 garlic clove, peeled and finely chopped

2 medium Hass avocados

juice of ½ lemon

1 tablespoon extra-virgin olive oil

1–2 teaspoons sherry vinegar or red wine vinegar

salt

**1.** Combine the tomatoes, scallions, bell pepper, and garlic on a cutting board, and chop them together briefly to mix. Make sure, however, not to turn the mixture into a mush: the pieces of each vegetable should remain identifiable. Transfer to a medium bowl.

**2.** Cut both avocados in half and remove the pits and skin. Cut the avocado into ½-inch pieces. Toss gently with the lemon juice, and then fold the avocado into the tomato mixture.

**3.** In a cup or small bowl, stir the oil and 1 teaspoon of the vinegar together with ½ teaspoon salt. Pour over the tomato mixture and stir gently to combine. Taste for seasoning. Sprinkle on some extra salt and more vinegar if desired.

**4.** Serve immediately.

# Romesco

MAKES ABOUT 1½ CUPS

Romesco is a classic sauce of Catalonia, a northern province of Spain. There dry hills are home to orchards of almond and hazelnuts, nuts that have been used in Catalonian sauces for hundreds of years. In addition, the sauce has tomatoes, garlic, and the local ñora peppers. In this country, a not-too-hot pepper, such as poblano, can take their place. The smoky Spanish paprika, called *pimenton*, also adds an authentic flavor note. Traditionally, romesco would be made by pounding the ingredients in a mortar; today a food processor or blender can do the job. Serve this as the Catalonians do, as a dip with grilled vegetables, especially leeks, or with fish.

¼ cup extra-virgin olive oil

3 large garlic cloves, peeled and halved

1 poblano pepper, seeded and cut into several pieces

½ cup skinned hazelnuts or additional almonds (see Note)

¼ cup blanched slivered almonds

1 slice white bread

4 medium-size ripe tomatoes, peeled and seeded

3–4 teaspoons Spanish paprika

sea salt

1–2 tablespoons red or white wine vinegar

**1.** Heat the oil in a medium skillet over medium heat. Add the garlic, lower the heat, and cook gently for about 2 minutes, until the garlic is golden and somewhat softened. (Take care it does not burn to a dark brown; if it does, it will taste acrid and both the garlic and the oil must be discarded.) Remove the garlic with a slotted spoon and set it aside on a large plate.

**2.** Add the pepper to the oil in the skillet and cook gently for 2 to 3 minutes. Remove and set aside with the garlic.

**3.** Add the hazelnuts and almonds to the skillet, raise the heat slightly, and cook the nuts for 1 to 2 minutes, until they are golden and smell toasty. Add them to the other ingredients on the plate.

**4.** Fry the bread in the oil for 1 to 2 minutes, turning once, until it is golden. Add to the other ingredients.

**5.** When the nuts have cooled, put them into a food processor and process until they resemble fine crumbs. Add half of the pepper and the garlic and half of the tomatoes, and then process again. Next add the bread, 2 teaspoons of paprika, and 1 teaspoon of salt; process again. Add the rest of the tomatoes and 1 tablespoon of the vinegar and process once more.

**6.** Taste the sauce. It should be mildly hot and taste richly of the paprika, peppers, nuts, and tomatoes. If necessary, add some or all of the remaining paprika and the rest of the pepper to achieve a good balance. You can also add the remaining vinegar if you want additional tartness, and more salt to taste. Serve at room temperature. Leftovers can be stored in a covered jar in the refrigerator for up to 3 days.

NOTE: To skin hazelnuts, place them in a single layer on a shallow pan and toast at 325°F for 10 to 12 minutes, or until the skins are very dark brown. Slide the hot nuts into a clean cloth towel, fold the towel over, and briskly rub the nuts. Most of the skins will loosen and flake off. Scrape off any remaining bits with a knife.

MAULE'S FIELD SEEDS.

# East India Tomato Sauce

## MAKES 2 CUPS

The author of *Murrey's Salads and Sauces,* published in 1884, writes that he found the recipe for this sauce in a book called *Domestic Economy of India* and that the sauce is excellent. The recipe calls for 15 cloves of garlic, but the author advises, "To please an American palate use half the quantity." The other ingredients are 36 tomatoes, 3 ounces of ground ginger, 2 ounces of salt, ¼ ounce of red pepper, and 2 wineglasses of tarragon vinegar. The following recipe is closely based on these directions and makes a fine hot sauce. Use it to marinate chicken or beef for barbecues or as a steak sauce, or add a tablespoonful or so to chili, stews, and any sauce in which you'd like a bit of heat.

3 pounds (15–18 large) plum tomatoes, peeled

1 tablespoon salt

10 garlic cloves (or more to taste), peeled and sliced

4 tablespoons ground ginger

1 tablespoon sugar

¼– ½ teaspoon cayenne pepper

½ cup tarragon vinegar, red wine vinegar, or cider vinegar

**1.** Slice the tomatoes in half horizontally. Seed the tomatoes by squeezing them or spooning out the seeds and juice, catching the seeds and juice in a sieve set over a bowl. Discard the seeds in the sieve and reserve the juice. Coarsely chop the tomatoes.

**2.** Combine the tomatoes and salt in a large skillet. Strain in about 1 cup of juice from the bowl. Cover the skillet and simmer over medium heat for 5 minutes.

**3.** Add the garlic to the tomatoes and cook over medium-high heat for 10 to 15 minutes, until about half the liquid has bubbled away. Stir in the ginger, sugar, and cayenne. Cook for 1 minute longer.

**4.** Purée the mixture in a food processor or blender, or pass it through a food mill or sieve.

**5.** Return the purée to the pan and stir in the vinegar. Bring to a boil again and cook over medium heat until the mixture is as thick as barbecue or steak sauce, about 10 minutes.

**6.** Serve warm or at room temperature. Store for up to 5 days in the refrigerator.

# Alan Kapuler
## PEACE SEEDS, *Corvallis, Oregon*

D r. Alan Kapuler is what you might call a maverick plant genius. He trained as a molecular biologist, studying DNA, viruses, and nucleotides, with prestigious stints at Rockefeller University and the University of Connecticut. One day he realized that the lab was too confining for him and, like many influenced by the 1960s, he "dropped out."

Traveling cross-country, he often ate meals consisting of French fries and ketchup, the only food available to vegetarians on the road in those days. He knew that the French fries didn't have much nutrition, but he started wondering about ketchup and tomatoes. That got him started on a lifelong study of food plants, nutrition, breeding, and the interrelationships between plants. He landed in Oregon and became an organic gardener.

Alan sought out open-pollinated and heirloom tomatoes to grow. Seeds were hard to find, but he managed to assemble a collection of 120 varieties. No longer having a lab at his disposal, he had to do his own testing. He found that they were full of important amino acids. Eventually, Alan went on to test hundreds of other varieties of vegetables in a professional lab. He published the results in the first five issues of *Peace Seeds Research Journal.* His work has implications for developing new medicines.

In 1973, he started Peace Seeds, a mail-order seed company, originally calling it Stonebroke Hippy Seeds. He helped draft the Oregon Tilth regulations for organic growers. When the Seed Savers Exchange began, Alan reintroduced the Brandywine tomato, among dozens of other varieties, to the commercial world. Alan is perhaps most well known for the development of his Peacevine cherry tomato. He believes in having gardens and farms that are a mix of many kinds of plants and crops. Under these conditions he always sees good harvests, little disease, and few pests. Alan does not believe in patents, or manipulating genes in the lab, or ownership of any form of living organism. He decries the current trends of genetic engineering because the scientists have too little understanding of what they are doing or what the long-term effects may be, and because the driving force behind genetic engineering is corporate profit.

# Tomato Marmalade

MAKES ABOUT 4 CUPS

This is definitely not a marmalade for your breakfast toast. "I love the sweet, sour, and spicy flavors with seafood and poultry," writes John Besh, executive chef at August's in New Orleans, where he creates dishes that marry inspirations from Louisiana with those of his training in France, in Germany, and at the Culinary Institute of America. It works particularly well as an accompaniment to oily fish, such as mackerel and salmon, and on pork, ham, or duck.

2 cups granulated white or organic evaporated cane sugar

3 cups red wine vinegar

20 tomatoes, peeled, seeded, and diced

4–8 jalapeño peppers, seeded and finely diced

1 tablespoon cumin seed

20 black peppercorns

zest and juice of 2 oranges

zest and juice of 2 lemons

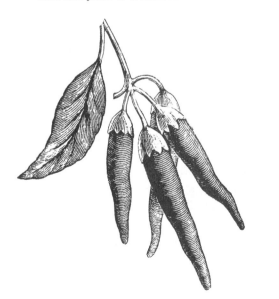

**1.** Combine the sugar and vinegar in a large saucepan and simmer over medium heat for 5 to 10 minutes, until the mixture reaches a syrup consistency.

**2.** Stir in the tomatoes, jalapeños, cumin seed, peppercorns, orange and lemon zest, and orange and lemon juices. Cook over low heat, stirring frequently, until the marmalade reaches a thick consistency, 20 to 25 minutes, depending on the juiciness of the tomatoes.

**3.** Pour into a jar or other container and store in the refrigerator. Serve cold.

# Tomato Ginger Vinaigrette

**SERVES 4–6**

Gary Danko, owner-chef of Gary Danko in San Francisco, shared this recipe with me. He loves using fresh local ingredients and mixing French and Asian themes, as this brightly flavored vinaigrette illustrates. Serve it over salads or cold poached salmon.

¼ cup minced fresh ginger

½ cup extra-virgin olive oil

1–2 tablespoons apple cider vinegar

1–2 tablespoons lemon or lime juice

1 tablespoon capers

½ cup peeled, seeded, and diced firm tomatoes

¼ teaspoon salt

1. Whisk the ginger, oil, 1 tablespoon of the vinegar, and 1 tablespoon of the lemon juice in a medium bowl for 1 to 2 minutes, until thoroughly blended. Gently stir in the capers, tomato, and salt.

2. Taste and add more vinegar, lemon juice, or salt if necessary. Serve immediately.

# Metro Bis Tomato Salad Dressing

**MAKES 2 CUPS**

Chris Prosperi, owner-chef at Metro Bis in Simsbury, Connecticut, created this all-purpose salad dressing for use on greens. He also uses it for a pasta salad (page 106) and a couscous salad (page 103).

1 cup tomato juice (page 235)

¼ cup red wine vinegar

1 small red onion, chopped (about ½ cup)

1 tablespoon Dijon mustard

1–2 teaspoons sugar

½ cup extra-virgin olive oil

salt and freshly ground black pepper

1. Combine the tomato juice, vinegar, onion, mustard, 1 teaspoon of the sugar, and the oil in a blender or food processor. Add salt and pepper to taste. Blend for 1 minute to mix well.

2. Taste and add additional sugar or more salt and pepper if needed. Process until combined, about 15 seconds. Serve immediately. Store leftovers in a covered jar in the refrigerator for up to 2 weeks.

# Seafood Cocktail Sauce

MAKES ABOUT 1¼ CUPS

Homemade cocktail sauce is far superior to cocktail sauces made from ketchup, which are usually too sweet. It's easy to make this fresh and vibrant sauce for serving with shrimp and other seafood. Homegrown tomatoes add such a bright flavor that you may never accept commercial seafood sauces again. For extra strength, make your own horseradish from a fresh root.

2 cups diced fresh tomatoes

½ cup finely chopped shallots or red onion

¼ cup tomato paste

½ cup prepared horseradish

1 teaspoon salt

2 teaspoons Worcestershire sauce

2 teaspoons white vinegar

1 tablespoon sugar

few drops of Tabasco (optional)

**1.** Combine the tomatoes, shallot, tomato paste, horseradish, and salt in a medium saucepan. Bring to a boil and cook over medium heat, stirring often, for 6 to 7 minutes, until the onion and tomato pieces are tender.

**2.** Stir in the Worcestershire, vinegar, and sugar. Cook for a minute longer, then take a teaspoonful, let it cool, and taste. Add more salt or sugar if you think it necessary, and a few drops of Tabasco if you want a fiery taste. The sauce at this point is quite chunky. You can serve it this way or, if you prefer it smoother, pour it into a blender or food processor and pulse a few times until it is the consistency you like.

**3.** Serve at room temperature or chill in the refrigerator for at least an hour and serve cold. Keep any leftovers covered in the refrigerator for up to 1 week.

# A BRIEF HISTORY OF TOMATOES IN THE NEW WORLD

Tenochtitlán (Mexico City) was the ancient imperial capital of the Aztecs, a city renowned for its beauty and architecture. In the nearby mountain valleys and slopes, farmers grew a rich variety of foods — many kinds of chiles, corn, beans, squashes, tomatillos, and amaranth. These were brought to the great city as a tribute to the king and to feed the growing urban population. This was one of the cradles of New World agriculture and civilization. Tomatoes were "tamed" near here, a significant New World contribution to the history of food development, which also includes plants as diverse as corn, potatoes, manioc (tapioca), cacao (chocolate), avocados, bananas, sweet potatoes, and peanuts.

Perhaps the first written record of tomatoes in Spanish comes from Bernard Díaz del Castillo, who was in Mexico at the time of the conquest in 1519. He says the Indians "had cooking pots ready with chili peppers, tomatoes, and salt," and further says that the Aztecs ate the limbs of their sacrificed people with a sauce made with chili peppers, tomatoes, wild onions, and salt. Yummy. You might call this the first written salsa recipe.

Most of the written record of tomatoes in Mexico does not begin until many years after the conquest of Mexico. Francisco Hernandez, commissioned by the king of Spain to catalog plants in the 1570s, first mentions *tomatl* — the word in the Aztec language, *Nahuatl*, meaning tomato — as well as the tomatillo. Hernandez gives a rough recipe for a dipping sauce from tomatoes mixed with chiles, which "stimulates the appetite" and is good with many other dishes.

Bernardino de Sahagún also wrote from Mexico in the sixteenth century. In his great work on Aztec life, *The General History of the Things of New Spain,* he writes about many types of tomatoes being sold in the marketplace, including large and small, green, sweet tomatoes, nipple-shaped tomatoes, and "yellow, very yellow, quite yellow, red, very red, quite ruddy, bright red, reddish, rosy dawn colored" tomatoes.

# Smoky Tomato Butter

### MAKES ABOUT 1½ CUPS

The Spanish paprika used in this recipe tastes smoky because the peppers are charred before they are ground into powder. Chris Douglass of Ashmont Grill in Boston teams it with charred tomatoes and garlic and whips them into butter, adding the sharp tang of lime to make a smoky rich topping for grilled fish. Any type of plum tomato will work in this dish, but Black Pear adds a special rich flavor. Or try Orange Banana for color.

1 pound (5–6 large) ripe plum tomatoes

3 large garlic cloves, unpeeled

1½ tablespoons extra-virgin olive oil

4 scallions, white and tender green parts, finely sliced; reserve the greens for garnish

1 cup (2 sticks) unsalted butter, at room temperature

juice of 1 lime

¼–½ teaspoon Spanish paprika (called *de la vera pimenton*)

sea salt

1. Preheat the oven to 475°F.

2. Place the tomatoes in a single layer in a baking dish and roast, turning them occasionally until the skins are blackened and the flesh is soft, 20 to 25 minutes. Let cool, and then peel and discard the blackened skins. Halve the tomatoes; scoop out and discard the seeds.

3. Meanwhile, toast the garlic cloves in a dry skillet over medium-high heat for 10 to 15 minutes, until the skins are blackened. Let cool, then peel and discard the skin.

4. Heat the oil in a medium saucepan over medium heat. Stir in the scallions and cook gently for about 4 minutes, until they are tender and translucent. Add the tomatoes and garlic and cook over high heat for 3 to 5 minutes, until any excess juices have simmered off and the mixture looks thick. Stir often to prevent scorching. Cool.

5. Transfer the tomato mixture to a food processor. Add 1 stick of the butter, the lime juice, ¼ teaspoon paprika, and ½ teaspoon sea salt. Process briefly to combine, and then add the remaining 1 stick butter and process until you have a smooth mixture. Taste and add additional paprika and salt if necessary.

6. Chill in the refrigerator for 30 minutes, or until the butter mixture is firm enough to handle.

CHAPTER THREE

# STARTERS

# Catalan Tomato Toasts

SERVES 6

When you have large super-juicy tomatoes and a terrific loaf of bread, consider making this Spanish favorite, known in its Catalonian home as *pan amb tomaquet*. It is often served as a midmorning snack or to start off the long late lunch that precedes the siesta. Of course, it is great as an appetizer or first course for any Mediterranean meal, and its preparation is so simple.

6 large slices country-style French or Italian-style bread or sourdough bread

3 large ripe juicy tomatoes

mild extra-virgin olive oil

6–12 slices cured serrano ham or prosciutto

1 (2-ounce) can anchovy fillets, packed in oil, drained, and soaked in water for 1 hour, then patted dry, or 1–2 (3.75-ounce) cans sardines, packed in olive oil, drained

1. Grill the bread in a lightly oiled cast-iron skillet over a wood-burning fire (if possible) or toast very lightly over medium-high heat.

2. Cut the tomatoes in thick slices and place them in a single layer on a large platter. Place the bread on top, pressing it down a little with your palms. Let it rest for 1 to 2 hours.

3. To serve, remove the bread from the tomatoes. It should have soaked up a lot of their juice. If any juice remains, drizzle it over the bread. Also drizzle very lightly with oil; serve the bread topped with the ham and anchovies. (Alternatively, you can omit the ham and/or anchovies and simply sprinkle the bread with sea salt and eat it with tomatoes.)

HUBBARD CURLED LEAF TOMATO

# Crostini with Tomatoes, Avocado, and Preserved Lemons

SERVES 4–6

Tomatoes and preserved lemons are a uniquely Moroccan combination. Here they are paired with cubes of avocado to make a flavorful topping for crostini. The same mixture can also be served as a salad on lettuce leaves. This recipe comes from Kitty Morse, who grew up in Morocco, where preserved lemons are chopped and added to many dishes, providing a sharp saltiness much appreciated in North African cooking. Look for jars of preserved lemons in gourmet food shops and stores specializing in Middle Eastern and Mediterranean ingredients. Kitty Morse has written many books, including *Cooking at the Kasbah: Recipes from My Moroccan Kitchen*.

3 large ripe tomatoes, peeled, seeded, and coarsely cubed

1 ripe avocado, pitted, peeled, and diced

2 teaspoons diced preserved lemon rind

¼ teaspoon salt

¼ cup extra-virgin olive oil

1 garlic clove, peeled and minced

1 baguette

1. Preheat the oven to 350°F.

2. Combine the tomatoes with the avocado, lemon rind, and salt. Set aside.

3. Combine the oil and garlic in a small bowl. Slice the baguette on a diagonal, and brush each piece with some of the oil mixture. Arrange the slices on a baking sheet and toast in the oven until lightly browned, 5 to 6 minutes on each side.

4. Remove the toasted bread from the oven and top each slice with a spoonful of the tomato mixture. Serve immediately.

# Tomato Antipasto Platter

An antipasto platter may contain many different ingredients. Feel free to add or subtract items as you like. This one serves as a healthful start to a meal or can stand on its own for a late-afternoon interlude with a glass of wine.

10 loosely packed cups (1-pound bag) spinach, washed but not dried, coarse stems removed

salt and freshly ground black pepper

2 tablespoons slivered almonds

4 tablespoons extra-virgin olive oil

1 garlic clove, peeled and thinly sliced

3 ripe firm tomatoes, preferably of different colors

4–6 basil leaves

2 cups Caponata (page 54)

1½ cups Greek Beans with Tomatoes (page 210)

2 (3½-ounce) cans sardines in olive oil, or 1 (7-ounce) can Italian tuna in olive oil, or 6 ounces thinly sliced Italian preserved meat, such as salami or cappacola

1 lemon, cut into 6 wedges

**1.** Put the spinach, with water clinging to the leaves, in a medium saucepan. Season lightly with salt and pepper, cover the pan, and cook over medium heat for 2 to 3 minutes, stirring once or twice, until all the leaves are limp. Drain. When cool enough to handle, squeeze out as much liquid as possible. Set aside.

**2.** Spread the almonds in a skillet set over medium heat. Stir until they are golden, 2 to 3 minutes. Watch carefully and remove the almonds quickly from the pan to make sure they don't burn. Set aside.

**3.** Heat 3 tablespoons of the oil in the same skillet over medium heat. Stir in the garlic, and then add the spinach, tossing it to separate the leaves. Season with salt and pepper to taste and cook for 2 minutes, until the spinach is heated through, stirring all the time.

**4.** Just before serving, slice the tomatoes. Season with salt and pepper and drizzle with the remaining tablespoon of oil. Place the tomato slices in the center of a large serving platter and garnish with the basil leaves. Arrange the spinach, caponata, beans, and sardines in piles around the outside of the platter. Squeeze one of the lemon wedges over the spinach and another over the beans. Sprinkle the toasted almonds on the spinach. Add the remaining lemon wedges to the platter for squeezing onto the sardines or vegetables. Serve at room temperature.

# REYNOLDSBURG TOMATO FESTIVAL
## REYNOLDSBURG, OHIO

The Reynoldsburg Tomato Festival is one of the largest tomato events in the United States, drawing upwards of 35,000 attendees. It is a four-day event for the whole family, starting the Wednesday after Labor Day.

The activities at the festival include the Tomato Queen Pageant, the Little Princess Contest, the Senior King and Queen Contest, the Tallest Tomato Plant Contest (17½ feet was the record winner), the Largest Tomato Contest (the prize is $200 per pound), tomato exhibits, fresh tomato sales, and free tomato juice. Tomato juice is the official beverage of Ohio, as decreed by the state legislature.

Additionally, there are souvenirs, food, rides, a car cruise-in, a pooch parade, arts and crafts, free entertainment, and more. Foods include many

items made from tomatoes, including ketchup (of course), caramels, tomato-shaped buckeyes, tomato cake, and tomato jam.

The idea for the Tomato Festival originated with the dedication of the plaque by the Franklin Historical Society in front of the Reynoldsburg Municipal Building, recognizing Alexander W. Livingston for his contribution to the creation of the "modern" tomato and thereby declaring Reynoldsburg the birthplace of the distinctly American tomato.

Livingston was a plant and seed merchant famous for the introduction of many tomato varieties. He lived and worked in Reynoldsburg for much of his life. In 1870, he introduced Livingston's Paragon variety, significantly one of the first introductions of the smooth-skinned types. It was grown in the fields of his Livingston Buckeye Farms at 1792 Graham Road in Reynoldsburg.

In 1965, the first event celebrating the development of the tomato was called the Tomato Fair and was held in conjunction with the Jaycees' Fourth of July celebration and the Firemen's Jubilee. The fair was located in the Kroger's parking lot. In September 1966, the Tomato Fair was separated from the Fourth of July celebration and became the Tomato Festival.

# Caponata

SERVES 8

Caponata comes from Sicily. It is one of the many Mediterranean dishes that team tomato with eggplant. Its unique feature is the refreshing sweet-sour flavor that comes from including capers and raisins as well as vinegar and sugar. Generally, caponata is served cold or at room temperature, often as an hors d'oeuvre, but you can also serve it warm as a side dish, in which case it will serve four.

2 pounds (2 medium or 1 very large) eggplant, cut into 3- to 4-inch cubes

2 tablespoons salt

¼ cup golden raisins

3 celery stalks, halved lengthwise and cut into ½-inch pieces

6 tablespoons extra-virgin olive oil, or more if needed

1 large onion, coarsely chopped

2 cups chopped fresh or canned tomatoes (3–4 large fresh tomatoes)

12 green olives, pitted and halved

2 tablespoons capers

2 tablespoons red wine vinegar, or more to taste

1 tablespoon brown sugar, or more to taste

salt and freshly ground black pepper

1 tablespoon tomato paste (optional)

1. Put the eggplant in a colander, sprinkle with the salt, and toss to mix well. Allow to drain for 45 to 60 minutes, until the eggplant is beaded with juice. Rinse briefly and pat dry with a kitchen towel.

2. Cover the raisins with warm water and set aside to plump.

3. Bring a medium pan of water to a boil. Blanch the celery for 5 minutes, drain, rinse in cold water to stop the cooking, and drain again.

4. Heat 2 tablespoons of the oil in a large skillet over medium heat. Add the onions and sauté until soft but not browned, about 4 minutes. Stir in the celery, tomatoes, olives, capers, vinegar, and sugar. Drain the raisins and add them to the mixture. Cover the pan and simmer for 10 minutes, stirring occasionally.

**5.** Heat the remaining 4 tablespoons oil in a large skillet over medium-high heat. Add a single layer of eggplant cubes and fry until golden on all sides, 6 to 8 minutes. Transfer the cooked eggplant to the skillet with the tomato mixture. Continue to fry the eggplant until it is all cooked, working in batches and adding more oil if needed.

**6.** When all the eggplant has been added to the tomato mixture, stir well. Season to taste with salt and pepper, bring to a simmer, and cook for 20 minutes, until the eggplant is tender. The sauce should be thick with the tomato mixture enrobing the eggplant and celery. If it is too thin (which may occur with very juicy tomatoes), stir in the tomato paste and raise the heat to evaporate the excess liquid. Taste and adjust the seasoning. As well as salt and pepper, you may want to add a little more vinegar or sugar to achieve a pronounced sweet-sour tang.

**7.** Let cool to room temperature or chill in the refrigerator to serve cold.

# Tomato-Orange Cocktail

### SERVES 4–6

Tomatoes and oranges make a terrific flavor pair, teaming up in a drink that can start the day brilliantly or brighten an afternoon that is leaving you faded. Kellogg's Breakfast or Earl of Edgecombe makes a beautiful color combination, while any of the large bicolors add sweetness.

> 3 stems pineapple mint or another kind of mint, plus 4–6 mint sprigs for garnish
>
> 3 cups tomato juice (page 235)
>
> 1 cup freshly squeezed orange juice
>
> salt
>
> sugar

**1.** Bruise the mint by rolling it with a rolling pin to release the flavor. Put the stems into a tall pitcher and add the tomato juice and orange juice.

**2.** Stir and taste. Season lightly with salt and sugar. Serve over ice cubes or chill for an hour before pouring. Garnish the glasses with mint sprigs or float them on the juice in the pitcher.

# Herbed Goat Cheese
# Broiled in Tomato Sauce

SERVES 6–8

With islands of gold-topped cheese rising from a scarlet sea of tomatoes, this imaginative dish looks as beautiful as it tastes. It comes from Josie Le Balch, owner-chef of Josie in Santa Monica, California. If you prefer, you can use an herbed cream cheese rather than the herbed goat cheese. Including an orange tomato variety, such as Earl of Edgecombe, further enhances the attractiveness of this dish. Serve with plenty of crusty bread, lightly toasted, for spreading with the cheese and dipping into the sauce.

### Herbed Goat Cheese

1 (8-ounce) package cream cheese, softened

1 (8-ounce) log fresh goat cheese, such as Montrachet, softened

2 tablespoons heavy cream

2 tablespoons olive oil, plus more if needed

1 garlic clove, minced

1 tablespoon chopped fresh basil

salt

### Tomato Sauce

2 tablespoons olive oil

4 garlic cloves, peeled and chopped

2 small white onions, finely chopped

1 (28-ounce) can whole plum tomatoes, with juice

4 cups peeled, seeded, and chopped fresh tomatoes

8 basil leaves, torn

salt and freshly ground black pepper

1. Combine the cream cheese, goat cheese, cream, oil, garlic, basil, and salt to taste in a large bowl. Mix with an electric mixer until smooth, about 2 minutes. Add more oil if needed for a smooth consistency. Cover with plastic wrap and refrigerate while you prepare the sauce.

2. For the sauce, heat the oil in a large skillet over medium-high heat. Add the garlic and sauté for 1 to 2 minutes, until lightly golden. Stir in the onion and sauté for 4 to 5 minutes, until the onion is soft and translucent. Stir in the canned and fresh tomatoes and basil and simmer over medium heat for 5 minutes, until the tomatoes have softened. Mash the tomatoes with a fork or whisk and continue simmering over low heat for 25 to 30 minutes, until the mixture thickens into a sauce. Season with salt and pepper to taste. Let the sauce cool. (The sauce may be covered with plastic wrap and stored in the refrigerator for 3 days or in the freezer for up to 1 month.)

**3.** To prepare the dish, preheat the broiler for 10 minutes.

**4.** Pour the tomato sauce into a shallow ovenproof serving dish. Using a small ice cream scoop or two spoons, scoop the goat cheese into balls and arrange them on the tomato sauce. Slide the dish close to the broiler and broil for 6 to 8 minutes, until the top of the cheese has golden brown patches and the tomato sauce is hot and bubbly.

**5.** Serve hot or warm.

 # Guacamole

**MAKES 2 CUPS**

This guacamole follows the Mexican tradition of including little chunks of tomato and onion to add substance. As a nontraditional alternative to the salt and citrus juice, substitute 4 teaspoons of umeboshi paste (Japanese salt plum).

> 2 ripe Hass avocados, pitted and peeled
>
> 2 tablespoons diced onion
>
> 1 garlic clove, peeled and finely chopped
>
> 4 small sprigs cilantro, coarsely chopped
>
> 2 teaspoons lemon or lime juice
>
> sea salt
>
> 1 large or 2 medium tomatoes, diced

**1.** Mash the avocado in a small bowl with a fork or a potato masher until reduced to a lumpy paste.

**2.** Gently fold the onion, garlic, cilantro, lemon juice, and about ½ teaspoon salt into the avocado. Combine thoroughly.

**3.** Fold in the tomatoes, leaving some of them visible rather than burying them in the mixture. Taste and adjust the seasoning.

# Peter Hoffman
## SAVOY RESTAURANT, *New York City*

The best way to be good to yourself and truly indulgent is to eat the freshest and most local food," according to Peter Hoffman, chef and co-owner with his wife, Susan Rosenfeld, of Savoy in Manhattan's SoHo. Peter combines the flavors and cuisines of the Mediterranean with local and seasonal ingredients, simply and unpretentiously prepared. This approach quickly won favor from the public and Savoy has a loyal following.

Peter opened Savoy in 1990. The restaurant is modest in size, seating 65. Café-style food featuring smaller plates is available, from noon to midnight. Full lunches and dinners are served, including a chef's tasting menu, utilizing fresh farmers' market ingredients. "What we buy, and where it comes from, is important, because then we support the right people, people who are making a difference in our lives and for the ecosystem." A complete renovation in 2002 created more warmth and natural light in the restaurant.

Peter's cooking style incorporates his multiple interests in cultural and historic traditions and the origins of food. His understanding of the regional cuisines of Europe comes from time spent working in the kitchens of Tuscany and the Languedoc, visiting the local markets on bicycle, and studying with Madeline Kamman, one of the greatest instructors of French cuisine.

Peter doesn't just stay in the kitchen, either. He was on the advisory board of the New York City Greenmarkets for 15 years. In 1995, he joined the fledgling Chefs Collaborative and two years later its board of directors. Concerned with dwindling fish populations, he organized and produced the collaborative's *Seafood Solutions* guide to sustainable fish procurement.

Peter decries modern changes that allow us to have the artificial luxury of consuming out-of-season foods throughout the year, because it puts us out of touch with our environment and ourselves. He is adamant that we should be eating *cucina povera*, using seasonal and local foods. "These are the best flavors you can savor anywhere."

Tomato, Watermelon, and Ricotta Salata Salad, *p. 91*

Insalata Caprese Verdura Style, *p. 98*

Tomato Tarts, *p. 108*

Tomato Basil Quiche, *p. 111*

# Spiced Tomato and Chickpea Dip

## MAKES ABOUT 4 CUPS

Chickpeas give this dip a texture like hummus, but with tomatoes and spices it sings in a higher key. Serve with pita bread, tortilla chips, or vegetable sticks. It is also good on bagels.

3 cups drained cooked or canned chickpeas

1¼ cups tomato purée (page 234)

1 small onion, coarsely chopped

3 garlic cloves, peeled

3 tablespoons extra-virgin olive oil

2 tablespoons lemon juice

2 teaspoons dried oregano

1 teaspoon ground coriander

1 teaspoon ground cumin

1 teaspoon ground ginger

1 teaspoon salt

¼ teaspoon cayenne pepper

1 medium-large ripe but firm tomato, peeled, seeded, and cut into small dice

1 tablespoon finely chopped parsley or chives

**1.** Combine the chickpeas, tomato purée, onion, garlic, oil, lemon juice, oregano, coriander, cumin, ginger, salt, and cayenne in a food processor and process for a few seconds until well blended.

**2.** Taste and adjust the seasoning by adding more salt or cayenne if you want a spicier mix. Process again until you have a purée.

**3.** To serve, garnish the dip with tomato and parsley.

### AUNT RUBY'S GERMAN GREEN

Seed saver Bill Minkey has a special attachment to this popular variety — he introduced it to the public and named it. A niece of Ruby Arnold from whom he got some of the seed lived in his hometown. He decided to add Aunt Ruby's to the name German Green and called Ruby. She said she thought it had a nice ring to it.

# Tomato Aspic

Traditionally, aspics are cold meat or fish dishes in a jelly made from bones and aromatic herbs. From scratch, they take hours of work; hence their luxury status. When powdered gelatin came along in the early twentieth century, aspic-style dishes suddenly became so easy that cooks ushered in the era of the dreaded gelatin salad by jellying anything they could lay their hands on. Tomato aspics belong to this period, but unlike many jellied salads, they taste delicious, especially at the start of a summer meal.

The only complicated part of this recipe is choosing the mold to use to form the aspic. If you want to serve cubes of tomato aspic in glass bowls for a look as cool as the taste, then simply chill the aspic in a rectangular or square pan and cut into cubes. Alternatively, you can mold the aspic in custard cups or other small molds and serve on individual salad plates, surrounded by sliced yellow and orange tomatoes. Or, if you happen to have copper gelatin molds on hand, choose any form you like. The recipe makes 2¼ cups of liquid.

2½ cups tomato juice (page 235), plus more if needed

6 basil leaves

1 small onion, peeled and quartered

1 large garlic clove, peeled and smashed

1 parsley sprig

leafy part of 1 celery stalk

½ teaspoon salt, or more to taste

1 packet unflavored gelatin

¼ cup cold water

½ teaspoon sugar (optional)

2–3 drops Tabasco (optional)

1. Combine the tomato juice, basil, onion, garlic, parsley, celery, and salt in a medium saucepan. Bring to a simmer over medium-low heat and cook gently for 10 to 15 minutes. Strain and discard the herbs and vegetables. Measure the strained juice. You should have 2 cups. Discard any additional; if necessary, bring the quantity up to 2 cups with additional juice.

2. While the tomato juice mixture is simmering, stir the gelatin into the water and let stand for 10 minutes to soften.

3. Stir the softened gelatin into the warm tomato juice mixture. Return the juice to medium heat and simmer for 1 minute longer,

stirring to make sure the gelatin is entirely dissolved. Taste for seasoning and add more salt to taste. Add sugar and Tabasco at this time if you think they will improve the flavor.

**4.** Rinse your aspic molds with cold water and leave damp (this helps free the aspic at serving time). Pour the warm mixture into the molds. Cover with plastic wrap and refrigerate for at least 4 hours before serving. The molds can be kept in the refrigerator for up to 3 days.

**5.** To unmold, fill a bowl slightly larger than the mold with hot water. Dip the outside of the mold into the water, taking care not to let water slosh onto the aspic. Leave the mold in the water for 30 to 45 seconds. Place a plate or serving dish on top of the mold and invert. Tap the bottom of the mold to help release the aspic. If it does not unmold, return it to the hot water for 20 to 30 seconds and repeat. Serve immediately.

# Bloody Bull

### SERVES 1

Odd as it sounds, this is a refreshing drink, best with a bitter India Pale Ale but also good with lager-style beers.

> 1 (12-ounce) bottle India Pale Ale (IPA), lager, or other beer
>
> ½ cup tomato juice (page 235)

**1.** Pour the beer into a tall glass, and while it is still frothing, pour in the tomato juice. Stir briefly and drink.

 # Spicy Tomato Cocktail

MAKES 2½–3 QUARTS

Here's a tomato drink that captures the flavors of the summer garden. It makes a great late-afternoon summer drink, perfect with hors d'oeuvres, crab, or lobster salad. Spiking it with vodka doesn't hurt a bit.

6 pounds very ripe tomatoes, coarsely chopped

3 celery stalks, leafy tops left whole, stems chopped

1 medium onion, peeled and sliced

1 medium green bell pepper, seeded and sliced

1 medium red bell pepper, seeded and sliced

1 garlic clove, peeled and crushed

1 jalapeño or other small hot pepper, seeded

2 teaspoons salt, or more to taste

½ teaspoon ground coriander

½ teaspoon black or white peppercorns

1 bay leaf

1 tablespoon sugar, or more to taste

2–4 tablespoons lemon juice, or more to taste

Tabasco or other hot sauce (optional)

**1.** Combine the tomatoes, celery, including the leafy tops, onion, green pepper, red pepper, garlic, jalapeño, 2 teaspoons of salt, coriander, peppercorns, and bay leaf in a large saucepan. Warm over low heat until the juice is running, about 5 minutes. Raise the heat and bring the mixture to a simmer. Simmer until all the vegetables are very soft, about 30 minutes.

**2.** Cool the mixture to lukewarm. Pass through a food mill fitted with the finest blade to remove the tomato seeds and other coarse material. Taste and add sugar and lemon juice to adjust the flavor. If desired, add a few drops of Tabasco.

**3.** Store in the refrigerator and use within 2 weeks. For longer storage, reheat the tomato juice until almost boiling. Then pour into either pint or quart canning jars, leaving ½ inch headspace. Seal and process for 40 minutes (or longer at altitudes above sea level) in a boiling-water bath, following directions on page 231.

# Stuffed Mussels with Tomatoes and Almonds

SERVES 6

Mussel shells make perfect minidishes to hold a mussel dressed with a tasty stuffing. Mussels like this could appear in cafés anywhere along the Mediterranean and in Turkey. Red tomatoes combine well with mussels, and almost any type will do. Stupice, Paragon, Livingston's Favorite, and Livingston's Beauty are all types I have enjoyed with mussels.

30 large mussels

freshly ground black pepper

1 cup chopped fresh or canned tomatoes

1 tablespoon chopped fresh parsley

¾ teaspoon herbes de Provence or dried oregano

1 garlic clove, peeled and finely chopped

salt

½ cup flaked almonds

⅓ cup breadcrumbs made from day-old bread

1–2 tablespoons extra-virgin olive oil

1. Preheat the oven to 350°F. Grease a shallow baking dish just big enough to hold the mussels in a single layer.

2. Wash the mussels in cold water, cutting off any stringy beards dangling from the shells. Mussels gape from time to time, but if they fail to close after being handled or tapped on a counter, discard them. Also discard those with broken shells. Put the cleaned mussels into a saucepan with water. Cover and bring to a gentle boil. Simmer for 3 to 5 minutes, or until the mussels have opened.

3. Drain and let the mussels cool until they are comfortable to handle. Break off and discard one shell from each. Loosen each mussel from the membrane that holds it in place, but leave it in its half shell. Arrange the shells open side up in a single layer in the baking dish. Grind the pepper over them.

4. Mix the tomatoes, parsley, herbes de Provence, and garlic in a small bowl. Season to taste with salt. Spoon a little of this mixture over each mussel.

5. In another small bowl, mix the almonds and breadcrumbs. Cover the mussels with this mixture. Drizzle with oil.

6. Bake for 8 to 10 minutes, until the almonds are toasted and golden. Serve hot.

# Salt Cod Ceviche
# with Tomatoes and Arugula

### SERVES 6

This recipe, a riff on the theme of the Mexican ceviche of fish or seafood "cooked" in lime juice, comes from Peter Hoffman, owner-chef of the Savoy Restaurant in New York. Salt cod is not traditional in ceviche, but it gives tremendous character to this dish. Use the thickest pieces of fish you can get, because the thin tail sections tend to be oversalted and never rehydrate quite as nicely as the main body of the fillets, though they can be used in a soup or stew.

**Ceviche**

1 pound salt cod, preferably thicker pieces from the center of the fillet

4 large heirloom tomatoes, such as Livingston's Beauty, Paragon, or Eva Purple Ball, seeded and cut into large dice

freshly ground black pepper

½ cup extra-virgin olive oil

¼ cup basil leaves, torn

few drops lemon juice (optional)

**Tomatoes and Arugula**

8 thick slices of country bread, toasted

3 large garlic cloves, peeled and halved

3–4 tablespoons extra-virgin olive oil

1 bunch arugula, washed and coarse stems removed

2 tablespoons vinaigrette or oil-and-vinegar salad dressing

**1.** Rinse the cod in cold water. Place it in a large pan or bowl and cover amply with cold water. Let soak for 36 to 72 hours, changing the water 2 or 3 times a day. The cod will gradually plump up and its texture will become similar to that of fresh fish, though somewhat firmer. The longer the fish remains in water, the less salty it will become. You can test the salinity level by tasting the water before you change it; the less salty the water, the less salty the fish. Once the cod is at the level of saltiness you desire, remove it from the water and use immediately or keep covered in the refrigerator for 1 to 2 days.

**2.** For the ceviche, scrape the fish with a spoon, separating the flesh from the fiber. This will give you pure muscle. Toss the fish in a medium bowl with the tomato. Marinate for 2 hours and then season with pepper and stir in the oil and basil. Add the lemon juice for an extra tang, if desired.

**3.** Rub both sides of the bread with the cut sides of the garlic. Arrange the slices on a baking sheet, drizzle one side of the bread with the oil, and then toast under the broiler until golden. Toss the arugula with the dressing. Serve as bruschetta with the cod on the toast and the arugula as garnish, or serve the ceviche with the dressed arugula as a salad, using the toast as croutons on the side.

# AMERICA'S LOVE AFFAIR WITH TOMATOES

If the preponderance of salsa, ketchup, and tomato sauce on store shelves is insufficient evidence of America's love affair with tomatoes, certainly statistics provide us with ample evidence.

Americans eat about 4.8 billion pounds of fresh tomatoes annually, or about 18 pounds per person. This does not include hothouse tomatoes grown and consumed within our borders, nor does it include the contributions of homegrown tomatoes. Roughly 27 million Americans, 25 percent of all households, have some type of vegetable garden, and of those, the majority grow tomatoes. In my experience, if people grow nothing else, they grow tomatoes. Often, even those who don't have a garden grow a few tomatoes in a pot or a planter. The real figure is probably closer to 22 pounds of fresh tomatoes consumed per person. About a third of the fresh tomatoes are imported.

In the United States, there are approximately 130,000 acres devoted to the outdoor cultivation of tomatoes, yielding $1.1 billion in annual sales.

The figures for processed tomatoes are even more amazing. There are about 300,000 acres under cultivation producing 23 billion pounds of tomatoes worth about $547 million. Processed tomatoes picked by machines are worth considerably less than fresh hand-harvested varieties; thus the huge discrepancy in annual sales. These production and sales figures do not include imported processed tomatoes, though statistically the United States is a net exporter. In total, the average American consumes 72 pounds of processed tomatoes each year, for a grand total of 90-plus pounds of tomatoes consumed annually. While tons of tomatoes are grown here, we are not the biggest producer of tomatoes. That distinction belongs to China.

# Scallops with Asian Noodle Salad and Tomato-Ginger Jam

### SERVES 4–6

This is a good dish when you want something requiring little last-minute attention. Both the noodles and the Tomato-Ginger Jam can be made ahead, and the scallops can be dusted in their spice mixture. When it's time to serve, the scallops need only 1 to 2 minutes' searing. Quickly settle them on the noodles and the dish is ready. The recipe comes from Susan Spicer, executive owner-chef of Bayona, a favorite restaurant in New Orleans.

**Tomato-Ginger Jam**

1 tablespoon peanut or canola oil

1 medium onion, finely chopped

1 tablespoon minced fresh ginger

1 teaspoon minced garlic

3 cups peeled, seeded, and diced ripe tomato

¼ cup rice wine vinegar, or more to taste

1 tablespoon honey, or more to taste

juice of 1 lime

1 teaspoon sambal oelek or other Asian chili paste

fresh mint, cilantro, or basil (optional)

**Asian Noodle Salad**

4 ounces linguine or Tung I brand noodles, cooked

1 tablespoon sesame oil

1 tablespoon canola oil

2 cups thinly sliced green or Napa cabbage

½ red onion, thinly sliced

2 scallions, white and tender green parts, thinly sliced

½ red bell pepper, thinly sliced

½ poblano pepper, thinly sliced

2 handfuls mizuna or mesclun (optional)

2 tablespoons soy sauce

**Scallops**

½ teaspoon freshly ground black pepper

½ teaspoon ground Szechuan peppercorns

½ teaspoon ground star anise

1 teaspoon salt

1 pound sea scallops

1 tablespoon canola oil

**1.** For the Tomato-Ginger Jam, heat the oil in a saucepan and sauté the onion, ginger, and garlic until wilted but not brown.

**2.** Stir in the tomato, vinegar, honey, lime juice, and sambal oelek and simmer for about 15 minutes, stirring from time to time, until thickened. Let cool and adjust seasoning with additional honey or vinegar to taste. Stir in the fresh mint, if desired. You can make this up to 2 days ahead and store covered in the refrigerator.

**3.** For the noodles, toss them with the sesame oil and set aside.

**4.** Heat the canola oil in a small skillet over medium-high heat and stir-fry the cabbage and red onion until they are slightly wilted but retain some crispness, 3 to 4 minutes.

**5.** Toss together the noodles, cabbage mixture, scallions, bell and poblano peppers, mizuna, if desired, and soy sauce. Divide among individual serving plates and set aside until the scallops are ready. (You can do this up to 1 hour ahead of time.)

**6.** For the scallops, combine the pepper, peppercorns, star anise, and salt. Pat the scallops dry with paper towels, then toss with the pepper mixture.

**7.** Heat the oil in a large skillet over high heat. Add the scallops a few at a time and sear for 1 minute on each side. They cook very quickly and carry over heat, so be sure you are ready to eat them almost as soon as you cook them. Serve immediately by placing the scallops on top of the prepared servings of Asian Noodle Salad. Offer the Tomato-Ginger Jam on the side.

# Heirloom Tomato Mosaic with Scallop Porcupines

### SERVES 6

Scallop mousse wrapped in julienned wonton skins sounds strange, and indeed magic happens when you drop them into hot oil: they sizzle into golden balls with quill-like strips of wonton pointing in all directions. That's why Daniel Wood, former chef at Stage Left in New Brunswick, New Jersey, and the conjurer who created this dramatic dish, calls them "porcupines." The fennel pollen that flavors both the scallop mousse and the accompanying sauce comes from wild fennel flowers gathered on the dry hillsides of Italy and California. Look for it at specialty food stores or check the Internet for mail-order suppliers.

## Fennel Pollen Butter Sauce

- 2 cups white wine
- 1 large shallot, minced
- 1 cup (2 sticks) unsalted butter, chilled, cut into 32 slices
- salt and white pepper
- ½ teaspoon fennel pollen

## Heirloom Tomato Mosaic

- 6 heirloom tomatoes of varied colors, peeled, halved, seeded, and cut into wedges or thick slices
- coarse sea salt and white pepper

## Scallop Porcupines

- 8 ounces scallops
- 2 egg whites
- ¼ cup heavy cream
- 1 teaspoon fennel pollen
- salt and white pepper
- 36 wonton skins, cut into ⅛-inch strips
- 4 cups (or more as needed) grapeseed oil or other oil for deep frying
- sprigs of opal basil and chervil for garnish

1. For the sauce, combine the wine and shallot in a heavy saucepan and bring to a boil over medium-high heat. Boil the mixture is reduced to 3 to 4 tablespoons. Whisk in 1 slice of butter. When it has blended in, add another slice and continue whisking in slices of butter 1 or 2 at a time until it is all incorporated. Season this

sauce with salt and pepper and stir in the fennel pollen. Keep warm.

**2.** For the tomato mosaic, cascade the multicolored tomato pieces onto one very large serving platter or arrange them in a 6-inch circle in the center of individual plates. Season the slices with sea salt and white pepper.

**3.** For the scallops, combine the scallops, egg whites, cream, and fennel pollen in a food processor. Season with salt and pepper. Purée for about 45 seconds, or until perfectly smooth.

**4.** Divide the wonton strips into two roughly equal portions. Working with one portion, make 12 piles on a chopping board. Top each pile with a heaping tablespoon of the scallop mixture. Cover this with strips from the second portion, making sure the scallop mixture is totally covered.

**5.** Meanwhile, in a deep fryer or tall saucepan, heat the oil to 400°F. Add 1 or 2 scallop porcupines (depending on the size of your pan; do not crowd). Fry until evenly browned, turning once in the process. The first side will take about 1 minute or a few seconds longer to brown and the second side will take about 30 seconds. In the process, some wonton strips may fall off; these can be lifted out of the pan with a slotted spatula, but be careful not to break off the wonton strips that flare off from the center of the scallop mixture, as these create the porcupine effect and are the charm of the dish. Drain

finished porcupines on paper towels and sprinkle with sea salt.

**6.** To serve on individual plates, drizzle sauce over each circle of tomatoes and place two warm scallop porcupines in the center. Garnish with an opal basil sprig and chervil. If you are using a single serving platter, drizzle the tomatoes with the butter sauce and arrange the scallop porcupines around them. Serve immediately.

# KETCHUP:
# AMERICA'S CONDIMENT OF CHOICE

Ketchup was probably made in the United States prior to 1800, but that early version would be unfamiliar to today's fast-food consumer. In the eighteenth century, ketchup was made with a number of different ingredients, including mushrooms, anchovies or nuts, vinegar, spices, and salt, but not tomatoes. The idea was to reproduce a soy-based fermented fish sauce that was well known in China and other parts of Asia.

In 1812, the first recipe for a tomato ketchup — called "Love Apple or Tomato Catchup" — was published by James Mease. Mease noted earlier, in 1804, that the French immigrants in Philadelphia made a "fine catsup from love apples." Mease's recipe departs from the earlier forms in that he uses tomatoes as the base and eliminates vinegar, fish, and many of the other ingredients. Six years later, another American recipe appeared. Soon tomato ketchup recipes appeared everywhere. Some used vinegar, some did not. A wide array of spices, including cloves, nutmeg, mace, mustard, black pepper, and cayenne, were utilized in fairly large quantities. By today's standards, the spices would have been overpowering. They helped preserve the ketchup and covered up the off tastes of spoiling foods.

Many of the old ketchup ingredients, such as anchovies, continued to be included while ketchup also continued in its forms without tomatoes at all. Recipes and the proliferation of homemade ketchup continued throughout the nineteenth century and into the twentieth.

Commercial bottling of ketchup began by 1830, gradually increasing in the 1850s and rapidly after the Civil War. Bottling technology had been developed in France and was known in the United States in 1812. Sugar began to be incorporated as a main ingredient before the Civil War. With sugar in the recipe, ketchup could remain on the shelf for a long time, since sugar acted as a preservative.

Heinz first sold its ketchup at the Philadelphia Centennial Exhibition in 1876. *The New York Tribune* reported in 1896 that ketchup had become the national condiment. At the turn of the century, there were more than 90 brands of ketchup available, and by 1915 at least 138 types. Some 20,000 acres of land were devoted to growing tomatoes for ketchup in 1907. The home production of ketchup, with its innumerable variations, unfortunately, became a thing of the past.

CHAPTER FOUR

# SOUPS

# Gazpacho

**SERVES 6**

Gazpacho, a chilled soup of fresh-from-the-garden tomatoes, is one of Spain's great culinary gifts to the world. The perfect pick-me-up on a hot, hot day, gazpacho may include other vegetables, which are sometimes served as relishes on the side. The use of bread is traditional, which makes this dish more of a meal. This version comes from Alice Waters, author of many cookbooks and internationally known chef and proprietor of Chez Panisse Restaurant and Café, where she has promoted her influential culinary philosophy of using only the freshest organic ingredients, picked in season.

## Soup

- 1 dried ancho chile, stemmed and seeded
- 1½ cups cubed crustless day-old bread
- 2–3 garlic cloves, peeled
- kosher salt
- 5 pounds vine-ripened tomatoes (preferably a mix of Cherokee Purple, Brandywine, and Early Girl), halved
- ⅓ cup extra-virgin olive oil

## Relish

- ½ pound vine-ripened tomatoes of mixed varieties and colors (preferably a mix of Green Zebra, Sun Gold, and Sweet 100 cherry tomatoes), quartered
- 1 small Mediterranean cucumber, peeled, seeded, and diced
- 1 gypsy pepper, cored, seeded, and diced
- ½ red onion, peeled and diced
- ½ bunch chervil, chopped
- ½ bunch basil, chopped
- 2 tablespoons red wine vinegar
- ¼ cup extra-virgin olive oil
- salt and freshly ground black pepper
- 6 slices Italian bread brushed with extra-virgin olive oil, toasted, and rubbed with 1 clove cut, peeled garlic

**1.** For the soup, soak the chile in a bowl of hot water for 30 minutes, until soft. Drain, peel, and crush it to a paste with a mortar and pestle; set aside.

**2.** Soak the bread in a medium bowl of cold water for 5 minutes, until soft. Drain and squeeze out excess water and set the bread aside. Use a mortar and pestle to crush the garlic and 2 tablespoons of salt to a paste. Add the soaked bread and grind until smooth; set aside.

**3.** Grate the cut side of the tomatoes on a box grater into a strainer set over a large bowl, straining out seeds and pressing through as much pulp as possible; discard the skins. Stir the reserved chile, the garlic-bread paste, and the oil into the tomato pulp, and season to taste with salt. Cover and refrigerate until chilled.

**4.** For the relish, combine the tomatoes, cucumber, gypsy pepper, onion, chervil, basil, vinegar, oil, and salt and pepper to taste in a medium bowl.

**5.** Divide the soup among 6 bowls; add a generous spoonful of relish and a slice of toast to each bowl.

## OF TOMATOES AND TURTLES

Botanists divide wild tomatoes into two groups: *L. esculentum* (the edible group) and *L. peruvianum.* Most of the tomatoes in the *peruvianum* group are green, barely look like tomatoes, and do not readily crossbreed with the common tomato. A notable exception is *L. cheesmanii,* which produce small seedy orange-red fruit with a thick pulpy skin, somewhat reminiscent of rose hips.

*Cheesmanii* actually occur in only one place in the world — on the shores of Galápagos Islands in the Pacific Ocean — while a subspecies grows farther inland. They have a very high vitamin C content, and they are very salt- and drought-tolerant, making them ideal breeding material for enhancing the cultivation of tomatoes in arid regions of the world. Seeds of *cheesmanii* require some special pretreatment in order to germinate. In the wild, the plants get around this requirement by having the fruits consumed by giant turtles that spread the seeds along the shoreline. As the seeds move through their digestive tract, the inhibitors to germination are removed. Without the turtles, *cheesmanii* would not reproduce, nor would there be genes for salt tolerance in tomatoes.

The complex relationships in nature are very delicate. All of us — people, plants, and animals — depend upon them for our survival.

# Chilled Sun-Gold Tomato Soup

Deborah Madison was happy to share this recipe from her book *Local Flavors: Cooking and Eating from America's Farmers' Markets,* which celebrates the good foods to be found in America's farmers' markets. It is a recipe that is intimately tied to the particular variety of tomato. While I admit I am often prejudiced against hybrid tomatoes, Sun Gold is a prolific and deliciously sweet cherry tomato, so sweet, in fact, that the flavor here is toned down with the addition of vinegar. You can substitute another cherry tomato, but it will in essence create a different soup. Try using Bicolor Cherry or Isis Candy if you can.

## Soup

    2 pints Sun Gold tomatoes, stems removed

    2 shallots, finely diced

    sea salt

    1 cup water

## Relish

    3 tablespoons Spanish Chardonnay vinegar or champagne vinegar

    2 teaspoons finely diced and seeded serrano chile (optional)

    2 tablespoons extra-virgin olive oil

    1 firm avocado, pitted, peeled, and finely diced

    1 tablespoon chopped basil or cilantro

**1.** Rinse the tomatoes and put them into a heavy saucepan with a tight-fitting lid. Add half the shallots, ½ teaspoon salt, and the water. Cook over medium-high heat, listening closely to the pot. Soon you'll hear the tomatoes popping. Take a peek after a few minutes to make sure there's sufficient moisture — you don't want the tomatoes to scorch. If the skins are slow to pop, add a few tablespoons of water. Once they release their juices, lower the heat and cook for 25 minutes.

**2.** Pass the tomato mixture through a food mill. You'll have about 2 cups of purée. Chill well, then taste for salt.

**3.** For the relish, combine the remaining shallots in a medium bowl with the vinegar, chile, if using, oil, avocado, and basil. Season with a pinch or two of salt and some pepper. Spoon the soup into small cups; divide the garnish among them and serve.

# Chilled Soup of Creole Tomatoes with Tapenade

SERVES 4–6

Louisiana-born John Besh, executive chef of August's in New Orleans, spends part of each summer in Provence. Describing this soup as one of his favorite ways to begin a dinner on a hot summer's night, he advises, "Remember, the riper the tomato, the better."

John intrigued me when he mentioned "Creole" tomatoes, a type unfamiliar to me. It turns out Creole tomatoes are simply tomatoes grown in Louisiana, not a specific variety. Big, ripe beefsteaks, such as Brandywine or Dr. Neal, add a subtle sweetness to the dish.

**Soup**

  3 garlic cloves

  ¼ cup extra-virgin olive oil

  3 pounds ripe Creole tomatoes, roughly chopped

  2 sweet red bell peppers, seeded and chopped

  1 small ancho chile pepper

  2 tablespoons sherry vinegar

  1 sprig fresh thyme

  1 handful fresh basil

    salt and freshly ground black pepper

1–2 teaspoons sugar (optional)

**Tapenade**

  4 garlic cloves, peeled

  ¾ cup pitted black olives

    juice of 1 lemon

  2 anchovies, rinsed (optional)

  1 cup extra-virgin olive oil

**1.** For the soup, heat the olive oil in a large pan over medium-high heat. Sauté the garlic, allowing it to cook for a moment without browning. Add the tomatoes and the bell and chile peppers and simmer for 15 minutes, and then stir in the vinegar, thyme, and basil.

**2.** Remove the pan from the heat and purée the soup in a food mill or food processor. Season to taste with salt and pepper and, if necessary, a teaspoon or two of sugar; however, most ripe Creole tomatoes have enough natural sugar to balance the acidity in this soup. Chill the soup for several hours.

**3.** For the tapenade, combine the garlic, olives, lemon juice, and anchovies, if desired, in a food processor. Purée into a paste while slowly adding the oil.

**4.** To serve, pour the soup into chilled soup bowls and drizzle with a spoonful of tapenade.

# Cream of Tomato Soup

**SERVES 4–6**

I favor using red, pink, or purple slicing tomatoes for this classic tomato soup, and any of them will work well. For a darker color and a slightly smoky flavor, try Cherokee Purple, Black from Tula, or Black Aisberg. White, yellow, and orange tomatoes make a milder but delicious tomato soup. For a special effect, make the soup in two batches by doubling or dividing the recipe in half and using two contrasting tomatoes, such as red and orange. To serve, using two ladles simultaneously ladle each into a flat soup plate for a two-colored soup. For those who are watching their diets, soy milk can be substituted for cream, but you won't get the incredibly rich flavor of a soup made with cream.

3 pounds (8–9 medium-large) ripe tomatoes, cored and halved

1 medium onion, chopped

1 celery stalk, chopped

2 garlic cloves, peeled and minced

1 tablespoon extra-virgin olive or canola oil

½ cup water

1 stem basil with about 8 leaves, plus small sprigs for garnish

1 stem parsley

salt

1–2 teaspoons sugar

1 cup heavy or light cream or soy milk

1. Combine the tomatoes in a large saucepan with the onion, celery, garlic, and oil. Add the water and cook over low heat for 30 minutes, or until the vegetables are very soft. Let cool.

2. Purée the mixture in a food mill in batches, discarding the skins and seeds of each batch. (If you don't have a food mill, peel, seed and chop the tomatoes before cooking them in step 1. Blend the cooked mixture in a blender until smooth.)

3. Return the tomato mixture to the pan and add the basil and parsley stems, salt to taste, and 1 teaspoon of the sugar. Simmer for 10 minutes, and then taste and adjust the seasoning, adding more salt and/or sugar as needed. Remove and discard the basil and parsley.

4. Just before serving, stir in ¾ cup of the cream. Pour the soup into bowls and add a little swirl of the remaining cream to each serving plus a sprig of basil.

# Yellow Tomato and Mussel Soup

**SERVES 4 AS A FIRST COURSE**

**B**lue-black mussel shells add drama to this vivid soup — a brilliant start to a summer supper. Clams can be substituted for mussels. The base of the soup uses yellow tomatoes because their milder flavor makes them the perfect match for seafood. Limmony is a fine match for this recipe, or any other yellow heirloom variety.

large pinch saffron (enough threads to cover a dime)

½ cup warm water

2 pounds juicy yellow tomatoes, peeled, seeded, and roughly chopped

4 ripe red plum tomatoes, peeled, seeded, and cut into 3 or 4 pieces

salt

1 teaspoon sugar (optional)

3 basil leaves, torn

¼ cup chopped fresh parsley

16 mussels

**1.** Put the saffron in a small bowl and cover with the warm water; steep, stirring once or twice, until the liquid is a deep orange-crimson, about 20 minutes.

**2.** Meanwhile, simmer the yellow tomatoes in a large saucepan over medium-low heat for 10 minutes, until tender. Stir in the saffron, its soaking liquid, and the plum tomatoes. Season to taste with salt and add the sugar if you think it is needed. Stir in the basil and half of the parsley and return to a simmer. If you would like a more liquid soup, add additional water and heat to a simmer.

**3.** Add the mussels and cover the pan. Simmer steadily for 4 to 5 minutes, until the shells have opened. Discard any that do not open.

**4.** To serve, divide the mussels among four shallow soup plates. Add the soup and dust with the remaining parsley.

#  Manhattan Clam Chowder

SERVES 6–8

**M**any New Englanders fire up at the thought of clam chowder with tomatoes, often claiming that their favorite milky chowders are the only authentic chowders around. In fact, chowder recipes have always varied, because the coastal people who invented them used whatever ingredients they had available. The earliest chowders had no potatoes, and eighteenth- and nineteenth-century chowders destined for the captain's table called for port or other red wine instead of milk. When people began growing tomatoes in their backyards in the 1900s, many naturally came up with the excellent idea of including their harvest in their chowder. Notably, tomato-based chowders come from southern New England and New York, where tomatoes ripened better than in the cooler climate farther north. As this history suggests, chowders, like other soups, are hospitable to a variety of ingredients, and exact quantities rarely matter. If possible, see if you can find some white- or yellow-fleshed heirloom potatoes, or fingerlings, such as Russian Banana. Even the modern Yukon Gold potatoes are darn good.

24 fresh cherrystone, mahogany, or other clams

3 cups water

2 teaspoons extra-virgin olive or canola oil

4 ounces pancetta or salt pork, cut into ½-inch pieces

2 large onions, chopped

2 celery stalks, chopped

salt

2 large potatoes, cut into ¾-inch dice

2 cups fresh or canned diced tomatoes, including their juice

1 (8-ounce) bottle clam juice

4 tablespoons chopped fresh parsley

1 bay leaf

1 teaspoon dried thyme

¼ teaspoon white pepper

about 1 cup tomato juice (page 235), (optional)

**1.** Wash the clams and put them into a large soup pot with 3 cups of water. Cover the pot and bring the water to a boil over high heat. Reduce the heat to medium-high and simmer for 3 to 4 minutes, until the shells open. Strain the liquid into a bowl and set it and the clams aside.

**2.** Rinse out and dry the pot. Over low heat, warm the oil and stir in the pancetta. Cook gently until it turns golden, 8 to 10 minutes. Stir in the onions and celery and season with salt. Cover the pot and let the vegetables sweat for 4 minutes. Stir in the potatoes and tomatoes. Add the reserved clam broth, the clam juice, and half the parsley. Stick the bay leaf in among the other ingredients; cover the pot and simmer for 15 minutes.

**3.** Meanwhile, remove the clams from their shells and coarsely chop them. Stir them into the pot along with the thyme and pepper. Check the seasoning. Add salt to taste, though you may find that the pancetta has seasoned the chowder enough. Simmer for 5 minutes longer, stirring in the remaining parsley during the final minute. Add the tomato juice if you want a thinner consistency. Serve hot.

# Tomato Dumplings

### SERVES 4–8

**D**rop these pillow-soft dumplings into soups such as Manhattan clam chowder, or into any hearty stew. The recipe comes from Lilla Weed, who contributed it to a cookbook called *Favorite Recipes of Wellesley Alumnae*.

> 1½ cups sifted all-purpose flour
> 1 tablespoon baking powder
> 1 teaspoon salt
> 1 egg
> 1 tablespoon melted butter
> ¾ cup tomato juice (page 235) or Spicy Tomato Cocktail (page 66)

**1.** Stir together the flour, baking powder, and salt in a mixing bowl. Make a well in the center.

**2.** Lightly beat the egg with the butter in a small bowl. Stir in the tomato juice. Pour this mixture into the well in the dry ingredients and quickly stir everything together with a fork.

**3.** Divide the mixture into 8 portions, forming each into a ball. Drop them into a pan of simmering soup or stew, taking care they don't touch, because they will swell during cooking. Put the lid on the pan and simmer for 12 to 15 minutes. Serve hot with the soup or stew.

# Tomato Salmon Bisque

S erve as a first course or add a salad and either Sun-Dried Tomato and Olive Bread (page 132) or a tomato focaccia (page 112) to make this summery tomato soup the highlight of a quick and satisfying supper.

3 large (about 1½ pounds) ripe tomatoes, peeled

3 cups chicken or vegetable broth

4 stems parsley, plus 3 tablespoons chopped

1 bay leaf

1 tablespoon lemon juice

1 (1-inch-thick) salmon steak (10–12 ounces)

1 tablespoon butter

1 teaspoon chopped summer savory

salt and freshly ground black pepper

**1.** Place a sieve over a bowl. Cut the tomatoes in half and squeeze the seeds, gel, and juice into the sieve. Stir, pressing lightly against the sieve with a spoon to make sure all the juice runs into the bowl. Discard the seeds and gel, but reserve the juice. Chop the tomatoes into ½-inch pieces and set aside.

**2.** Combine the broth, parsley stems, bay leaf, and lemon juice in a medium-large saucepan over medium heat. Add the salmon. Bring to a simmer and simmer for 5 minutes. Remove the salmon from the broth and set aside. Reserve the salmon broth.

**3.** In another medium-large saucepan, melt the butter over low heat and stir in the tomatoes. Add the reserved tomato juice. Strain the salmon broth onto the tomatoes, discarding the celery and herbs. Add half the chopped parsley and the savory to the salmon broth and tomato mixture. Season with salt and pepper to taste. Bring to a simmer and cook for 5 minutes.

**4.** Meanwhile, break the salmon into large flakes, discarding the skin and bone. Add the salmon flakes to the tomato mixture and simmer for 2 minutes longer to finish cooking. Serve immediately; garnish each serving with a little of the remaining parsley.

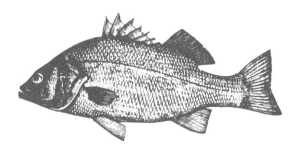

# Summer Minestrone

SERVES 4–8

When tomatoes are shining forth in the garden, so, too, is a host of other good vegetables, zucchini, summer squash, peppers, and Swiss chard among them. Here's a minestrone recipe that features these and other summer crops.

2 tablespoons extra-virgin olive oil

1–2 garlic cloves, peeled and finely chopped

1 medium carrot, cut into ½-inch rounds

1 celery stalk, coarsely chopped

4 cups (12–15 large) chopped ripe plum tomatoes

4–6 cups chicken or vegetable broth

1 teaspoon chopped fresh oregano

1 teaspoon fresh thyme

1 stem basil, plus extra sprigs for garnish

salt and freshly ground black pepper

1 cup (4 ounces) penne, elbow macaroni, small shells, or other medium-size pasta

12 green beans, washed, trimmed, and cut into 1-inch pieces

1 medium green or yellow bell pepper, seeded and cut into 2-inch by ¼-inch strips

1 medium leek, washed, white and tender green parts cut into ½-inch pieces

8 stems Swiss chard, stalks and leaves cut into 1-inch strips

1 medium zucchini, sliced

1 medium yellow summer squash, sliced

½–1 teaspoon sugar (optional)

**1.** Warm the oil in a large saucepan over medium heat; stir in the garlic and let it soften for 1 to 2 minutes, and then stir in the carrot and celery. Cook for 2 minutes. Add the tomatoes, 4 cups of the broth, the oregano, thyme, basil, and salt and pepper to taste. Stir. Cover the pan, bring to a simmer, and simmer for 10 minutes.

**2.** Increase the heat and bring the soup to a brisk boil over high heat. Stir in the pasta, followed by the green beans, bell pepper, and leek. Cook briskly, stirring often, for 3 minutes.

**3.** Reduce the heat so the soup is simmering and add the chard, zucchini, and summer squash. If the mixture is thicker than you like, add some or all of the remaining broth. Return to a simmer and cover the pan. Continue cooking the soup for 5 minutes, until the pasta and the vegetables are tender. Serve immediately or cool and reheat as needed. Garnish with basil leaves. Check for seasoning before serving and add more salt and pepper and sugar to taste, if desired.

# Tomato, Lentil, and Almond Soup

SERVES 6–8

Americans have been interested in vegetarianism since the early nineteenth century, and none more so than the Kellogg family of Battle Creek, Michigan, who began to produce breakfast cereals to wean people away from their traditional meaty breakfasts of bacon, sausages, and steaks. This recipe is adapted from one that Mrs. E. E. Kellogg included in her 1897 book, *Science in the Kitchen*. It is an outstanding hearty vegetarian soup. The combination of lentils, tomatoes, and almonds is surprisingly delicious. Served either puréed or chunky, it's ideal for a cold day.

1 cup green or brown lentils, rinsed and picked over

1 bay leaf

⅓ cup almond butter (available in natural food stores)

2 tablespoons extra-virgin olive oil

1 large onion, chopped

1 garlic clove, peeled and chopped

1 cup diced celery

3 cups peeled and chopped fresh or canned tomatoes

salt

½ teaspoon ground coriander

¼ teaspoon freshly ground black pepper

1 cup water

⅓ cup flaked almonds

1½ cups chopped fresh parsley or cilantro

1 large red tomato, diced (peeling and seeding are optional)

1. Soak the lentils in plenty of cold water for 1 hour. Drain, rinse, and put them into a large pan with the bay leaf and enough cold water to cover by 1 inch. Simmer for 30 minutes or until the lentils are soft. Discard the bay leaf. Stir the almond butter into the lentils, and then purée the mixture in a food processor or by passing it through a food mill or sieve.

2. Heat the oil in a soup pot over low heat. Soften the onion and garlic in the oil for 2 to 3 minutes, and then add the celery, chopped tomatoes, 1 teaspoon of salt, coriander, pepper, and the puréed lentil mixture. Add the water and simmer for 10 minutes, stirring from time to time, until the celery and tomatoes have softened. At this point, you can either purée the soup again to make it smooth or omit this step if you prefer it chunky. Add more water to thin the soup, if desired. Taste and add salt if needed.

**3.** While the soup is cooking, prepare the almonds and the tomato for the garnish. Preheat the oven to 300°F. Place the almonds in a single layer on a pie plate and toast for 5 minutes, until golden and fragrant.

**4.** Just before serving, stir half the parsley into the soup. Serve the soup in bowls and garnish each serving with a spoonful of the diced tomato, sprinkles of almond flakes, and parsley.

# Tomato Bouillon

**SERVES 2**

Bouillon is now most often used as a broth for stews and sauces. But it used to be served as a drink, most famously on luxury ocean liners whose passengers needed a fortifying midmorning brew. Tomato bouillon is a good drink in winter, especially for skiers or woodchoppers or anyone else coming in from the cold. You can also serve it as a light soup, in which case you may want to add a swirl of cream or a sprinkle of parsley and chives to each serving.

1½ cups beef bouillon

1½ cups tomato juice (page 235) or Spicy Tomato Cocktail (page 66)

Worcestershire sauce or Tabasco

**1.** Heat the bouillon to a simmer. Pour in the tomato juice and reheat.

**2.** Pour into mugs for serving. Sprinkle with Worcestershire or Tabasco according to taste.

 # Tomato Consommé Martini

My first taste of this cocktail was shortly before giving my introductory talk at the beginning of the Epicurean Tomato Fête in 2002. I had been told there was barely any vodka in it. The drink was so good, so distinctive, cooling, and mildly savory, I had to have another. I had just rounded the corner of the old Georgian mansion when the vodka kicked in. The martini was served with a peeled Green Grape tomato slightly pickled to resemble an olive. The consommé makes a delightful chilled soup without the addition of vodka.

5–6 pounds (about 10 large) tomatoes, cored and quartered

1 cup dry white wine

5 garlic cloves, peeled

4 shallots, sliced

8 stems parsley

4 stems tarragon

4 stems fresh thyme

1 small bay leaf

2 teaspoons sea salt

1 teaspoon black peppercorns

water

vodka

ice cubes

**1.** Put the tomatoes, wine, garlic, shallots, parsley, tarragon, and thyme into a large saucepan. Knead and squish them together with your hands. Add the bay leaf, salt, peppercorns, and 1 cup of water, or enough to cover the mixture.

**2.** Place on medium-high heat and let the mixture just come to a bare simmer. Be extremely careful not to let it boil; the key to clarifying the consommé is to slowly release the natural pectin in the tomato. The pectin, much like albumin in protein, will extract the impurities, thereby making a clear liquid.

**3.** After the liquid has cooked for 15 minutes, turn off the heat and gently ladle and strain the liquid through a sieve lined with damp cheesecloth or a damp cotton or linen napkin. Take your time and be gentle. If the liquid needs more seasoning, add salt to taste. Cool.

**4.** To make martinis, put the tomato consommé and vodka into a glass in a ratio of 2 measures of consommé to 1 of vodka. Add ample ice and stir or shake. Pour into chilled martini glasses and serve immediately.

CHAPTER FIVE

# SALADS

# Heirloom Tomato Salad with Balsamic Miso Dressing

**SERVES 4**

This salad with its unusual dressing comes from Michel Nischan. Renowned for his work in support of organic agriculture and a former board member of the Chefs Collaborative, he is also a cookbook author and former chef of the Heartbeat Restaurant in New York City.

Miso, a thick paste made from salting and fermenting soybeans and rice or barley, comes in several colors, some pale, some dark. Chickpea miso is a good substitute for white miso in this recipe. If you don't have access to the particular tomatoes called for in the recipe, substitute other red, yellow, and green (ripe) tomatoes.

2 Cherokee Purple tomatoes

2 Limmony tomatoes

2 Evergreen tomatoes

⅔ cup snipped fresh fennel fronds

2–4 teaspoons aged balsamic or malt vinegar

2 teaspoons shiro miso (white miso)

1–2 teaspoons extra-virgin olive oil

cracked black pepper

**1.** Cut each tomato into ¼-inch slices. Sprinkle each slice with a small amount of fennel.

**2.** Whisk the vinegar, miso, and oil together in a small bowl, and then drizzle over the tomato slices. Lightly sprinkle pepper over each slice.

**3.** Stack the slices, alternating colors, on four chilled plates. Sprinkle with the remaining fennel and serve immediately.

RED APPLE TOMATO

# Tomato, Watermelon, and Ricotta Salata Salad

**SERVES 4**

The three main ingredients in this salad from Chef William S. Webber create a wonderful dance of sweet, tart, and salt flavors.

Ricotta salata is a firm, salted form of ricotta, not the soft kind that comes in plastic tubs. Here it contrasts brilliantly with the juiciness of the crisp watermelon and tender tomatoes. You can easily mix and match colors for a vibrant presentation, using yellow and/or red tomatoes and yellow and/or red watermelon.

¼ cup sherry vinegar

1 shallot, peeled and minced

1 teaspoon Dijon mustard

¾ cup extra-virgin olive oil

   sea salt and freshly ground black pepper

1 pound (1–2 thick half-moon slices, including the rind) seedless watermelon

1 pound (about 3 large) vine-ripened tomatoes

10 ounces ricotta salata

1 fennel bulb, thinly sliced

8 large mint leaves

**1.** For the vinaigrette, whisk together the vinegar, shallot, and mustard in a small bowl; slowly add the oil. Season with salt and pepper to taste.

**2.** For the salad, peel the watermelon and slice into wedges about ⅛ inch thick. Slice the tomatoes and the ricotta salata into wedges. (If your piece of cheese is small, shave it with a vegetable peeler.)

**3.** To serve, layer slices of melon, tomato, ricotta salata, and fennel on each of four salad plates, spiraling upward until you have built small towers about 3 inches high. Drizzle with the vinaigrette.

**4.** Just before you serve the salads, cut the mint leaves into thin strips and sprinkle them evenly over the plates.

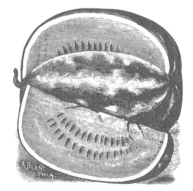

# Village Farm Greenhouse Tomato, Feta Cheese, and Basil Salad

### SERVES 4–6

Onions, feta cheese, and lots of fresh herbs make a delicious combination in this recipe from David Garrido, former executive chef of Jeffrey's Restaurant and Bar in Austin, Texas, and winner of numerous awards for both cooking and community service. David uses locally grown tomatoes in his salad, and any sun-ripened slicing tomato will work. Try using some of the uniform heirlooms like Magnus, Eva Purple Ball, Redfield Beauty, or Trucker's Favorite.

1 Texas 1015 onion or other sweet onion

½ cup extra-virgin olive oil

¼ cup sherry vinegar

6 ripe red tomatoes, cut into wedges

2 celery stalks, finely chopped

½ cup basil, torn or cut into ¼-inch strips

½ cup chopped fresh marjoram

   salt and freshly ground black pepper

1 cup crumbled feta cheese

**1.** Slice the onion, separate it into rings, and cut each ring into matchsticks. Mix the oil and vinegar. Put half the mixture into a small bowl with the onion and marinate for 30 minutes.

**2.** Toss the tomatoes, celery, basil, and marjoram in a salad bowl and season lightly with salt and pepper. (Feta is a salty cheese, so use salt sparingly at this point.)

**3.** Dress the tomato mixture lightly with the remaining oil and vinegar dressing. Scatter the marinated onions on top, using the marinade only if you want more dressing. Finally, scatter on the feta. Check the seasoning and add more salt and pepper if desired.

# Tomato and Buffalo Mozzarella Salad

### SERVES 4–6

Simplicity is the key to this great salad. A good extra-virgin olive oil is essential, as is a light application of vinegar. Other vinegars, such as sherry or red wine vinegar, may be substituted for the balsamic, but they will not be as sweet. Buffalo mozzarella is made from the milk of water buffalo. The fresh mozzarella typically seen in the United States is mixed with cow's milk. The "real" all-buffalo-milk mozzarella is a creamier and softer cheese. Since part of the appeal of the salad is in its appearance, choose a beautiful oblong platter to serve it on. It looks especially lovely on black pottery.

1 pound buffalo mozzarella, sliced ¼ inch thick

1 very large tomato, such as Brandywine or Winsall, or 3 medium-size tomatoes, cored and sliced

15 fresh basil leaves

2–3 tablespoons extra-virgin olive oil

2 tablespoons balsamic vinegar

sea salt

edible flowers, such as violas, nasturtiums, marigold petals, borage blossoms, or cilantro blossoms (optional)

**1.** Arrange the mozzarella alternating and overlapping with the tomatoes on an oblong platter or large dinner plate. Slip some basil leaves between the slices along the sides so they are protruding halfway out.

**2.** Drizzle or spoon the oil over the tomatoes. Do the same with the vinegar. Lightly sprinkle salt on the tomatoes. Distribute the flowers on the slices and plate, if desired. Let sit for a few minutes and serve.

VARIATIONS: Mayonnaise may be substituted for extra-virgin olive oil, producing a slightly different effect. Spread ½ teaspoon on top of each tomato slice as you arrange them on the plate and let sit for 10 minutes. Very thinly sliced rings of red or sweet white onion may be scattered on top of the cheese and tomatoes.

# Red and Yellow Tomato Salad with Lentils, Basil, and Goat Cheese

**SERVES 8**

Famed for his seafood dishes, Robert Kinkead, owner-chef of Kinkead's in the Foggy Bottom area of Washington, DC, is just as talented in other culinary fields. His food reflects the cooking techniques of the American South and Northeast, as well as Europe and Asia. This salad combines the tiny green Le Puy lentils of France with the red lentils typical of Indian cooking and a vivid array of heirloom tomatoes. Circles of walnut-crusted goat cheese make a tasty garnish.

1½ cups French green lentils

  salt

1½ cups red lentils

  ½ cup extra-virgin olive oil

  ½ carrot, cut into ⅛-inch dice

  ½ cup celery, cut into ⅛-inch dice

  ½ cup onion, cut into ⅛-inch dice

  4 garlic cloves, minced

  ¼ cup, plus 1 tablespoon red wine vinegar

  freshly ground black pepper

  4 large ripe red heirloom tomatoes, such as Brandywine or Cherokee Purple, peeled

  4 large ripe yellow heirloom tomatoes, such as Manyel or Limmony, peeled

 12 fresh basil leaves, cut into ribbons

  1 medium red onion, thinly sliced

  2 teaspoons sugar

  1 (12-ounce) log fresh goat cheese

⅔ cup crushed walnuts

**1.** Rinse and pick over the green lentils. Put them in a medium saucepan, cover plentifully with water, bring to a boil, add 1 teaspoon of salt, and cook for 10 minutes. Taste for doneness and, if necessary, cook 1 or 2 minutes longer, but take care not to overcook them. Drain and set aside.

**2.** Meanwhile, bring 1 quart of water to a boil. Rinse and pick over the red lentils; place them in a heatproof bowl. Pour the boiling water over the lentils and let stand for 40 minutes, or until tender. Drain and combine with the green lentils in a large mixing bowl.

**3.** Heat 2 tablespoons of the oil in a medium skillet. Add the celery, carrots, and onion, and sauté for 2 minutes, or until the onion is translucent. Add this mixture to the lentil mixture, along with 2 of the garlic cloves, ¼ cup of the remaining oil, and the ¼ cup vinegar. Season with salt and black pepper to taste.

**4.** Core and slice the red and yellow tomatoes and marinate in the remaining 2 tablespoons oil, the 1 tablespoon vinegar, half the basil, and the red onion, with a pinch of sugar, salt, and pepper, for 30 minutes or so.

**5.** Roll the goat cheese in the walnuts and cut into 8 rounds.

**6.** Preheat the oven to 375°F. Chill 8 salad plates by placing them in the freezer for a few minutes.

**7.** Just before serving, place the goat cheese on a cookie sheet. Warm it in the oven for 2 to 3 minutes.

**8.** To serve, divide the lentil salad among the salad plates. Top with alternating red and yellow tomato slices in overlapping circles. Garnish with the remaining basil and a round of warm goat cheese.

# Heirloom Tomato and Goat Cheese Salad

### SERVES 6

A delightful savory complex of flavors will greet you when you make this recipe from *Daniel Boulud's Café Boulud Cookbook*, by Daniel Boulud and Dorie Greenspan. The pesto dressing is fantastic, uniquely combining the marinade for the tomatoes with the rich, dark pesto and contrasting with the soft, sweet goat cheese and, of course, heirloom tomatoes. Use a number of different tomatoes for the salad. After all, variety is the spice of life.

4 large ripe, juicy heirloom tomatoes, peeled and cored

18 small tomatoes, such as cherry, grape, or pear tomatoes

1 shallot, finely chopped, rinsed, and dried

1 tablespoon finely chopped oregano

1 tablespoon finely chopped Italian parsley

2 teaspoons salt, plus more for seasoning

freshly ground white pepper

pinch of crushed red pepper flakes

2 tablespoons balsamic vinegar

1 tablespoon sherry vinegar

2 bunches (about 8 ounces) basil, leaves only, washed

½ garlic clove, peeled and germ removed

1 teaspoon finely grated Parmesan cheese

1 teaspoon pine nuts, very lightly toasted

½ cup extra-virgin olive oil

1 cup (6 ounces) soft fresh goat cheese

1. Cut the large tomatoes in half lengthwise. Working over a strainer set in a large bowl, seed the tomatoes, discarding the seeds and saving the juice. Cut the seeded tomatoes into 8 wedges and add them to the bowl with the juice. Cut the small tomatoes in half and add them to the bowl of tomatoes. Gently mix in the shallot, oregano, parsley, salt, a pinch of white pepper, red pepper flakes, balsamic vinegar, and sherry vinegar. Allow the mixture to sit at room temperature for 30 minutes. (If you need to leave the tomatoes up to an hour or an hour and a half, that's okay.)

2. For the pesto dressing, boil a pan of lightly salted water. Plunge the basil into the boiling water and blanch for 2 minutes. Drain the leaves and run them under cold water to stop the cooking and cool the leaves. Drain, and then squeeze the leaves free of excess moisture between your palms.

**3.** Combine the basil, garlic, Parmesan, pine nuts, and oil in a food processor and process until smooth. Transfer to a bowl, cover with plastic wrap, and set aside. (The pesto dressing can be made a day ahead and kept tightly covered in the refrigerator. Stir the pesto and bring it to room temperature before using.)

**4.** To finish the salad, drain the tomatoes, reserving the juice, and arrange them on a large serving platter or in a shallow bowl. Pour up to

¾ cup of the reserved juice into the pesto and mix well. You may want a little less tomato juice, but you probably won't want more: You're looking for a fairly thin, very tasty pesto. Taste as you mix; season with salt and white pepper if needed.

**5.** To serve, top the tomatoes with dollops of goat cheese and drizzle the entire salad with some of the pesto. Pass the extra pesto in a sauceboat at the table.

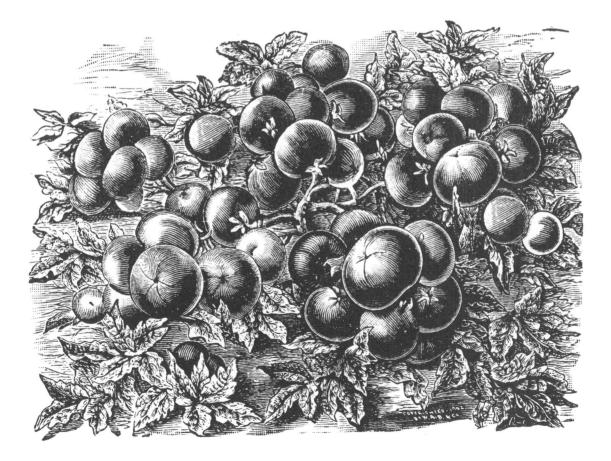

# Insalata Caprese Verdura Style

**SERVES 4–6**

A t Verdura, his now-closed Tuscan-style restaurant in Great Barrington, Massachusetts, chef William S. Webber was committed to supporting local farmers and artisans by using only the freshest seasonal ingredients when possible. Here he shares his recipe for the classic tomato-mozzarella salad, which he makes with fresh buffalo-milk mozzarella and opal basil. If you don't have access to these premium ingredients, any fresh mozzarella and basil will still produce delicious results. Using a mix of black, red, pink, and yellow tomatoes really lights up this simple salad.

2 (8-ounce) lobes fresh buffalo mozzarella

4 stems opal basil

1½ pounds (about 4 large) fresh vine-ripened organic tomatoes

zest and juice of 2 organic lemons

3–4 tablespoons extra-virgin olive oil, or more to taste

sea salt and freshly ground black pepper

2 cups organic baby arugula

**1.** With your fingers peel and tear apart the mozzarella into rough 1-inch chunks. Set aside.

**2.** Gently tear the leaves from the stems of the basil and set them aside, discarding the stems.

**3.** Slice the tomatoes in half, and then slice into ¼-inch half-moons. Set aside.

**4.** Mix the mozzarella, basil, tomatoes, and lemon zest and juice together with 2 tablespoons of the oil. Season with salt and pepper and add more oil, if desired.

**5.** Arrange the arugula on individual salad plates. Pile the tomato salad on top and serve.

# ALEXANDER LIVINGSTON
# "FATHER OF THE MODERN TOMATO"
## 1821–1898

Entrepreneur, showman, promoter, and plant breeder wrapped up in one, Alexander Livingston was largely responsible for changing the tomato, and the tomato industry, through his plant-breeding and selection efforts. Yet he generally lies in obscurity — unless, that is, you are very much into tomatoes.

Livingston was born and raised in Reynoldsburg, Ohio. At the age of 10 he saw his first tomatoes, which were supposedly wild, red, yellow, and, purple. He gathered some but was told not to eat them, because they were poisonous. From then on the tomato intrigued him. By the age of 21, Livingston was working for a seed grower and learning the trade. At that time tomatoes were ruffled and uneven in shape. For years Livingston tried, without much success, to produce an improved tomato. In 1852 Livingston was able to purchase his own land and a few years later greatly expanded his seed business with the purchase of Buckeye Garden Seed Company.

By the late 1850s and early 1860s, a few improved tomato varieties had been developed, including Trophy, which was relatively round and smooth compared with its predecessors. These tomato developments spurred Livingston to double his efforts to develop new tomato varieties. He introduced the red Paragon tomato in 1870. While not the first round tomato, it rapidly became one of the most popular and a favored canning tomato in places such as New Jersey. Five years later he released Acme, a red tomato with a tinge of purple.

The seed company went bankrupt with the crash of 1876–1877, but his son Robert organized a new company under the name of A. W. Livingston and Sons. They moved it from Reynoldsburg to Columbus in 1880, and Livingston introduced Perfection. Three years later he developed Livingston's Favorite, an even better canning variety, from a field of Paragons. His "crown jewel of them all" was Livingston's Beauty, a pinkish purple tomato he introduced in 1886. Alexander Livingston died in 1898; the company continued as Livingston Seed Company, run by his sons and grandsons, who continued to introduce varieties such as Magnus, Dwarf Stone, and Globe. The Livingstons introduced 31 varieties of tomatoes altogether.

# Spiced Tomato Salad

SERVES 4–6

Floyd Cardoz, executive chef of Tabla in New York City, loves mixing European methods with the ingredients and flavorings of his native India. This vivid salad, full of vibrant savory and hot flavors, is based on a demonstration he gave to New England farmers who grow organic and specialty vegetables for New York chefs. Floyd Cardoz emphasizes, "In India, if you eat tomatoes, you eat chiles, you eat cilantro, you eat black pepper." These are crucial ingredients, but Indian cooks vary their salads by matching their favorite spices with whatever ingredients are in season. Made with tomatoes of various colors, this salad looks spectacular.

½ cup balsamic vinegar

1 teaspoon black peppercorns

1 teaspoon coriander seeds

1 teaspoon cumin seeds

3 pounds ripe tomatoes of various colors and varieties

2 teaspoons chat masala (available where Indian foods are sold)

1-inch piece fresh ginger, peeled and grated or slivered

1 jalapeño or other chile pepper, finely chopped

1 tablespoon coarsely torn Thai or other basil, plus sprigs for garnish

3 tablespoons coarsely chopped cilantro

coarse sea salt such as Maldon salt

about 2 tablespoons extra-virgin olive oil

**1.** Bring the vinegar to a boil in a small saucepan and boil for 10 minutes, until it is reduced to about half its volume and is thick and syrupy.

**2.** Combine the peppercorns, coriander, and cumin in a small nonstick skillet. Stir them over high heat for about 1 minute, until they are a shade darker in color and very fragrant. Grind them in a spice grinder or mortar and pestle.

**3.** Cut the tomatoes into large chunks and arrange them in a single layer on a shallow dish. Sprinkle with the seed mixture and the chat masala. Add the ginger and jalapeño. (Use only half the jalapeño if you want to hold down the heat.) Add the basil, 1 tablespoon of the cilantro, and sea salt to taste. Toss gently.

**4.** Drizzle the vinegar syrup over the top; drizzle on the oil. Toss gently and briefly. Add a final sprinkling of salt and the remaining cilantro, and garnish the platter with the basil sprigs.

# Fresh and Sun-Dried Tomato Salad with Parmesan

SERVES 4

Diana Kennedy, author of *The Cuisines of Mexico* and several subsequent books on Mexican and other foods, describes her favorite tomato salad as "sliced, unskinned heirloom tomatoes dotted with strips of sun-dried tomatoes (the real things, not those round unsalted affairs), olive oil, a mere touch of balsamic and some very thin slices of Parmesan." Here it is formalized into a recipe. Serve with whole wheat bread. Alternatively, this is a good salad for stuffing into pita pockets.

6–8 large ripe tomatoes, either all red or a mixture of colors, washed and sliced

sea salt and freshly ground black pepper

⅔ cup ½-inch strips of oil-packed sun-dried tomatoes

1 tablespoon oil from the jar of sun-dried tomatoes

about 1 tablespoon balsamic vinegar

4 ounces Parmesan cheese

1. Arrange the tomato slices in a single layer on four salad plates and season to taste with salt and pepper.

2. Scatter the sun-dried tomatoes on top. Drizzle with oil and vinegar.

3. Using a swivel-bladed vegetable peeler to get very thin slices, slice the Parmesan and lay the pieces on top of the salad. Serve immediately.

LIVINGSTON'S GLOBE TOMATO

# Astor Tomato and Parmesan Salad

## SERVES 2–4

The anonymous author of *Murrey's Salads and Sauces* (1884) identifies himself only as a professional caterer who had worked at the Astor House Hotel in New York, whence comes this salad with its unusual Rhine wine dressing. The quantities are left vague, though "a liberal quantity of grated Parmesan" is specified. But is that the powdery Parmesan we sprinkle on pasta? Or is it shredded on the coarser teeth of a grater? Both of these are fine, but even better are skinny slices of Parmesan made by using the widest shredder on a box grater, a flat cheese slicer, or a swivel-bladed vegetable peeler. The thin slices of Parmesan partner with the tomatoes perfectly, and the light wine-based dressing enhances the fruitiness of the tomatoes and suits the cheese much better than more strident conventional dressings of oil and vinegar. If you are going to use finely grated Parmesan, use cheese you have grated yourself in a food processor, not the stuff that comes in canisters.

2 large ripe red tomatoes, washed and sliced

2 large ripe yellow or orange tomatoes, washed and sliced

½ teaspoon sea salt

white pepper

3 ounces Parmesan cheese, thinly sliced or shredded, or 4 tablespoons finely grated Parmesan

1 tablespoon olive oil

3 tablespoons Rhine-type wine, such as Riesling or Gewürztraminer

**1.** Arrange the tomatoes in rows on a serving platter. Sprinkle with salt and pepper and arrange the Parmesan slices on top and among them or sprinkle with Parmesan if using the grated sort.

**2.** Drizzle the oil on top, then pour on the wine. Serve at room temperature or lightly chilled.

# Tomato Couscous Salad

### SERVES 4

Couscous salads are quick to make and satisfying to eat. Try this simple version from Chris Prosperi of Metro Bis in Simsbury, Connecticut, as an alternative to potato or pasta salad with a summer meal.

1 cup couscous

   salt and freshly ground black pepper

2 cups boiling water

1 tablespoon extra-virgin olive oil

1 cup diced tomato (¼-inch pieces)

½ cup chopped parsley

1–3 tablespoons fresh lemon juice

2–3 dashes Tabasco

   about ½ cup Metro Bis Tomato Salad Dressing (page 45)

**1.** Mix the couscous with 1 teaspoon of salt in a large bowl. Pour in the water and the oil. Cover and let sit for 10 minutes.

**2.** Lightly fluff the couscous with a fork, and then add the tomato, parsley, 1 tablespoon of lemon juice, Tabasco, and the tomato dressing. Stir gently with a fork. Check seasonings and adjust by adding salt, pepper, Tabasco, lemon juice, and tomato dressing to taste.

**3.** Cover and chill in the refrigerator for 2 hours or up to 6 hours. Before serving, check the seasonings and adjust with salt, pepper, and lemon juice as needed.

## PARSLEY

# Heirloom Tomatoes with New Potatoes, Herbs, and Melted Taleggio Cheese

SERVES 4

When executive chef Sarah Stegner cooked at the Ritz-Carlton hotel in Chicago, her food reflected both her deep roots in the Midwest — she was born in Evanston, Illinois — and her training in classical French cuisine. The combination of earthy new potatoes and runny rich Taleggio cheese in this salad makes a wonderful contrast to the juicy acid-sweet tomatoes. An unusual combination of vegetables, this dish should be served as a first course — all by itself — to fully appreciate the striking flavors. The flavor of Taleggio is unique, but if it's unavailable, you can substitute fontina, a sort of Asiago, or even a Saint André cheese. As for the tomatoes, a meaty red, such as Dr. Neal, Brandywine, or Olena Ukrainian, is perfect.

1 pound new potatoes

salt and freshly ground black pepper

¼ cup minced shallots

2 tablespoons butter

1 tablespoon extra-virgin olive oil

2 teaspoons red wine vinegar

¼ teaspoon Dijon mustard

12 small basil leaves, chopped

2 tablespoons fresh chives, snipped ¼ inch in length

1 tablespoon roughly chopped chervil

1 tablespoon roughly chopped parsley

16 heirloom tomatoes, cut into ½-inch slices

4 ounces Taleggio cheese, rind removed, sliced

1. In a medium saucepan, cover the potatoes with cold water and salt generously. Bring to a boil, and then simmer for 20 to 25 minutes, until the potatoes are tender but not mushy when pierced with a fork. Drain, plunge into cold water to stop the cooking, and drain again. Peel and cut the potatoes into quarters.

2. Cook the shallots in the butter in a medium skillet over medium-low heat. When the shallots are tender, add the potatoes and warm through. Season with salt and pepper and set aside.

3. Turn the broiler to high.

4. For the salad dressing, whisk the oil, vinegar, mustard, basil, chives, chervil, and parsley in a small bowl. Season to taste with salt and pepper.

5. Place some slices of tomato in the center of four heatproof plates. Put one-quarter of the potatoes on top of each plate of tomatoes. Place the cheese over the top of the potatoes and put the plate under the broiler. Brown for 2 to 4 minutes; remove promptly from the heat. The plate will be very hot.

6. Sprinkle the salad dressing over the melted cheese and serve immediately.

# THE FIRST RECIPES

The first known written recipes utilizing tomatoes appeared in Antonio Latini's *Lo Scalco alla Moderna*, printed in Naples in 1692. What is particularly significant about these two recipes is that they would seem to indicate that tomatoes are assumed to be available as an ingredient. The sauces are both Spanish in style, and we have our first recipe for tomato sauce and ratatouille.

### Minestra of Eggplants

Cut [the eggplants] in small pieces, with minced onions, fresh pumpkins cut small, and small pieces of tomatoes. Underfry everything together with fragrant herbs, with sour grapes. You will produce a very good minestra, Spanish style.

### Tomato Sauce, Spanish Style

Take half a dozen tomatoes that are ripe, and put them to roast in the embers, and when they are scorched, remove the skin diligently, and mince them finely with a knife. Add onions, minced finely, to discretion; hot chile peppers, also mince finely; and wild thyme [or dittany] in a small amount. After mixing everything together, adjust it with a little salt, oil, and vinegar. It is a very tasty sauce, both for boiled dishes or anything else.

# Tomato Pasta Salad

When I put out a call for simple home-style recipes using tomatoes, Chris Prosperi of Metro Bis in Simsbury, Connecticut, developed this pasta salad. He suggests cooking pasta for salads a minute or so longer than usual. He also emphasizes the importance of tasting the salad and adjusting the salt, pepper, and lemon juice before serving it.

8 ounces orecchiette or any other shape of medium pasta

salt and freshly ground black pepper

2 cups diced tomatoes (1-inch pieces)

¾ cup diced red onion (about ½ onion)

½ English cucumber, cut into ½-inch dice

½ cup pitted olives

¼ cup chopped fresh cilantro

1–2 teaspoons ground cumin

1–3 tablespoons lemon juice

¼–½ cup Metro Bis Tomato Salad Dressing (page 45)

**1.** Bring 3 quarts of water to a boil in a large saucepan. Add the pasta and 2 tablespoons of salt. Stir, and then boil for 8 to 10 minutes. Drain the pasta into a colander and let sit for 5 minutes (do not rinse).

**2.** Combine the tomato, onion, cucumber, olives, cilantro, 1 teaspoon of cumin, 1 tablespoon of lemon juice, and salt and pepper to taste in a large bowl. Mix well.

**3.** Add the pasta to the bowl of vegetables and mix well. Add ¼ cup of the tomato dressing and mix again.

**4.** Taste the salad and adjust seasonings by adding additional cumin, lemon juice, salad dressing, and salt and pepper as needed. Serve immediately.

CHAPTER SIX

# PIZZAS &
# SANDWICHES

# Tomato Tarts

### MAKES TWO 8-INCH OR SIX 3-INCH TARTS

Josie Le Balch grew up in the restaurant business in Los Angeles. With her husband, she now owns Josie in Santa Monica, where she has created an inventive menu that has won rave reviews. In the words of the *Los Angeles Times Magazine*, "Le Balch moves from American to Italian to French with the aplomb of a lounge pianist." If you make the pastry for these tomato tarts ahead of time, they are a quick last-minute fix. A large tart can be the centerpiece of a summer lunch or supper. Think of the smaller sizes for a first course. The quick final baking draws out the lush summery flavors of the tomato topping.

## Tart Dough

- 3⅓ cups all-purpose flour
- 2 tablespoons sugar
- 1½ teaspoons salt
- ⅔ cup vegetable shortening, at room temperature
- 2 tablespoons butter, at room temperature
- 2 tablespoons milk
- ½ cup water

## Filling

- 4 ounces herbed cream cheese
- 1 pound tomatoes of assorted colors and sizes
- ¼ cup extra-virgin olive oil
- 1 tablespoon balsamic vinegar
- salt and freshly ground black pepper

**1.** Combine the flour, sugar, and salt in a large mixing bowl. Add the shortening and butter to the dry ingredients in small bits and rub them in. (Alternatively, if you have an electric mixer, you can mix them with the paddle attachment.)

**2.** Add the milk and water and mix again until just incorporated into a dough. Turn the dough onto a sheet of plastic wrap and wrap it into a flat package. Refrigerate for 30 minutes or until ready to roll it out.

**3.** When you are ready to make the tarts, preheat the oven to 350°F.

**4.** Roll out the tart dough to a thickness of about ⅛ inch. Line two 8-inch or six 3-inch tart pans with dough. Prick the bottom all over with a fork. Line the tart shells with parchment paper and then baking weights or dried beans and blind-bake the shells for about 10 minutes. Remove the weights or foil and bake 2 to 3 minutes longer to allow the crust to brown evenly on the bottom.

**5.** Let the shells cool to room temperature, and then spread the cheese on the bottom.

**6.** Cut the tomatoes into bite-size pieces (or leave grape tomatoes whole). Toss them with the oil and vinegar and season with salt and pepper to taste. Fill the tart shells with tomatoes. Return the tarts to the oven and warm for 3 to 4 minutes. Serve immediately.

## AN ACT OF DEATH-DEFYING COURAGE

Undoubtedly the most famous story surrounding the introduction of the tomato to America took place in Salem, New Jersey, on the courthouse steps, in September 1820, at the height of the tomato season. Robert Gibbon Johnson publicly announced that he would eat raw tomatoes and defy death. A large crowd of onlookers gathered around Johnson and his basket full of tomatoes, awaiting the results. Johnson ate the tomatoes and did not die, nor did he even fall sick. Dramatically he had proved to dozens of people that tomatoes were safe to eat, and thus he is often credited with the introduction of tomato consumption to America. Unfortunately, the story just isn't true and rightfully belongs in the great genre of American myths, along with Paul Bunyan and his Blue Ox and Pecos Bill.

PIZZAS & SANDWICHES

# Josie Le Balch
## JOSIE, *Santa Monica, California*

Josie Le Balch is a third-generation chef. Her father and grandfather were both chefs. In order to be close to her father as a kid, she spent lots of time alongside him in the kitchen at his acclaimed Chef Gregoire restaurant. That early and enduring exposure to food was a significant help in learning her trade. But Josie firmly believes that being a chef is a natural ability, an innate love — "Either it's in your heart or it isn't."

Clearly, being a chef is a passion for her — she loves cooking and food. Running a restaurant operation requires extensive management skills, but Josie just shrugs and says that she accepts all these roles; they are what it means to be a chef. She figures one or two of the would be chefs she meets have the innate talent and/or the drive to really make it. "I think some real-world kitchen training combined with schooling is what is required. And then lots of hard work with a few quality chefs."

Josie's heritage is French, and she was trained by her father in classical French haute cuisine. She went on to train with various chefs, including Wolfgang Puck at Ma Maison and Jean Betranou at L'Ermitage. In 1986, she became head chef of the Saddle Peak Lodge, one of the first restaurants in Los Angeles to feature game on its menu, a specialty for which she has become well known. She was executive chef at Remi Restaurant in Santa Monica for five years, during which time she won several awards.

Josie characterizes her food as "rustic-progressive American with French and Italian influence." But she does not combine the French with the Italian. And while she will use different ingredients in her food from the influences of other cuisines, she sticks close to home, buying seasonal and local ingredients, especially from the Santa Monica Farmers' Market. Fusion cuisine is definitely not a term she uses, and she decries the cuisine of "the weirder the better." Her food uses simple flavors, not more than five to a plate. "My food starts from an earth base, sustaining and supporting small farms." Having grown up with the tyranny of the classical kitchen, Josie now wants to "have fun, enjoy all the creative aspects and keep evolving with our food heritage."

# Tomato Basil Quiche

Quiches can have a variety of fillings. Traditionally Gruyère is the cheese used in a quiche, but any type of hard cheese can be substituted. I like using a sharp cheddar, because it goes very nicely with the tomatoes and is a cheese still being produced in many of the dairy states in America. Thus, in some places you can make this quiche entirely out of local ingredients, except the port. The port combines well with red tomatoes, adding a subtle winey flavor. It can be omitted, if you desire, but reduce the baking time by 5 minutes. Any red slicing tomato will work nicely: Paragon, Earliana, Abe Lincoln, and Cardinal are among many.

2 medium or 1 large (about 10 ounces) tomato, sliced ¼ inch thick

8 ounces sharp white cheddar or Gruyère cheese, shredded (about 2 cups)

1–2 garlic cloves, peeled and finely chopped

1 unbaked 9-inch pie shell

1 small onion, thinly sliced

leaves from 3 stems basil, torn if large

4 eggs

1⅔ cups light cream

6 tablespoons aged port or sherry

½ teaspoon freshly ground black pepper

1. Preheat the oven to 425°F. Place the tomato slices on a paper towel to absorb excess moisture.

2. Toss the cheese with the garlic in a small bowl. Sprinkle 1½ cups of the cheese mixture evenly on the bottom of the pie shell. Arrange the onion on top of the cheese. Arrange the tomato slices in a single layer on top of the onion. Distribute the basil on top of the tomato and in the crevices between the rounds. Sprinkle the remaining ½ cup cheese mixture on top.

3. Beat the eggs thoroughly in a medium bowl. Add the cream, port, and pepper and beat well. Slowly pour the egg mixture into the pie shell.

4. Bake for 20 minutes. Lower the oven temperature to 350° and bake for 35 minutes longer, until the quiche is lightly browned on top.

5. Cool the quiche on a wire rack for a few minutes before serving.

# Tomato, Potato, and Olive Focaccia with Rosemary

### SERVES 4–6

Eat this focaccia for lunch or serve it with drinks before a meal. You can use Yellow or Red Pear or King Humbert tomatoes. A few capers or thinly sliced red onion add variety to the topping.

## Dough

- 1 package (1 tablespoon) active dry yeast
- 1 cup lukewarm water
- 4 cups bread flour or all-purpose flour
- 1 teaspoon salt
- 3 tablespoons extra-virgin olive oil

## Topping

- 1 medium potato, peeled and cut into ¾-inch cubes
- 1 tablespoon extra-virgin olive oil
- 1 teaspoon rosemary leaves
- 1 clove of garlic, peeled and coarsely chopped
- 18 cherry or small pear tomatoes
- 1 teaspoon coarse sea salt, such as Maldon salt
- 12 black or green olives, pitted

1. For the dough, stir the yeast into ½ cup of the water in a small bowl and let stand for 10 minutes, until dissolved and slightly frothy. In a warmed bowl or the bowl of a food processor, mix the flour with the salt. Make a well in the center and pour in the yeast mixture and the remaining water. Mix briefly, and then add 1 tablespoon of the oil and knead or process to make a firm but not sticky dough, adding more tepid water, a little at a time, if necessary, to achieve this. Developing the dough takes 5 to 7 minutes with a food processor or electric mixer, 10 to 12 minutes if kneading by hand.

2. Shape the dough into a ball and set it in a large, lightly greased bowl. Cover with a plastic bag or plastic wrap and a clean cloth and set in a warm draft-free spot. Leave until it has doubled in bulk, about 1½ hours, depending on the room temperature.

3. Knock down the dough by punching it vigorously or slamming it on the counter. Grease a pizza pan or baking sheet. Stretch the dough on the pan until it fits the pan's shape. Don't worry about an exact fit, because the dough will rise again; however, if the dough is hard to spread, and shrinks back to its original shape, roll into a ball again, bang it firmly on the counter to "shock" it, and let it stand covered with a towel for 10 to 15 minutes. This will help it relax and make it easier to spread.

**4.** Cover the dough once more and let it rise again until it looks puffy — about 25 minutes. Dent the dough by poking it with your fingertips. It will now look dimpled. Brush with the remaining 2 tablespoons oil, letting some collect in the dimples. The dough is now ready for topping.

**5.** While the dough is resting, preheat the oven to 425°F.

**6.** For the topping, bring a medium pan of lightly salted water to a boil. Cook the potato in the boiling water for 7 to 8 minutes, until just tender. Drain.

**7.** Combine the olive oil, rosemary, and garlic in a medium bowl. Add the potato and tomatoes. Stir gently to lightly coat the vegetables with the oil, and then scatter the mixture over the prepared dough. Sprinkle with salt. Dot the olives here and there. Drizzle on any oil remaining in the bowl.

**8.** Bake for 12 to 15 minutes, until the edges of the dough are golden and the tomatoes and potatoes are beginning to brown.

**9.** Let rest 5 minutes (or longer if more convenient) before serving. To serve, cut into large rectangles or squares.

 # Chaiwalla Savory Tomato Pie

SERVES 4–6

**M**ary O'Brien created this pie for Chaiwalla, her teashop in Salisbury, Connecticut. When I was in the restaurant, a customer — a stranger to me — walked in, turned to me, and said, "You have to try her tomato pie." What can I say? It's scrumptious, and after you are done with your dinner, you will want to keep picking away at it. Try it with a farm-produced extra-sharp cheddar and a nice tart tomato, such as Paragon. Excellent!

2 cups all-purpose flour

4 teaspoons baking powder

½ teaspoon salt

4 tablespoons butter, cut into several pieces

about ⅔ cup milk

1 pound ripe tomatoes, skinned and sliced

salt and freshly ground black pepper

2 tablespoons torn basil leaves

1 tablespoon snipped chives

6 ounces sharp cheddar cheese, shredded (1½ cups)

2 tablespoons mayonnaise

**1.** Preheat the oven to 400°F.

**2.** Mix the flour, baking powder, and salt in a large mixing bowl. Cut the butter into the flour mixture until it looks like crumbs. Stir in the milk to make a springy dough. Use a little more milk if the dough feels too dry.

**3.** On a floured board, roll out half the dough and fit it into a 9-inch pie plate. Top with tomato slices, sprinkle with the basil and chives, and then with half the cheese. Spread the mayonnaise on the cheese, and then add the remaining cheese.

**4.** Roll out the remaining dough and cover the pie with it. Bake for 20 minutes, or until the surface looks golden and a cake tester inserted into the center comes out clean. Serve warm.

# Basic Pizza Dough

Pizza dough is really fairly easy to make, but it does require some planning, since the entire process takes a couple of hours. Small amounts of herbs such as rosemary or basil can be added to the dough mixture after adding the water and oil.

1 package (1 tablespoon) active dry yeast

    about 1 cup lukewarm water

4 cups all-purpose flour

2 teaspoons salt

2 teaspoons extra-virgin olive oil

1. Mix the yeast with ½ cup of the water. Set aside for 10 minutes, until slightly frothy.

2. Mix the flour and salt in the bowl of an electric mixer or food processor or in a large mixing bowl. Stir in the yeast mixture and combine well. Add the remaining ½ cup water and the oil and mix or process for 4 to 5 minutes, until you have a smooth elastic dough that does not stick to your hands or the sides of the bowl. (If you are mixing by hand, mix the dough, and then knead for 10 minutes on a floured board until the dough is no longer sticky.) Form the dough into a ball and place it in a bowl. Cover the bowl with plastic wrap and leave it in a nondrafty spot until the dough has doubled in bulk, about 1½ hours.

3. Grease a pizza pan or large baking sheet.

4. Knock down the dough by slamming it on the counter. Let it rest for about 5 minutes, and then stretch it into a circle with your hands. (It won't be a perfect circle, but that doesn't matter.) Place it on the pan, cover, and leave for 15 minutes longer, until the dough looks slightly puffy.

5. The dough is now ready for topping.

 # Pizza Middle Eastern Style

SERVES 4–8

If you wanted to enjoy this Middle Eastern pizza in Lebanon, you would order *lahma bi ajeen*. The spiced topping of tomatoes and lamb makes these individual pizzalike pies favorites for lunch and snacks in Lebanon and other countries around the Mediterranean and Black Sea. The strong flavor of the lamb demands a full-flavored red, pink, purple, or black tomato. Paste types work best and require less cooking, but other tomatoes will do.

Basic Pizza Dough (page 115)

2–3 tablespoons extra-virgin olive oil

2 tablespoons chopped onion

1 garlic clove, chopped

2 cups coarsely chopped cooked lamb or ½ pound raw ground lamb

salt

¾ teaspoon ground allspice

½ teaspoon ground cinnamon

½ teaspoon cumin seeds

freshly ground black pepper

2 cups chopped fresh or canned tomatoes, with juice

tomato paste

**1.** Make the pizza dough according to the recipe directions through step 2.

**2.** While the dough is rising, make the topping. Heat 1 tablespoon of the oil in a skillet and soften the onion and garlic for 3 to 4 minutes. Add the lamb and cook until it is lightly browned. Pour off any excess fat, leaving about 1 tablespoon in the skillet. Stir in salt to taste and the allspice, cinnamon, cumin, and ½ teaspoon pepper.

**3.** Drain the tomatoes, reserving the liquid. Stir the tomatoes, half the reserved liquid, and 1 teaspoon tomato paste into the lamb mixture. Simmer for 5 minutes. Taste for seasoning and add more salt or pepper if needed. The topping should be as thick as spaghetti sauce. If it is thicker, thin with a little reserved tomato liquid (or water as needed); if it is too thin, add a little more tomato paste.

**4.** When the dough has doubled in bulk, preheat the oven to 375°F and grease two large baking sheets.

**5.** Knock down the dough by slamming it on the counter, and then divide it into 8 portions. Let them rest for about 5 minutes, and then use your hands to stretch the 8 portions into circles. (They won't be perfect circles, but that doesn't matter.) Place them on the baking sheet, cover, and leave for 15 minutes longer, or until the dough looks slightly puffy.

**6.** Spread some of the topping on each dough circle, leaving a ¾-inch border. Use a pastry brush to brush the border lightly with the remaining oil.

**7.** Bake for 6 to 7 minutes, until the crust is golden and the topping is heated through. Serve hot.

GOLDEN STRIPED TOMATO

# Pizza Margherita

SERVES 4

Among the simplest and freshest-tasting pizzas, Pizza Margherita was created to honor Queen Margherita of Italy in 1889. In patriotic style, the red tomatoes, white cheese, and green basil symbolize the red, white, and green bands of the Italian flag.

Basic Pizza Dough (page 115)

3 tablespoons extra-virgin olive oil

1 garlic clove, peeled and slivered

1½ pounds (3–4 large or 8–9 plum) ripe tomatoes, peeled, seeded, and each cut into 4–6 pieces

2 stems basil, plus sprigs for garnish

1 tablespoon chopped fresh oregano or 2 teaspoons dried

salt and freshly ground black pepper

½ cup freshly grated Parmesan cheese

8 ounces fresh mozzarella, thinly sliced

1. Make the pizza dough according to the recipe directions through step 2.

2. While the dough is rising, make the tomato sauce and topping. Warm 1 tablespoon of the oil in a medium saucepan over low heat. Add the garlic and cook for 1 minute without browning. Stir in the tomatoes and all their juice. Add 1 stem of the basil and 1½ teaspoons of the oregano. Cover the pan and simmer over low heat for 4 to 5 minutes, until the tomatoes have softened but remain bright red and chunky.

Season with salt and pepper to taste and remove the basil stem. Set aside until the dough is ready.

3. Preheat the oven to 400°F. Grease a 14-inch pizza pan or heat a 15- by 12-inch pizza stone. (Most pizza stones do not need greasing.)

4. After the dough has risen once, knock it down by slamming it on the counter, and then knead it a few times. Let it rest for 5 minutes, and then form the dough into a ball, place it in the center of the pizza pan or pizza stone, and use your knuckles to stretch it to cover the surface. If the dough shrinks back or tears, cover it with a cloth towel or a sheet of plastic wrap and let it rest for 5 to 10 minutes longer, then try spreading it again.

5. Brush a 1-inch border all around the dough with oil. Tear 3 large leaves from the remaining basil stem into big pieces and stir them into the sauce. Pour the sauce into the center of the prepared dough, leaving the oiled border uncovered. If any oil remains, drizzle it on top of the sauce, then sprinkle on the Parmesan.

**6.** Bake for 12 to 15 minutes, until the crust is golden and feels firm when you lift it from the pan with a spatula. Scatter the mozzarella evenly over the surface. (Some patches of sauce will not be entirely covered; that's fine.) Sprinkle the cheese with the remaining 1½ teaspoons oregano. Return the pizza to the oven and bake 5 minutes longer, until the cheese has melted and the exposed crust is a rich brown.

**7.** Transfer the pizza pan to a cooling rack and cool for 4 to 5 minutes. (If you baked the pizza on a stone, remove it with a pizza peel and let the peel rest on a cooling rack.) Take an attractive sprig of basil and put it in the center of the pizza. Scatter 4 to 5 small or medium basil leaves or a few small sprigs of basil over the surface. Slice and serve while still hot.

# Heirloom Tomato Pizza with Grilled Vidalia Onions, Fresh Ricotta, and Aceto Balsamico

SERVES 4–5

From chef Melissa Kelly, owner of Primo Restaurant in Rockland, Maine, come these personal-size pizzas with a difference. Garlic purée replaces tomato sauce on the crust, while sliced heirloom tomatoes and halved cherry tomatoes share the limelight with slices of sweet Vidalia onions in the topping. The roasted garlic gives the pizza a uniquely savory, buttery, caramelized flavor that combines beautifully with the melding of the various cheeses and heirloom tomatoes.

### Dough

- ¾ cup lukewarm water
- 2 teaspoons active dry yeast
- ¼ cup whole wheat flour
- 1 tablespoon milk
- 2 tablespoons olive oil
- ½ teaspoon salt
- 2 cups all-purpose flour
- 2 tablespoons honey

### Topping

- 1 head garlic
- 2 tablespoons extra-virgin olive oil
- 2 Vidalia onions, cut into ¼-inch slices
- salt and freshly ground black pepper
- ¼ cup grated pecorino cheese
- ¼ cup grated fontina
- ½ cup grated mozzarella
- ¼ cup grated provolone
- 2 heirloom tomatoes, such as Brandywine and Rose de Berne, sliced
- ½ cup fresh ricotta
- ½ pint heirloom cherry tomatoes, cut in half
- 15-year-old balsamic vinegar
- 1 tablespoon chopped fresh marjoram

**1.** To prepare the dough, mix ¼ cup of the water with the yeast and whole wheat flour. Set the bowl in a warm draft-free spot for 15 to 20 minutes, until it is bubbly on the surface.

**2.** Add the milk, oil, salt, flour, honey, and remaining ½ cup water. Mix into a dough, and then knead by hand or in an electric mixer until it is smooth and does not stick to your hands or the bowl. (If the dough is dry, add more lukewarm water, 1 to 2 tablespoons at a time, to get the right consistency.) Cover and let rest 40 to 60 minutes, until double its original size.

**3.** Divide the dough into 4 pieces for individual thin pizzas. Shape them roughly into 8- to 9-inch circles with your hands. If the dough shrinks back after you have shaped it, let it rest for a few minutes, then try again. Let the prepared pizza crusts sit in a warm spot for 20 to 30 minutes. Keep them covered with plastic wrap.

**4.** Preheat the oven to 350°F.

**5.** While the dough is rising, roast the garlic: First, slice off the stem end so that the tips of the cloves are visible. Wrap the whole bulb loosely in foil and bake for 30 to 45 minutes, until it is soft when squeezed. Cool the garlic until it can be handled, and then squeeze out all the soft garlic cloves and mash them with 1 tablespoon of the oil.

**6.** Also while the dough is rising, preheat the broiler. Season the onions with salt and pepper and brush with the remaining 1 tablespoon oil, then broil or grill them for about 4 minutes, until somewhat tender and very golden on one side.

**7.** To assemble the pizzas, raise the oven temperature to 475°F and place a pizza stone in the oven. Brush the garlic over the surface of each pizza crust and sprinkle with pecorino. Combine the fontina, mozzarella, and provolone and sprinkle some on each crust. Place the tomatoes and the onions, pale side up, on top. Dot with ricotta, and sprinkle with the cherry tomatoes. Bake on the stone or on a preheated baking sheet lined with parchment paper until the edges are golden and crisp, 5 to 6 minutes.

**8.** Top with a sprinkle of salt, a drizzle of vinegar, and the marjoram and serve immediately.

# Robert Gurvich's Pizza with Fresh Tomato Sauce

### MAKES TWO 8-INCH PIZZAS

**H**ere is a classic pizza recipe made special with homemade dough and a fresh tomato sauce from Robert Gurvich, chef at Alison Restaurant in East Hampton, New York. He suggests a topping of your choice, and with pizza the sky is the limit, though some toppings get a bit too far-out for me. Slices of fresh mozzarella are the classic. Or try a couple of cups of cooked spinach, squeezed dry and scattered on top, or steamed broccoli florets with a few tablespoons of walnuts. Various hard cheeses create interesting variations, but I prefer a fresh chèvre dabbed on top, with or without the mozzarella. Button mushrooms, sliced and sautéed in olive oil and a little white wine, are good. For a touch of the exotic, wild mushrooms, such as native fresh porcini (boletes), chanterelles, or black trumpets, are excellent. Meat lovers enjoy sautéed spiced sausage or prosciutto. Fruit can be weird on pizza, but slices of dried figs go very well with prosciutto and ham.

## Fresh Tomato Sauce

- 2 tablespoons extra-virgin olive oil
- 1 small onion, minced
- 3 garlic cloves, peeled and minced
- 1 tablespoon tomato paste
- 2 pounds (about 10) Roma or other plum tomatoes, peeled, seeded, and diced
- 1 cup sun-dried tomatoes (packed in oil)
- 6–8 fresh basil leaves, washed, dried, and cut into ⅛-inch strips
- salt and freshly ground black pepper

## Dough

- 1 package (1 tablespoon) active dry yeast
- 1 teaspoon honey
- ¾ cup warm water, or as needed
- 2¾ cups all-purpose flour
- 1 teaspoon salt
- 2 tablespoons olive oil, plus extra for brushing

1. For the tomato sauce, heat the oil in a medium saucepan. Sauté the onion over medium-high heat for about 5 minutes, until soft. Add the garlic and cook a minute longer. Add the tomato paste and the Roma and sun-dried tomatoes; simmer for about 15 minutes, until the sauce reduces to a thick mass. Let cool to room temperature, then purée in a blender or a food processor or pass through a food mill.

2. Stir the basil leaves into the sauce. Season to taste with salt and pepper, and then chill.

3. For the dough, dissolve the yeast and honey in ¼ cup of the water. Let sit for 5 to 10 minutes, until frothy on the surface.

4. In a mixer fitted with a dough hook, combine the flour and salt. Pour in the oil and, when absorbed, stir in the prepared yeast. Add the remaining ½ cup of water — or a little more if necessary to form a dough — and knead on low speed about 5 minutes. (If working manually, knead for about 10 minutes.) The dough should be smooth and firm. Let it rise in a draft-free spot, covered with a plastic bag and a kitchen towel, until doubled in bulk, 40 to 75 minutes, depending on the temperature of the room.

5. Divide the dough into 4 pieces. Work each ball by pulling down the sides and tucking them under the bottom of the ball. Repeat 4 or 5 times. On a smooth unfloured surface, roll the ball under your palm until it is smooth and firm. Cover with a sheet of plastic wrap and a towel and leave for 20 minutes. At this point, the balls can be loosely covered with plastic wrap and refrigerated for a day if you like.

6. Preheat the oven to 525°F. Place a pizza stone in the oven.

7. To prepare each pizza, place a ball on a lightly floured surface. Press down the center, spreading out the dough into a 7- to 8-inch circle, with the outer border a little thicker than the center. Brush lightly with oil and coat evenly with the tomato sauce. Add your favorite toppings at this point, or simply add some strips of mozzarella.

8. Transfer the pizza to the baking stone and bake for 15 to 20 minutes, until nicely browned. Transfer to a firm surface. Cut with a pizza cutter and serve immediately.

# Bruschetta with Tomatoes and Smoked Trout

**SERVES 4–8**

**B**ruschetta — made from good-quality bread flavored with garlic and olive oil, then topped with ripe tomatoes — is one of the best ways to enjoy tomatoes. Often bruschetta is served as an appetizer, but this version, with smoked trout and avocado, makes a quick meal. And if you love smokiness, you can even spread a little Smoky Tomato Butter (page 48) on the bread before piling on the tomato topping. A mixture of Green Zebra, Garden Peach, Golden Queen, Paragon, and/or Eva Purple Ball tomatoes is just about perfect here.

8 large pieces crusty country-style bread, sliced about ¾ inch thick

2 large garlic cloves, peeled and halved

3 tablespoons extra-virgin olive oil

3 medium-size (1–1¼ pounds) juicy ripe tomatoes, seeded and chopped

2 tablespoons chopped fresh parsley, plus a few sprigs for garnish

1 tablespoon snipped fresh chives

1 teaspoon drained capers

salt

4 ounces smoked trout or mackerel

½ teaspoon freshly cracked black pepper

1 small Hass avocado

½ teaspoon lemon or lime juice

3–4 tablespoons Smoky Tomato Butter (page 48), optional

**1.** Broil or grill the bread slices: place them about 4 inches from the heat source and cook for 2 to 3 minutes on each side, until golden brown. While the bread is still hot, rub the surfaces with the garlic and drizzle with the oil.

**2.** For the topping, mix the tomatoes with the parsley, chives, and capers and season to taste with salt.

**3.** Break the trout into flakes, season with the pepper, and gently mix with the tomatoes.

**4.** Peel and pit the avocado and mash the flesh. Season with salt, stir in the lemon juice, and set aside.

**5.** To finish the bruschetta, spread the toasted bread slices with Smoky Tomato Butter, if desired, then pile the tomato mixture on top and garnish with a dollop of the avocado and a sprig of parsley. (Alternatively, you can spread the mashed avocado onto the bread before adding the tomato mixture.) Serve immediately.

# Panini of Heirloom Tomatoes, Pancetta, and Basil Mascarpone

Walter Pisano, executive chef and owner of Tulio, the flagship restaurant for Hotel Vintage Park in downtown Seattle, created this recipe for a chunky Italian-style variation on America's BLT. The sandwich is typical of Pisano's style: rustic yet refined Italian cuisine using fresh local ingredients.

⅛ cup fresh basil with no black marks

½ cup mascarpone

salt and freshly ground black pepper

12 pieces pancetta cut into ⅛-inch slices

8 slices focaccia or other firm flavorful bread

2–3 tablespoons extra-virgin olive oil (optional)

1 bunch arugula, washed and dried

4 heirloom tomatoes cut into ½-inch slices

1. Preheat the oven to 375°F.

2. Process the basil in a blender for 10 seconds, add the mascarpone, and season with salt and pepper. Process a few seconds longer, until just mixed. Remove from the blender and set aside.

3. Lay the pancetta on a baking sheet and crisp in the oven for about 12 minutes, until it is golden on both sides. Drain the pancetta on paper towels. Toast the bread either on a grill or in the oven, brushing it with oil if you wish.

4. Spread a small amount of basil mascarpone on the top half of the bread and place the arugula on top. On the bottom half, place the tomatoes and crispy pancetta, then season with salt and pepper. Put the sandwiches together and serve immediately.

# GARY IBSEN'S TOMATOFEST

Gary Ibsen's Carmel TomatoFest takes place each year in mid-September at the Quail Lodge Resort and Golf Club in Carmel, California. This festival features tastings of three hundred varieties of tomatoes, making it the largest annual tomato-tasting event anywhere. It started as a small get-together of family and friends to celebrate the tomato harvest. It has turned into a major tomato festival, attracting as many as 1,800 attendees.

The TomatoFest is a fund-raiser for local youth charities and has donated more than $100,000 to them. It features a buffet of great tomato dishes prepared by 50 central California chefs, with dishes such as Green Heirloom Tomato Pie; Brandywine Tomato, Peach, and Pear Compote in Merlot Sauce; and a Swiss Tomato Fondue.

There is a Salsa Showcase, with 90 tomato salsas from various parts of the United States, plus tastings of specialty food products made from tomatoes, and an Italian Pavilion, with a tasting and display of Italian foods. The International Olive Oil Tasting features extra-virgin olive oils from eight countries and California. The TomatoFest's location in wine country enables it to feature tastings of 75 types of premium Monterey County wines.

There is a country barbecue, plus live music and dancing, making the festival an all-around family party. Seeds and tomatoes are also offered for sale.

In 2009, Gary transferred management of the TomatoFest to Harvest Farm-to-Table. The event still takes place at Quail Lodge Resort, but it now showcases a broader range of farm-fresh products.

Heirloom Tomato Pizza, *p. 120*

Panini of Heirloom Tomatoes, Pancetta, and Basil Mascarpone, *p. 125*

Pasta with Tomatoes, Garden Vegetables, and Crumbled Blue Cheese, *p. 137*

Prawns with Garlic, Heirloom Tomatoes, and Lemon, *p. 156*

# Bacon, Lettuce, and Tomato Sandwiches

It is almost as American as apple pie or ketchup. Any type of bacon will work, but if you can find a preservative-free, applewood-smoked bacon, that's the best. And if by some chance you have a local farmer raising and processing heirloom pigs such as Tamworth, you'll have a real taste sensation. I like a nice juicy red slicing tomato such as Ponderosa, Abe Lincoln, Paragon, or Mortgage Lifter in this sandwich.

1 pound sliced applewood-smoked bacon

1 large garlic clove, peeled and minced (optional if you are using aioli)

½ cup mayonnaise or aioli (page 174)

1 tablespoon capers

8 slices multigrain sourdough bread

4 lettuce leaves, torn

2 medium or 1 large tomato, sliced

¼ teaspoon freshly ground black pepper

1. Fry the bacon in a single layer in a heavy skillet over medium heat until almost crisp but still flexible, about 6 minutes, turning often. Drain the bacon on paper towels or in a clean brown paper bag. Continue cooking in batches until all the bacon is cooked.

2. Stir the garlic, if desired, into the mayonnaise. Add the capers and mix gently.

3. Toast the bread until lightly browned. Do not let it get too crunchy. Or grill it in a very lightly oiled cast-iron pan over high heat for about 2 minutes on each side, until lightly browned.

4. Spread a heaping teaspoon of mayonnaise on one side of each piece of bread. Lay the lettuce down on 4 of the slices of bread. Lay tomato slices on the other 4 slices. Add the bacon on top of the tomatoes, about 4 slices per sandwich. Grind pepper on both open-faced sides of the sandwich. Place the bread slice with the lettuce on top of the bacon and tomato. Gently press down on the sandwich, slice in half on a diagonal, and serve.

NOTE: Instead of frying the bacon, you can roast it. Preheat the oven to 400°F. Arrange the bacon in a single layer on a meat rack in a roasting pan. Roast for about 30 minutes (check every 5 minutes or so). This method takes much longer but drives off more fat.

# Sun-Dried Tomato and Olive Bread

## MAKES 2 LOAVES

**D**ramatically studded with red tomatoes and black olives, this bread is colorful and delicious.

1 large garlic clove, peeled and finely chopped

1 small onion, finely chopped

2 tablespoons olive oil, preferably from a jar of sun-dried tomatoes

2 teaspoons salt

1 package (1 tablespoon) active dry yeast

½–1 cup lukewarm water

4–5 cups all-purpose flour, or more as needed

¼ teaspoon rosemary leaves

½ cup coarsely chopped oil-packed sun-dried tomatoes

12 kalamata or other black olives, pitted and cut into 3 or 4 pieces

2 teaspoons butter, melted (optional)

**1.** Mix the garlic and onion with 1 tablespoon of the oil and about ¼ teaspoon of the salt in a small pan. Cover and cook over low heat for 4 to 5 minutes, until the onion is tender but not browned. Remove the lid and set the pan aside to cool.

**2.** Stir the yeast into ½ cup of the lukewarm water and let stand for about 10 minutes, until frothy.

**3.** Mix 4 cups of the flour and the remaining salt in a large bowl, in a food processor, or in the bowl of an electric mixer. Stir in the yeast mixture and the remaining ½ cup lukewarm water and briefly mix. Add the garlic and onions, the remaining 1 tablespoon oil, the rosemary, about one-third of the sun-dried tomatoes, and about one-third of the olives. Mix by hand or in a food processor or electric mixer, adding more lukewarm water, a little at a time, as needed to create a dough. Knead the dough, by hand or by machine, adding the rest of the tomatoes and olives a few at a time to distribute them evenly. Knead for about 5 minutes longer with a processor or mixer, or 10 to 15 minutes longer by hand, until the dough has a silky texture and does not stick to your hands or the bowl. Shape the dough into a ball and place it in a greased bowl. Cover the bowl with plastic wrap or a large plastic bag and let stand in a draft-free spot for 1½–2 hours, until doubled in size.

**4.** Knock the dough down by punching it or slapping it on the counter. Knead for 2 to 3 minutes longer, and then divide into two equal portions and form them into balls or ovals. Grease and flour a baking tray or line the tray with parchment paper. Place the loaves on the tray and let stand until almost doubled in size, 45 to 65 minutes.

**5.** Preheat the oven to 425°F.

**6.** Make 3 to 4 evenly spaced quick slashes across the surface of the loaves with a straight-edged razor or very sharp knife. Cover the loaves again and let stand for about 10 minutes, during which time the slashes will open as the dough continues to rise.

**7.** Bake for 10 minutes, and then reduce the oven temperature to 375° and bake for 15 minutes longer. Test the loaves for doneness by rapping them on the bottom with your knuckles; if they sound hollow, they are done.

**8.** Transfer the loaves to a cooling rack. If a tender crust is desired, brush lightly with the butter while the bread is still hot. Cool completely on a rack before slicing.

# Green Tomatoes on Toast

SERVES 4

No nineteenth-century cookbook was without recipes for "toasts," which were served either as breakfast dishes or as after-dinner savories. Tomatoes were a favorite topping. This green tomato version provides a welcome use for unripe tomatoes. The topping is also excellent as a dip. The recipe is based on one in an anonymous book of 1890 titled *Preserving and Canning Fruits and Vegetables.*

> 2 pounds green (unripened) tomatoes, peeled and thickly sliced
>
> salt
>
> ¼ cup cream or 3 tablespoons butter
>
> freshly ground black pepper
>
> 4 slices thick bread, toasted and hot

**1.** Put the tomatoes in a medium saucepan and sprinkle with salt. Cover and cook over low heat until the juices have run a little, then raise the heat slightly and cook for 7 to 8 minutes longer, until the tomatoes are soft.

**2.** Stir in the cream. If using butter, cut it into small pieces and stir them into the hot tomatoes. Season generously with pepper and pour over the toast. Serve immediately.

# Dru Rivers
## FULL BELLY FARM, *Guinda, California*

Full Belly Farm is a diversified organic fruit and vegetable farm located in Guinda, northwest of Sacramento and northeast of San Francisco in the Capay Valley. Twelve acres are devoted to heirloom tomatoes and produce upwards of 150,000 pounds each year. The farm was started 20 years ago with Dru Rivers and her three partners renting and cultivating 50 acres. In time they were able to purchase an entire 200-acre farm and cultivate the whole area.

The farm produces lots of vegetables: heirloom and hybrid potatoes; sweet corn; many kinds of melons, including heirloom varieties; broccoli; greens; mesclun; and more. The orchards produce apricots, peaches, nectarines, apples, Asian pears, and citrus fruits.

Full Belly sells to a variety of markets, including some of the best San Francisco restaurants. They also run a CSA (community supported agriculture) farm, one of the largest in the country, with seven hundred members. Putting together the weekly boxes of produce for each family is a monumental task, which Full Belly generally accomplishes with aplomb. According to Dru, "Marketing through the CSA is a tremendously stabilizing force for any farm. Because people pay for at least a portion of their shares up front, it creates cash flow for the farmers when we need it the most — before the season has started. People get to know us, we get to know them, and it becomes more personalized." Every year they have a cooking class for members and a Farm Day for member visitation. Annually they put on the Hoes Down Harvest Festival, which attracts more than four thousand people.

The farm started growing heirloom tomatoes in the mid-1990s, like many other farms on the West and East Coasts. Rivers and her partners were somewhat familiar with them from being members of the Seed Savers Exchange. They tested 15 or so varieties a year until they settled on those that did the best for them. They continue to test new varieties yearly.

Full Belly also grows about two acres of hybrid tomatoes. Why so few compared with the heirlooms? "It's the taste. Everyone wants taste, and the heirlooms are hands-down better."

CHAPTER SEVEN

*Mostly Vegetable*

MAIN
DISHES

# Nell Newman's Organic Tomatoes and Basil with Fusilli

### SERVES 2–3

Nell Newman, daughter of Paul Newman and Joanne Woodward, is founder of the New-man's Own Organics division of Newman's Own. An ardent supporter of sustainable agri-culture, she is a frequent speaker on organic foods, defining her niche as "supporting the envi-ronment through the growth of organic agriculture." This recipe exemplifies her enthusiasm for flavorful organic products. Use a mix of currant tomatoes and cherries, such as Pink Ping Pong, Sarah Goldstar Cherry, and red, pink, yellow, orange, and black tomatoes, such as Dr. Wyche's Yellow, Limmony, Black Krim, Black from Tula, Abe Lincoln, and June Pink.

6 cups chopped very ripe organic tomatoes of various types and colors

¼ cup organic extra-virgin olive oil

2–4 garlic cloves, peeled and minced

1 cup basil leaves, julienned

salt and freshly ground black pepper

⅓ cup pine nuts

12 ounces organic fusilli or other pasta

1 cup organic corn cut from the cob

**1.** Cut large tomatoes into pieces and halve cherry tomatoes. If you have any tiny tomatoes, they can be left whole. Put them in a large bowl with the oil, 2 cloves of garlic (or up to 4 if you like), the basil, and a light seasoning of salt and pepper. Toss gently to mix. Cover the bowl with plastic wrap and leave for 4 hours, or all day.

**2.** Just before serving time, bring a large pot of salted water to a boil. Toast the pine nuts in a small skillet over medium heat, stirring them until they are golden and fragrant. Set aside.

**3.** Cook the pasta in the boiling water, follow-ing the package directions. Drain the pasta and return it to the hot pan; return the pan to the turned-off burner.

**4.** Pour the tomatoes onto the hot pasta and toss gently. Add the corn and the pine nuts and toss again. Serve immediately.

# Pasta with Tomatoes, Garden Vegetables, and Crumbled Blue Cheese

### SERVES 4

Blue cheese brings extra panache to this popular team of summer garden vegetables.

2 (7- to 8-inch) Chinese or Japanese eggplants, diagonally cut into 1-inch slices

salt

12 ounces rotelle, penne, or other medium-size pasta

2 tablespoons extra-virgin olive oil

2 green or red bell peppers, seeded and cut into ½-inch strips

1 large onion, quartered and sliced

2 garlic cloves, peeled and slivered

10 plum or paste tomatoes or other firm tomatoes, peeled, seeded, and quartered

2 medium summer squash, diagonally cut into ½-inch slices

1 medium zucchini, diagonally cut into ½-inch slices

1½ teaspoons chopped summer savory

6 basil leaves, torn, plus 3 or 4 small sprigs for garnish

freshly ground black pepper

2 teaspoons balsamic vinegar

4–6 ounces Roquefort, Stilton, Danish Blue, or other blue cheese, crumbled

1. Layer the eggplant slices in a colander, sprinkling them with 2 tablespoons salt as you do. Leave the slices standing in the sink for 45 minutes, then rinse off the salt and pat dry.

2. Bring a large pot of water to a boil. Add a tablespoon of salt and then stir in the pasta. Boil the pasta for 8 minutes, or according to the package directions, until just al dente. Drain and keep warm.

3. While the pasta is cooking, heat the oil in a large skillet over high heat. Add the eggplant, peppers, onion, and garlic. Reduce the heat to medium and sauté the vegetables for 2 minutes. Stir in the tomatoes, summer squash, and zucchini. Add the summer savory and basil and season to taste with salt and pepper. Sauté for 5 to 6 minutes, until the vegetables are tender, stirring and raising the heat if necessary to cook the vegetables briskly. Stir in the vinegar and cook for 1 minute longer.

4. Serve the pasta on a large platter with the sautéed vegetables piled on top. Scatter the blue cheese over the vegetables. Garnish with the basil sprigs.

# Spaghetti with Slow-Roasted Tomatoes, Basil, and Parmesan Cheese

### SERVES 4

Since 1994, when she opened her restaurant, Rialto, in Cambridge, Massachusetts, chef Jody Adams has been winning awards for her interpretation of the classic regional foods of the Mediterranean. Adams wrote *In the Hands of a Chef: Cooking with Jody Adams of Rialto Restaurant* with her husband, Ken Rivard. This is one of her favorite dishes — full of bright flavors and rich tastes, yet unfussy in conception. If you do not like arugula, substitute baby spinach leaves. The slow roasting both caramelizes and concentrates the flavor of the tomatoes, thus enhancing more ordinary commercial varieties. If you start with a full-flavored cherry, such as Peacevine or Matt's Wild Cherry, all the better.

¼ cup extra-virgin olive oil, plus more for roasting

1 large white onion, cut into ½-inch dice

6 garlic cloves, smashed and peeled

18 basil leaves

⅛ teaspoon crushed red pepper flakes

48 ripe cherry, grape, or sweet tomatoes, rinsed and dried

3 teaspoons kosher salt

2 teaspoons sugar

1 pound spaghetti

2 cups lightly packed arugula

¼ cup basil, cut into thin ribbons

½ cup finely grated Parmesan cheese

1. Preheat the oven to 250°F.

2. Heat ¼ cup of the oil in a large skillet over medium heat. Add the onion and garlic and cook, stirring occasionally, until tender, about 5 minutes. Remove from the heat; add the basil leaves and red pepper and stir well.

3. Toss the tomatoes with 1 teaspoon of the salt and the sugar and place them in a roasting pan with sides. The pan should be large enough to hold the tomatoes in a single layer. If they won't fit, use an additional roasting pan and more oil. Spoon the onion mixture over the tomatoes. Add enough oil to come halfway up the tomatoes. Roast until the tomatoes are tender but not falling apart, about 3 hours. Stir once, gently, during the roasting. (You can roast the tomatoes up to 6 hours ahead of time, if convenient.)

**4.** To finish the dish, bring a large pot of water with the remaining 2 teaspoons salt to a boil. Add the spaghetti and stir constantly until the water returns to a boil. Cook until the pasta is al dente, about 7 minutes.

**5.** Meanwhile, heat the tomatoes with the onions and oil in a large shallow saucepan over low heat. When the pasta is done, drain it and transfer to the saucepan with the tomatoes. Add the arugula. Toss well. Add the basil and toss again.

**6.** Serve in a warm shallow bowl with Parmesan sprinkled over the top.

**Onion, Yellow Danvers**

## WORLD-TRAVELING TOMATOES

In France, while tomatoes may have been used in the southern areas adjacent to Italy in the seventeenth century, it was not until the late eighteenth and early nineteenth centuries that they appeared in cooked dishes. The Vilmorin seed company, one of the most important French seed companies and still in existence today, listed tomatoes as ornamental plants at least as late as 1760. It was not until 1778 that tomatoes were identified as vegetables. In 1805, a French seed seller, Tollard, refers to tomatoes as "thomate," indicating their cultivation had "multiplied greatly," but it was not until 1830 that commercial production was large enough to supply the Paris market. In northern France, tomatoes were not generally used until 1900.

Tomatoes may have reached Poland early on but were apparently not widely adopted until more recently. The Turks probably spread tomatoes to the eastern Mediterranean, northwest Africa, and parts of the Mideast during the Ottoman Empire, beginning in the sixteenth century. Tomatoes certainly were cultivated in Africa by the second half of the seventeenth century, and by the end of the nineteenth century were throughout the continent. It is believed tomatoes reached China and the Philippines in the late 1500s but became widely used in China only during the twentieth century.

# Risotto of Heirloom Confit Tomatoes and Roasted Mushrooms

SERVES 2–3

Slow roasting intensifies the flavor of confit tomatoes, making them delicious partners to mushrooms in this risotto devised by Peter Platt, owner-chef at the Old Inn on the Green in New Marlborough, Massachusetts. Peter's cooking always delights me and, I imagine, all of his clients. This risotto is no exception. It is great as a course by itself or an accompaniment to chicken or pheasant.

### Confit Tomatoes

- 3 tablespoons ollve oll
- 6 large heirloom plum tomatoes, such as King Humbert, or any thick-fleshed heirloom tomato, such as Winsall or Ponderosa, peeled
- 2 garlic cloves, peeled and sliced
- 2 teaspoons fresh thyme leaves

### Risotto

- 6 tablespoons extra-virgin olive oil
- 1 cup sliced fresh mushrooms, wild-style varieties or regular white
- 2–3 cups simmering chicken or vegetable stock
- 2 large shallots, finely chopped
- 1 cup arborio, Carnaroli, or Vialone Nano rice
- ⅔ cup dry white wine
- ½ teaspoon sea salt
- 2 tablespoons mascarpone cheese

- ½ cup freshly grated Parmesan cheese
- 1 tablespoon finely chopped basil
- 1 tablespoon chopped chervil
- 1 tablespoon finely snipped chives
- freshly ground black pepper

1. For the confit tomatoes, preheat the oven to 250°F and grease a baking sheet or shallow pan with a little of the oil.

2. Cut each tomato into 6 wedges and remove the seeds. Arrange the wedges in a single layer on the baking sheet and scatter the garlic and thyme over them. Drizzle the remaining oil on top and bake for 1½ to 2 hours, until the tomato juice has evaporated and the wedges have shrunk. Baste with the oil two or three times during the baking, and make sure that the tomatoes don't brown. Set aside while you make the

risotto. (You can make the tomatoes up to 3 days ahead of time and keep them covered in the refrigerator if that is more convenient.)

**3.** For the risotto, heat 3 tablespoons of the oil in a large skillet over high heat. Add the mushrooms and cook briskly, stirring often, for 2 to 3 minutes, until the edges are browned. Remove from the pan with a slotted spoon and set aside. Reserve the pan juices.

**4.** Set the stock to simmering on a back burner. Heat the remaining 3 tablespoons oil in a large saucepan over medium heat. Stir in the shallots and cook for 3 to 4 minutes, until tender but not browned. Stir in the rice for a minute, until it is glistening with the oil. Pour in the wine, letting it sizzle over high heat until it has all evaporated, 5 to 7 minutes.

**5.** Add a ladle of the hot stock to the rice and stir it in over medium-low heat. Season lightly with salt. When the stock has been absorbed, in about 3 minutes depending on the variety of rice, add another ladle and stir it in. Proceed in this way, adding the simmering stock a ladleful at a time and cooking for a total of 15 to 18 minutes, until the rice is tender and coheres in a soupy mass. (You may not need an entire 3 cups of stock to achieve this, but you should have 3 cups available, as different brands and types of rice absorb the liquid in varying amounts.)

**6.** Stir in the mascarpone and Parmesan. Reserve a few tomato pieces and a few mushroom pieces for the garnish. Stir the remaining tomatoes and mushrooms into the risotto, along with the basil, chervil, and chives. Cook over gentle heat for another couple of minutes to reheat the vegetables and melt the cheese. Add pepper to taste. Serve on warmed plates and garnish with the reserved tomato and mushroom pieces. Drizzle the reserved mushroom juices on top and serve immediately.

# Hominy Arepas with Roasted Yams, Sun-Dried Tomato Salsa, and Chipotle Tofu Cream

SERVES 4

Arepas are hominy pancakes that hail from the Andes in South America, but this particular combination comes from Greg Higgins, owner-chef of Higgins in Portland, Oregon, where he features locally grown and produced food and offers a menu that includes many vegetarian dishes. The dish sails with bursts of flavorful contrasts of hot and cool, savory and tart, sweet and earthy. If you can find a source of heirloom corn, such as Iroquois white flour corn, all the better.

## Sun-Dried Tomato Salsa

1½ cups sun-dried tomatoes, cut into matchstick strips

1 cup onion, cut into ¼-inch dice

2 jalapeño peppers, seeded and minced

1 bunch cilantro, chopped

1 tablespoon garlic, minced

1 tablespoon New Mexico chili powder

1 teaspoon coriander seed, toasted and ground

1 teaspoon cumin seed, toasted and ground

½ teaspoon sugar

¼ cup lime juice

salt and freshly ground black pepper

## Chipotle Tofu Cream

½ pound soft organic tofu

¼ cup lime juice

1 chipotle chile packed in adobo, plus 1 tablespoon of adobo sauce from the can

salt and freshly ground black pepper

## Roasted Yams

4 medium garnet yams, peeled and cut into 1-inch thick slices

¼ cup olive oil

salt and freshly ground pepper

## Hominy Arepas

1 (29-ounce) can hominy, or 3 cups cooked white corn hominy

¼ cup extra-virgin olive oil

salt and freshly ground black pepper

½–¾cup fine or medium-ground white cornmeal

½ cup sliced scallions (white and tender green parts)

4–6 tablespoons vegetable oil

**1.** For the sun-dried tomato salsa, put the tomatoes in a medium bowl and cover with warm water. Leave for an hour or until they are tender, then drain. In a medium bowl, mix the tomatoes with the onion, jalapeños, cilantro, garlic, chili powder, coriander, cumin, sugar, and lime juice. Season with salt and pepper to taste. Set aside until serving time.

**2.** For the chipotle tofu cream, put the tofu, lime juice, chipotle chile, and adobo sauce in a blender or food processor and blend to a purée. (Alternatively, mix by hand in a mixing bowl.) Season to taste with salt and pepper. Set aside until serving time.

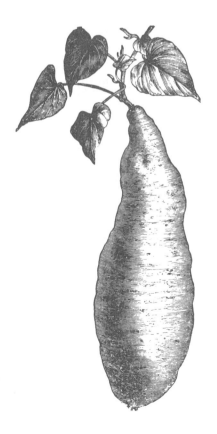

**3.** For the roasted yams, preheat the oven to 375°F. Toss the yams with the oil and season them with salt and pepper. Place them in a single layer on a cookie sheet and roast for 30 to 40 minutes, until tender and slightly browned at the edges.

**4.** For the hominy arepas, drain the hominy, reserving a cup of the liquid from the can. If you cooked the hominy yourself, reserve one cup of the cooking liquid. Put the grains into a food processor with the olive oil. Season with salt and pepper, then process, adding some of the reserved liquid as needed, until the mixture is smooth and creamy.

**5.** Combine the puréed hominy with the cornmeal, scallions, and a seasoning of salt and pepper in a medium mixing bowl. Knead in the bowl to form a smooth dough. Taste and adjust the seasoning with more salt and pepper if necessary. Divide the dough into 12 equal portions, round them into balls, and then flatten until they are ¾ inch thick and 2½ to 3 inches in diameter.

**6.** Heat 3 tablespoons of the vegetable oil in a large skillet and cook the arepas, turning them once or twice, until they are golden brown and crispy. You will need to make two batches, adding additional oil to the pan as needed. Serve the arepas with the roasted yams on the side or on top. Drizzle with the chipotle tofu cream. Serve the salsa on the side.

# Greg Higgins
**HIGGINS**, *Portland, Oregon*

Greg Higgins likes to think of his food as "home cooking," and while that is a modest description, it says much about his philosophy and his roots. Higgins was brought up in rural upstate New York, just south of Buffalo. With five kids to feed, Greg's mother had a big home garden and cooked on a daily basis. Greg learned to love both working in the garden and preparing recipes from *The Fannie Farmer Cookbook*. He worked on farms and, as a teenager, apprenticed in a small local cheese plant.

Eventually, Higgins found the lure of cooking compelling and traveled to the Alsace and Burgundy regions of France to hone his craft. Back in the United States, he traveled westward, finally settling in Portland, where he spent nearly a decade as the executive chef at the Heathman Hotel. Greg opened Higgins in 1994. He serves up a varied menu that largely reflects the ever-changing availability of ingredients from the Pacifc Northwest. Fifty varieties of regional mushrooms may grace the menu through the course of a year, and home-cured meats range from salami to dry-cured sausage. He admits he is obsessive about ingredients, even making his own heirloom tomato ketchup.

Greg believes firmly in commitment to the community. Supporting farms and farmers is critical, and almost everything he buys is locally and sustainably or organically grown. When he's not cooking, you can find Greg in his raised-bed trial garden, evaluating the best heirloom tomatoes and other varieties for home use, the education of his staff, and farmers.

Higgins's role as a chef is that of a "catalyst and educator," someone who helps "connect people to the continuum of a clean and protected environment, a strong, sustainable farm and local food system, and healthy eating." And yet when one is eating at Higgins, this message is subtle. "You want people to experience and enjoy their food. That is the most compelling way to win people over. We're interested in nourishing and sustaining not only our customers' appetites but also the land and the quality of life we all enjoy," he says.

# Eggplant Parmigiana

When tomatoes are in season, so are eggplants. This dish is a partnership of three equal ingredients: eggplant, tomatoes, and cheese.

2 pounds eggplant, cut into ¼-inch slices

salt

about ¾ cup all-purpose flour

about ½ cup olive oil

4 cups Marinara Sauce (page 19) or other well-seasoned tomato sauce

freshly ground black pepper

¾ pound mozzarella, shredded or thinly sliced

¾ cup freshly grated Parmesan cheese

½ cup chopped parsley

2 teaspoons dried oregano or 2 tablespoons fresh basil

**1.** Layer the eggplant slices in a colander, sprinkling them with salt as you do (use a total of about 3 tablespoons salt). Let stand for 45 minutes, until beaded with moisture, and then rinse and pat dry with paper towels.

**2.** Preheat the oven to 375°F and grease a 9- by 13-inch baking dish.

**3.** Dip the eggplant slices in the flour and shake off any excess. Heat half the oil in a large skillet and brown the eggplant slices, a few at a time, over medium heat, for 3 to 5 minutes per side, until golden on both sides. Drain the cooked slices on paper towels while you proceed. Replenish the oil in the skillet as needed.

**4.** To assemble the parmigiana, put just enough tomato sauce into the baking dish to cover the surface. Add a layer of eggplant and season it with pepper and a little salt. (You won't need much salt, because the cheese is already salty.) Sprinkle on about one-third of the mozzarella, one-third of the Parmesan, half the parsley, and half the oregano. Add about half the remaining tomato sauce and another layer of eggplant, seasoning, herbs, and half the remaining cheeses. Cover with the last of the tomato sauce and a final layer of Parmesan and mozzarella.

**5.** Cover the dish with foil and bake for 20 to 25 minutes, until bubbly. Remove the foil and bake for 5 minutes longer.

**6.** Let the dish rest for 4 to 5 minutes before serving.

NOTE: You can assemble the dish 4 to 6 hours ahead and bake later if you like.

# Huevos Rancheros

The breakfast of Mexico and the Southwest, huevos rancheros spice up the early morning. The basic version is simple: an egg on a tortilla topped with a ranchero sauce of lightly spiced tomatoes. For something zingier, replace the sauce with Rick Bayless's Essential Quick-Cooked Tomato-Chipotle Sauce on page 31. To make a heartier dish, pile some beans or seasoned cooked ground meat onto the tortilla before adding the egg.

1 pound (2–3 large) ripe tomatoes, peeled and coarsely chopped

2 serrano chiles, halved and seeded

1 tablespoon lard or canola oil

1 medium onion, chopped

1 garlic clove, minced

½ teaspoon salt

4 soft 5-inch corn tortillas

4 extra-large eggs

1. Put the tomatoes and chiles in a food processor or blender and process until they are puréed.

2. Heat the lard in a small pan and stir in the onion. Cover and cook gently over low heat for 4 to 5 minutes, until the onion has softened.

3. Stir in the garlic, cook for a minute, and then stir in the tomato mixture and salt and simmer 4 to 5 minutes to make a sauce.

4. Warm the tortillas either by placing them in a lightly greased nonstick skillet over low heat for 2 to 3 minutes or by placing them in a steamer set over boiling water for 2 to 3 minutes.

5. In another lightly greased nonstick skillet over low heat, crack the eggs. Cover the pan and cook over low heat for 3 to 4 minutes, until the whites are completely set and the yolks are still slightly runny.

6. To serve, put an egg onto each tortilla and top with sauce.

# Tomato Pancakes

**W**hy do we add only dessert fruit to our pancakes? Tomatoes and bacon go so well together. This is an old recipe that should never have been forgotten. The secret of these delicious pancakes is to use chunks of fresh summer tomato thoroughly drained of juice. Yellow Brandywine or a bicolor such as Regina's adds a bit of fruity flavor that works particularly well. Bacon or sausage makes a perfect accompaniment, or just serve with maple syrup or a zingy chutney, such as the Green Tomato Chutney on page 238 or the Tomato, Orange, and Ginger Chutney on page 240.

2 cups chopped drained tomatoes

2 eggs, beaten

1–1½ cups milk

2 teaspoons dried oregano

2 cups all-purpose flour

4 teaspoons sugar

2 teaspoons baking powder

1 teaspoon salt

1–2 tablespoons light olive or vegetable oil, or butter

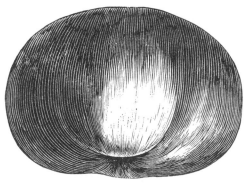

DWARF ORANGEFIELD

**1.** Preheat the oven to 250°F.

**2.** Stir together the tomatoes, eggs, 1 cup of the milk, and the oregano.

**3.** Mix the flour, sugar, baking powder, and salt in a large bowl. Make a well in the center and stir in the tomato mixture to make a thick batter. If the batter is too thick, add some or all of the remaining milk to achieve a thick, smooth batter that pours slowly from a spoon or pitcher.

**4.** Grease a griddle with oil and set it over high heat. When the oil is hot, lower the heat to medium and spoon on portions of batter to form pancakes about 4 inches in diameter. Flip the pancakes when the edges are dry (the centers will still be wet), after 3 to 4 minutes. Cook the other side for 3 minutes, until both sides are golden. Keep the first pancakes warm in the oven while you continue making pancakes until all the batter is used. Serve immediately.

# Frittata with Tiny Tomatoes and Sweet Potatoes

### SERVES 4

Frittatas are a kind of Italian omelet, but unlike the better-known French-style omelet, they are cooked slowly and without folding, so they emerge from the pan like large pancakes. Traditionally, most frittatas are turned so both sides brown, but with yellow eggs, orange sweet potatoes, and bright tomatoes, this one looks lovely served sunny-side up — a presentation that means you don't have to deal with the tricky business of inverting the frittata from a hot pan onto a serving dish and then sliding it back into the pan.

2–3 tablespoons extra-virgin olive oil

1 small sweet potato, peeled and cut into ½-inch cubes

salt

1 tablespoon water

1 tablespoon butter

6 eggs, thoroughly beaten

2 cups grape or other tiny tomatoes, such as Santa

4 scallions, white and tender green parts, chopped

1 teaspoon fresh thyme or ½ teaspoon dried

¼ cup grated Parmesan cheese

freshly ground black pepper

**1.** Heat 1 tablespoon of the oil in a small saucepan over medium heat and toss in the sweet potato cubes. Season lightly with salt, add the water, cover the pan, and let the potatoes sweat over low heat for 5 to 6 minutes, until just tender — but not soft or mushy — when poked with a knifepoint.

**2.** When the potatoes are ready, heat another tablespoon of the oil and the butter in a medium skillet over medium heat. Pour in the eggs and cook for 1 minute. Lower the heat to low, and then scatter the sweet potatoes, tomatoes, scallions, and thyme on top, arranging them so they are distributed evenly. Sprinkle on the Parmesan and lightly season with salt and pepper.

**3.** Cook the frittata gently for 8 to 10 minutes, until the underside is brown and the top is lightly set. Using a palette knife or spatula, ease it from the pan onto a warmed serving platter. Cut into wedges and serve.

NOTE: If you prefer to brown both sides, invert the serving platter over the skillet and tip the frittata onto it. Return the pan to the heat, add the remaining tablespoon of oil, then slide the frittata back into the pan so what was the topside is now the bottom. Cook 2 to 3 minutes longer, then slide it back onto the serving platter and serve cut into wedges.

# Bloody Mary

### SERVES 1

**B**loody Marys are most often made with vodka, but they can also be made with gin or rum. Tequila is an option, too, in which case the lemon juice is replaced with lime juice and the drink is called Bloody Maria. When sake is the base, the name becomes Bloody Mary Quite Contrary. Here's my recipe for one drink. For a crowd, make a jug of Bloodies by multiplying the amounts as appropriate.

1½ ounces vodka

2 ounces tomato juice (page 235) or Spicy Tomato Cocktail (page 66)

½ teaspoon lemon juice

salt and freshly ground black pepper

ice cubes

slug of Worcestershire sauce

half a lemon slice

6-inch stalk of tender celery with leafy top (optional)

**1.** Shake or stir the vodka with the tomato juice, lemon juice, salt and pepper to taste, and 2 to 3 ice cubes in a cocktail shaker. Pour into a glass.

**2.** Add Worcestershire to taste. Garnish with the half lemon slice nicked so that it sits on the rim of the glass. Stick the celery stalk into the glass, if desired, where it can act as a stirrer.

# Winter Bean Stew

SERVES 8

Canned tomatoes carry the flavor of summer into winter. Usually they are far better than out-of-season fresh tomatoes from far away, especially if you can your own. Here canned tomatoes team with canned beans and winter vegetables to make an easy vegetarian stew that will feed a crowd. Ginger flavors the beans and aids digestion.

2 tablespoons extra-virgin olive oil

1 large onion, chopped

2 garlic cloves, peeled and chopped

2 carrots, sliced into thin disks

2 stalks of celery, cut into ½-inch pieces

2 tablespoons grated fresh ginger

salt

1 (15½-ounce) can chickpeas, drained

1 (15½-ounce) can kidney beans, drained

1 teaspoon cumin seeds

4 cups canned whole plum tomatoes

1 bay leaf

1 (19-ounce) can cannellini beans (do not drain)

1 cup frozen peas

½ cup Tomato Purée (page 234), or more to taste

freshly ground black or red pepper

**1.** Warm the oil in a large pan over low heat. Stir in the onion, garlic, carrots, celery, and ginger. Season with salt, and then cover and cook over low heat for 3 to 4 minutes, until the vegetables are fragrant.

**2.** Add the chickpeas and kidney beans. Sprinkle the mixture with the cumin seeds, and then gently stir in the tomatoes and bay leaf. Cover and simmer 5 minutes longer.

**3.** Add the cannellini beans, peas, and tomato purée, stirring gently so as not to break up the beans. Season with pepper. Taste and add more salt, pepper, or tomato purée as necessary. Simmer 5 minutes longer. Serve immediately or refrigerate overnight and reheat to serve on the second day.

THE CARDINAL

## *William Woys Weaver's*
## **Top 10 Tomatoes**

William Woys Weaver is a food historian who has written numerous books on food and plants.

### Aunt Ruby's German Green

### Hartmann's Yellow Gooseberry
A good tomato for nibbling and salads

### Governor Pennypacker
An old Pennsylvania variety from the early 1900s; nice for cooking

### Omar's Lebanese

### Brown Flesh
Very handsome; one of Tom Wagner's creations

### Trophy

### Shah
Essentially a white version of Brandywine, though I am not sure of the lineage

### Teton de Venus
Finicky, but the fruit is truly sweet

### Chalk's Early Jewel
Well, it is from Norristown, only a few miles away from where I live, so it does great for me and is always the first to ripen.

### Dr. Lyle
A good competitor for Brandywine

MOSTLY VEGETABLE MAIN DISHES

# Imam Bayildi

SERVES 4–6

Imam Bayildi is almost certainly a Turkish dish, though Greeks, who often call it simply "Imam," sometimes claim to have invented it during the centuries when the Ottoman Turks ruled their land. Still others claim it was originally Armenian. Certainly it is popular in both countries and, indeed, throughout the Balkans and the Middle East. The name refers to an Imam — a Muslim religious leader — who supposedly swooned when he tasted the dish. The explanation of the swoon varies: some say the Imam was aghast at the liberal use of so much expensive olive oil; others, that the dish was so delicious that he fainted with delight. Indeed, it is a perfect marriage of tomatoes and eggplant, and an ideal do-ahead dish, since it is best served at room temperature and can easily be made the day before you plan to serve it.

4 (8-inch) eggplants

2 tablespoons salt, plus more for seasoning

½ cup extra-virgin olive oil, plus more as needed

4 medium-large (about 1½ pounds) onions, peeled, halved, and sliced

15 garlic cloves, peeled

4 cups peeled, seeded, and diced tomatoes

1 cup chopped fresh parsley

1–2 teaspoons honey or sugar

4 whole unpeeled tomatoes, thickly sliced

1. Cut the eggplants in half lengthwise. Slash them across the flesh side 3 or 4 times and scoop out enough flesh from the center to leave a space about as big as an egg. Sprinkle the eggplants and the scooped-out pieces with 2 tablespoons of salt and let them stand for 1 hour (or longer if more convenient), until the eggplants are plentifully beaded with liquid. Rinse them and pat dry with paper towels.

2. Heat ¼ cup of the oil in a large skillet over high heat. Put in 3 or 4 eggplant halves, cut side down, and cook over medium heat until browned, 5 to 6 minutes. Turn them over and cook 1 to 2 minutes longer, until golden. Place the prepared eggplants in a shallow baking dish that will hold them all in a single layer. Add more oil to the skillet as necessary and fry all the eggplant halves in the same way. Finally, fry the bits you cut from the center, turning them until they are golden on all sides, about 5 minutes.

3. If the eggplant has absorbed all the oil in the skillet, add 2 tablespoons. Sauté the onions and garlic over low heat for 10 minutes, until

the onions are soft and golden. Stir in the diced tomatoes, parsley, and honey. Add the reserved eggplant bits and season lightly with salt. Cover the pan and cook, stirring occasionally, for 10 to 15 minutes, until the mixture is tender.

**4.** Preheat the oven to 375°F.

**5.** Stuff the eggplants with the tomato mixture, pushing some of it into the slashes you made before salting and covering the entire top surface of the halves. Place 2 or 3 tomato slices on top of each half. Season the slices lightly with salt. Cover the dish with foil and bake for 40 minutes, until the eggplant halves are tender but not mushy. (Test them by inserting a knifepoint.) Remove the foil and bake for 10 to 15 minutes longer; the tomato slices will brown and wrinkle a little. Serve warm or at room temperature.

**Black Pekin**   Pkt., 10 cts.

## THE LIVINGSTON LEGACY

Along with the Paragon and Livingston's Beauty, Alexander Livingston and his sons introduced 31 varieties of the tomato. Other introductions included his Potato Leaf, New Stone, Royal Red, Buckeye State, New Dwarf Aristocrat, Large Rose Peach Tomato, Honor Bright, and two yellow types, Gold Ball and Golden Queen. The latter he claimed to have developed from a variety he obtained at a county fair. By the 1930s half of all the major tomato varieties on the market were Livingston introductions or bred from them. Livingston wrote up some of his history in *Livingston and the Tomato*, which, while largely self-promotion, was one of the first books on growing tomatoes and included a number of tomato recipes.

Fortunately, many of the Livingston varieties still exist, and they remain some of the most classic eating tomatoes.

# Egg in a Tomato Nest

### SERVES 1

Recipes for eggs baked in tomatoes appear in many nineteenth-century American cookbooks. They are also favorites in parts of Italy and in Greece. This easy dish makes a perfect Sunday-morning treat, accompanied by toast, smoked fish or bacon, a dash of hot sauce, and a cup of estate-grown coffee. If you are cooking for one or two persons only, the easiest way to make the dish is to sit the tomatoes in ramekins or custard cups. For a larger group, arrange the required number of tomato nests in a shallow baking dish.

1 medium-large (7–8 ounces) ripe but not soft tomato

1 egg

salt and freshly ground black pepper

**1.** Preheat the oven to 375°F. Lightly grease a ramekin or other dish.

**2.** Cut a slice from the stalk end of the tomato. Using a knife and a teaspoon, scoop out the center of the tomato, leaving a hollow nest. Pat the interior dry with a paper towel. Place the tomato in the prepared dish and bake for 8 to 10 minutes, until it is thoroughly heated.

**3.** Remove the tomato from the oven. Crack the eggshell and gently drop the egg into the tomato. Season the egg with salt. Return the dish to the oven and bake 8 to 10 minutes longer, until the egg whites are set. If you want the yolk hard, bake a minute or two longer. Grind the pepper on top and serve immediately.

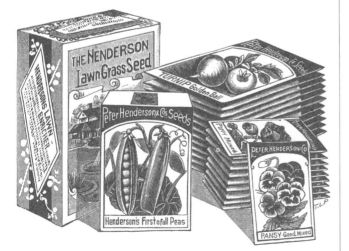

# CHAPTER EIGHT

# MAIN DISHES

## *with Seafood, Chicken, and Meat*

# Prawns with Garlic, Heirloom Tomatoes, and Lemon

**SERVES 2–4**

From Sarah Stegner, co-chef at the Prairie Grass Café, comes this delectable combination of shrimp and tomatoes. In Europe, the word "prawns" refers to particular members of the shrimp family; in this country, it refers to the larger sizes of shrimp — in this case the size marketed as colossal shrimp, which run 12 to a pound. Sarah Stegner recommends serving this dish with toasted French bread and a fresh green salad. Rice pilaf or pasta also makes a good partner.

2 tablespoons extra-virgin olive oil

1 pound (about 12) prawns (colossal-size shrimp), shelled and deveined

salt and freshly ground white or black pepper

1 tablespoon chopped fresh garlic

1 cup chopped fresh peeled and seeded heirloom tomatoes

juice from ½ lemon

2 tablespoons butter, at room temperature

1 tablespoon snipped chives

1 tablespoon chopped flat-leaf parsley

**1.** Heat the oil in a large skillet over medium heat. Lightly sear the prawns on both sides, 45 to 60 seconds. Season with salt and pepper. Add the garlic and cook 2 to 4 minutes, until it just begins to brown.

**2.** Remove the prawns from the pan and set aside. Add the tomatoes to the pan and simmer until they begin to break down — 4 to 7 minutes, depending on their ripeness. Add the lemon juice and stir in the butter, and then stir in the chives and parsley.

**3.** Taste and adjust the seasoning. Return the prawns to the sauce and cook for 1 minute longer to reheat them. Serve hot.

# Sarah Stegner
## THE PRAIRIE GRASS CAFÉ, *Northbrook, Illinois*

S arah Stegner's cooking style reflects both her deep roots in the Midwest and her training in classical French cuisine. A native of Evanston, Illinois, she has never strayed too
far from home. That is, unless you count her stints in France with chefs Pierre Osi in Lyon
and Bertolli and Gerard Bessin in Paris.

Sarah has what you might call staying power. Her first real job in the kitchen was at
the Ritz-Carlton Chicago; she stayed there for almost twenty years before opening the Prairie
Grass Café in 2004.

Her cooking style evolved over time to become what it is today, "French influenced
with Midwestern roots." That means bigger portions than seen at many East and West Coast
gourmet restaurants. More important, it is strongly based in local foods.

For years Sarah was content to obtain her food from the usual food distributors, rarely
local and often not seasonal. Local growers were few and hard to find in the Midwest, but
gradually they began to appear. Once she started finding local and sustainably produced
vegetables, cheese, and meats, there was no turning back. She became dedicated to seeking
and promoting local farmers and food.

Sarah helped organize the Chicago Green City Market and joined the steering com-
mittee, which created standards for a market composed of farmers dedicated to sustainable
production. The farmers found a steady market in the Chicago chefs, and Sarah found "farmers who stood behind what they believed and knew what they were doing and could convey
that to me, the chef."

Now, from May to October, Sarah is engaged in "a continual process of trying to source
local products and expand what I cook for my guests to eat." And because of this dedication,
parts of her menu change daily, depending on what is available at the market. She is "just as
enthused as when I started. It's a great job which allows me to have the freedom and creativity
to cook. . . . You continue to learn when you love what you do; it doesn't matter where you are."

# Shrimp Creole

## SERVES 4

A classic old-style Louisiana dish, relatively simple to make, with a delicious piquant seafood flavor. You can omit the hot seasoning altogether, but a little bit really makes the dish and you can go all the way if you want. Any kind of tomato will do nicely here, but I like the bicolor tomatoes, such as Regina's, which add a bit of sweetness and combine well with shrimp.

1½ pounds uncooked medium (20–24 to the pound) shrimp

1 bay leaf

3 tablespoons vegetable oil

1 large onion, coarsely chopped

2 garlic cloves, peeled and finely chopped

2 celery stalks, washed and cut into ½-inch pieces

2 pounds (5–6 medium-large) tomatoes, peeled, seeded, and coarsely chopped

1 large green bell pepper, seeded and cut into ¼-inch strips

1½ teaspoons fresh thyme leaves or ¾ teaspoon dried

¼–½ teaspoon cayenne pepper

1 teaspoon paprika

1 teaspoon salt

1 tablespoon Worcestershire sauce

several drops Tabasco (optional)

4 cups cooked long-grain white rice

**1.** Bring 3 cups of water to a boil. Drop the shrimp in and cook for 1 minute, until they have turned pink. Strain the water into a bowl and reserve. Rinse the shrimp under cold running water. When cool enough to handle, peel them, adding the shells to the reserved cooking water. Refrigerate the shrimp.

**2.** Return the cooking liquid and shells to the pan, add the bay leaf, and cover. Cook over medium heat for 5 minutes, and then strain again. Discard the shells and bay leaf, but reserve the liquid.

**3.** Heat the oil in a large saucepan over medium heat; stir in the onion, garlic, and celery. Sauté for 4 to 5 minutes, until the vegetables have softened slightly.

**4.** Stir in the tomatoes and half the bell pepper. Add the thyme, ¼ teaspoon cayenne, the paprika, salt, and Worcestershire. Finally, add 2 cups of the reserved shrimp cooking liquid. Simmer the mixture over low heat for 20 minutes, by which time some of the liquid should have evaporated, leaving a thick mixture. If the sauce is not thick and rich, raise the heat and cook a few minutes longer.

**5.** Taste the sauce and check for seasoning and flavor. Add the additional cayenne and Tabasco, if desired. Season with additional salt, if needed. Stir in the remaining bell pepper, cover the pan, and simmer for 5 minutes longer. Finally, stir in the reserved shrimp and cook over medium heat for 2 to 3 minutes, until the shrimp is heated through. Serve immediately over warm rice.

## TOMATO REMEDIES AND FOLK USES

Tomatoes have long been used in a variety of folk cures. Tomatoes mixed with buttermilk relieve the pain associated with sunburn. Tomatoes have been used to heal sores and wounds, and supposedly in New Guinea, tribes used crushed tomato leaves for the same purpose. One tomato aficionado told me he cleans the bottom of his copper pots with half of a tomato and they shine like new. A tomato-juice bath is a well-known remedy for exposure to skunk spray.

 # Roast Lobster with Tomato, Corn, and Fines Herbes

Tomato, corn, and lobster make up the quintessential perfect summer dinner. This recipe by Gary Danko illustrates his love of French and regional American cooking and his enthusiasm for fresh ingredients. Danko won numerous awards as chef at Beringer Vineyards in the 1980s, then at The Ritz-Carlton in San Francisco and at Viognier in San Mateo. When he opened Gary Danko in San Francisco in 1999, he was greeted with accolades in the press and honored with the James Beard Foundation's Best New Restaurant award. His lobster is delicious served with mashed potatoes or in the Maine style, with boiled new potatoes and a bit of butter, salt, and parsley.

¾ cup corn cut from the cob

3 (1¼-pound) live lobsters

1–2 tablespoons olive oil

½ cup broth from cooking the lobsters

½ cup clam juice

½ cup dry white wine, such as a Fumé Blanc

1 shallot, finely minced

1 bay leaf

1 sprig thyme

¼ cup heavy cream

½ cup (1 stick) cold butter, cut into 16 pieces

2 tomatoes, peeled, seeded, and diced

2 tablespoons chopped chives

1 tablespoon chopped Italian parsley

½ teaspoon chopped chervil

1 teaspoon lemon juice

salt

1. Bring a small saucepan of water to a boil. Add the corn and cook for 2 minutes. Drain, submerge in ice water until cool, and set aside.

2. Bring to a boil a pan of water large enough to hold the lobsters.

3. To kill the lobsters humanely, fill a large bowl or the sink with warm water. Submerge lobsters upside down. Run hot tap water into the bowl or sink, progressively raising the temperature. The lobsters will fall asleep. Slide the sleeping lobsters into the boiling water and leave them for 4 minutes. Reserve ½ cup of the cooking broth for use in the sauce.

4. With tongs, remove the lobsters from the pan and submerge in ice water for 5 to 10 minutes, until completely cold.

**5.** Cut the lobsters in half through the back, taking care to preserve the shells whole. Remove the meat from the claws and tail. Clean the carcass. Replace the meat in the shells. Put the filled shells into a shallow baking dish that will just hold them. Brush the surface of the lobster meat with oil. Cover and reserve in the refrigerator while you prepare the sauce.

**6.** Preheat the oven to 350°F.

**7.** Combine the lobster broth, clam juice, wine, shallot, bay leaf, and thyme in a nonreactive saucepan. Simmer to reduce the liquid to half the original volume. Add the cream and return

to a boil. Lower the heat. Whisk in a bit of the butter. When it has dissolved, whisk in another bit. Continue this way, keeping the pan on very low heat while all the butter bits are being whisked in, until the sauce thickens and all the butter has been used. Stir in the tomato and corn. Season with the chives, parsley, chervil, lemon juice, and salt to taste. Cover the saucepan and stand it in a larger pan filled with very hot water to keep it warm.

**8.** Put the lobsters in the oven and roast for 6 to 7 minutes. Remove them to a serving dish or plates and spoon the sauce over each lobster. Serve at once.

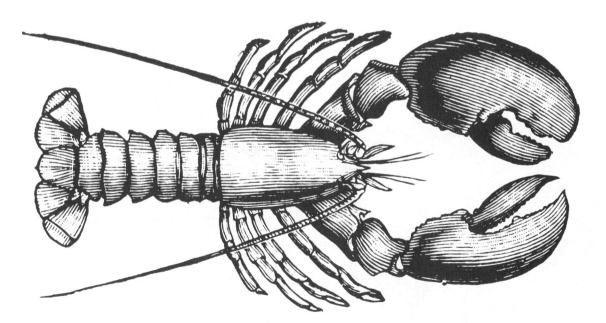

MORE MAIN DISHES

# Angel-Hair Pasta with Sun-Dried Tomatoes, Lemon, and Shrimp

SERVES 4

**H**ere's a dish you make in minutes from Anita Dafonte, a dedicated home-style cook and gardener who lives and gardens with her husband, Vincent Laurence, in Newtown, Connecticut. Quick, bright, flavorful — it's the perfect weeknight supper. The lemon complements the delicate angel-hair pasta. Scallops work well in this dish, too.

12 ounces angel-hair pasta

2 tablespoons extra-virgin olive oil

1½ pounds shrimp, peeled and deveined

1 cup oil-packed sun-dried tomatoes, cut into ¼-inch strips (see page 230 for instructions on drying your own)

zest of one lemon

1 tablespoon fresh thyme leaves

**1.** Bring a large pot of salted water to a boil. Add the pasta and cook for 5 minutes, or according to the package directions, until al dente.

**2.** While the pasta is cooking, heat 1 tablespoon of the oil in a skillet over high heat. Add the shrimp and cook for 2 to 3 minutes, tossing them, until they begin to turn pink. Stir in the tomatoes, half the lemon zest, and half the thyme. Remove the pan from the heat and keep the contents warm.

**3.** Drain the pasta. Toss it with the shrimp and tomatoes and the remaining tablespoon oil. Transfer to a serving platter or individual plates. Top with the remaining lemon zest and thyme and serve hot.

BONNY BEST EARLY TOMATO.

Rosemary-Roasted Cod with Confit Tomatoes and Green Beans, *p. 168*

Trio of Stuffed Tomatoes, *p. 196*

Tomato and Potato Casserole, *p. 209*

Green Tomato Chocolate Cake, *p. 226*

# Mussels with Tomato-Saffron Sauce

### SERVES 4

Saffron, the dried stamens of a fall-blooming crocus, has a slightly honeyed, mildly bitter flavor quite unlike any other spice. It is one of the most expensive ingredients in the world, but fortunately you do not need much to flavor a dish. In Mediterranean cooking, saffron is often  combined with tomatoes. The saffron combines well with yellow tomatoes, if available. Serve over pasta or rice, with French bread.

4 pounds mussels in their shells

1 large pinch saffron (enough to cover a quarter)

½ cup warm water

2 tablespoons extra-virgin olive oil

1 large onion, chopped

1–2 garlic cloves, peeled and finely chopped

1 celery stalk, chopped

1½ cups white wine

4 cups seeded and chopped fresh or canned tomatoes, with juice

⅔ cup chopped fresh parsley

1 bay leaf

salt and freshly ground black pepper

1. Wash the mussels in cold water, cutting off any stringy pieces (the beard) hanging from the shells. Mussels gape open from time to time, but if they fail to close their shells after being handled or tapped on a counter, discard them. Also discard those with broken shells. Set the cleaned mussels aside.

2. Put the saffron in a small bowl and stir in the water. Set aside for 10 minutes.

3. Warm the oil in a large pan over medium heat. Stir in the onion, garlic, and celery. Lower the heat, cover the pan, and cook gently for 3 to 4 minutes, until the vegetables are fragrant and slightly softened.

4. Raise the heat, pour in the wine, and let it bubble for 7 to 8 minutes, until the vegetables are tender and the liquid has reduced by about half. Add the saffron mixture, the tomatoes, half the parsley, the bay leaf, and salt and pepper to taste. Bring to a brisk boil, and then add the mussels. Cover the pan and simmer for 4 minutes. Peek inside. If the mussels have opened, quickly stir in the remaining parsley and serve immediately; if they are closed, put the lid back on and cook for another minute until they open before adding the parsley.

# Rosemary-Roasted Cod with Confit Tomatoes and Green Beans

**SERVES 4**

The vivid flavors of rosemary, olives, and confit tomatoes — roasted tomatoes preserved in oil — highlight the cod in this dish. Try using a mild yellow such as Yellow Brandywine, or orange or bicolor like Marizol Gold, or Regina's. You can substitute other mild, white-fleshed fish in this dish. Rice or potatoes make a fine accompaniment.

4 cod fillets (about 6 ounces each)

1 (6-inch) stem rosemary

salt and freshly ground black pepper

3 tablespoons extra-virgin olive oil

½ pound green beans, trimmed and cut into 3-inch pieces

1 large garlic clove, peeled and sliced

16 confit tomatoes (page 251)

1 teaspoon capers, drained

8–12 niçoise or kalamata olives, pitted and roughly chopped

1 lemon

**1.** Preheat the oven to 400°F. Grease a baking dish large enough to hold the cod in a single layer.

**2.** Strip the leaves from the rosemary stem and scatter some on the baking dish, then place the cod fillets on top. Season with salt and pepper. Scatter on the remaining rosemary. Drizzle with 1 tablespoon of the oil. Set the dish aside for 20 to 30 minutes while you prepare the vegetables.

**3.** Bring a medium saucepan of lightly salted water to a boil. Drop the beans into it and cook for 5 minutes. Drain, and then plunge the beans into a bowl of cold water to stop the cooking. Drain again and set aside.

**4.** Bake the cod for 8 minutes.

**5.** While the cod is baking, heat the remaining 2 tablespoons oil in a large skillet over low heat. Stir in the garlic. Raise the heat to medium and stir in the beans and tomatoes. Cook over medium heat for 5 minutes, and then add the capers and olives. Grate the lemon zest, and then halve the lemon and squeeze the juice of one half. Stir the zest and juice into the pan. Toss the vegetables together and continue to simmer the mixture while you place a piece of cod on each of 4 plates. Top each plate with one-quarter of the vegetables. Cut the remaining lemon half into 4 pieces and add a wedge to each plate. Serve immediately.

# Spanish-Style Fish with Tomatoes and Potatoes

**SERVES 4**

This hearty Spanish dish is usually made with monkfish, a firm-fleshed fish that needs longer cooking than flakier fish. Swordfish is an alternative, but do not substitute tender-fleshed fish such as sole, flounder, or even cod, because it will disintegrate in the sauce. Potatoes add another substantial element to the dish, making it perfect for colder days. If you canned your own tomatoes in summer, here is a chance to use them. Serve with crusty bread or a salad, or both.

1–1½ pounds monkfish or swordfish, cut into 3-inch chunks

    salt and freshly ground black pepper

2–3 tablespoons all-purpose flour

   3 tablespoons extra-virgin olive oil

   ¾ cup (1 medium) chopped onion

   1 small garlic clove, peeled and chopped

   2 cups coarsely chopped fresh or canned tomatoes

   2 large potatoes, peeled and cut into ½-inch slices

   about 1 cup fish stock or water

   2 tablespoons chopped fresh parsley

   ½ cup roasted red pepper strips

**1.** Season the fish with salt and pepper and dust with flour.

**2.** In a pan that can be taken to the table or in a large skillet, heat the oil over high heat. Add the fish and cook until lightly browned, turning as needed, about 3 minutes per side. Remove the fish from the pan and set aside.

**3.** Add the onion, garlic, and tomatoes to the pan. Lower the heat and sauté for 2 to 3 minutes, until slightly softened. Add the potatoes, season with salt and pepper, and then add enough stock to come up to the level of the vegetables. Cover with a lid and cook gently over low heat for about 12 minutes, until the potatoes have softened slightly.

**4.** Return the fish to the pan and simmer for 5 minutes, covered. Remove the lid and cook 5 minutes longer. During the final minutes, add the parsley and arrange the pepper strips over the top. When they have heated through, take the pan to the table and serve.

NOTE: Unfortunately, many of the delectable firm-fleshed fish, such as swordfish and tuna, are overfished. Try to use them sparingly.

# Caribbean Red Fish Sauce with Red Snapper

### SERVES 3–4

I love this dish — lime and tomato are such great, tangy companions, and lots of lime works here. It can be prepared with almost any meaty fish, including tuna, and the heat from the hot pepper can be adjusted to taste. Shellfish such as scallops or shrimp can be substituted for, or combined with, the fish. I recommend a good slicing tomato — try Paragon, Abe Lincoln, or Earliana.

1 tablespoon extra-virgin olive oil

⅔ cup chopped onion

3 tablespoons finely chopped garlic

1⅔ cups Canned Tomato Purée (page 234)

⅔ cup lime juice

½ teaspoon finely chopped dried hot pepper, or 1 teaspoon red pepper flakes

1 teaspoon sea salt

1 pound red snapper fillet, sliced into several large chunks

**1.** Heat the oil in a large skillet over medium heat; sauté the onion and garlic for 3 to 4 minutes, until softened. Add the tomato, lime juice, hot pepper, and salt, and simmer for 5 minutes.

**2.** Add the fish and simmer for 8 to 12 minutes, until the fish is tender and opaque. Do not overcook. Serve immediately.

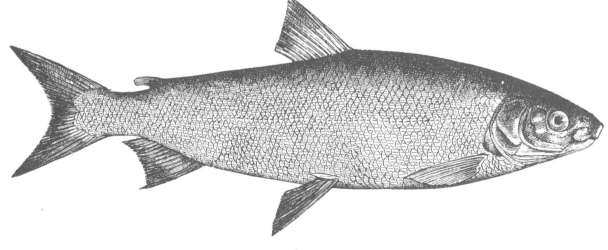

# Striped Bass with Roasted Tomatoes with Caper Sauce

### SERVES 4

**N**ora Pouillon, owner-chef of Nora's and Asia Nora's in Washington, DC, is a longtime advocate of using organic, seasonal, locally produced ingredients. Nora serves this fish with creamy mashed potatoes and a simple salad. The recipe also works well with other firm, flavorful white fish.

## Caper Sauce

- 1 cup parsley
- 1 teaspoon capers
- ⅛ teaspoon chopped garlic
- 1 tablespoon Dijon mustard
- ½ cup water, or more as needed
- 1 teaspoon lemon juice
- ⅓ cup extra-virgin olive oil, or more as needed

## Fish and Tomatoes

- 4 plum tomatoes, cut in half
- 2 tablespoons extra-virgin olive oil
- 1 teaspoon minced garlic
- 1 teaspoon chopped fresh thyme
- salt and freshly ground black pepper
- 4 striped bass fillets (4–6 ounces each), skinned
- 1 teaspoon capers

**1.** For the caper sauce, purée the parsley, capers, garlic, mustard, water, and lemon juice in a blender. With the blender running, add the oil slowly until the sauce is smooth and creamy. If it is too thick, add more water; if too thin, add more oil.

**2.** Preheat the oven to 450°F. Grease a baking dish large enough to hold the tomatoes in a single layer.

**3.** Arrange the tomatoes in the baking dish. Brush them with 1 tablespoon of the oil and sprinkle with the garlic, thyme, salt, and pepper. Roast for 10 minutes, until softened (though not collapsed) and lightly caramelized.

**4.** Meanwhile, heat the remaining 1 tablespoon oil in a large skillet over high heat. Season the fish with salt and pepper and sear on each side for 4 minutes. (Alternatively, sear each side for 2 minutes, and then put the fish into the oven with the tomatoes for 5 minutes to finish.)

**5.** To serve, nestle the fish next to mashed potatoes. Add the roasted tomatoes and garnish with the caper sauce and additional capers.

# Swordfish Plaki

SERVES 4–6

**P**laki is a Greek dish of fish covered in a sauce of tomatoes, onions, and peppers. Fish of many kinds are used, with smaller ones invariably served whole, head and tails intact. The proportions of tomatoes and peppers also vary. Some cooks add spinach to the mix. You can feel free to make this dish with any flavorful white-fleshed fish and with whatever mix of tomatoes and other vegetables suits you. In Greece, this dish, like most others, is often served lukewarm. Rice is the usual accompaniment. Orzo — the rice-shaped pasta often used for soups — is another option.

¼ cup extra-virgin olive oil

1 medium or large onion, thinly sliced

1–2 garlic cloves, peeled and minced

1 medium green bell pepper, or other sweet green pepper, seeded and cut into ½-inch strips

1 medium red bell pepper, seeded and cut into ½-inch strips

1 pound (3–4 medium-large) tomatoes, peeled and coarsely chopped

½ cup chopped fresh parsley

1 teaspoon dried oregano

salt and freshly ground black pepper

1½–2 pounds swordfish or other firm white fish

2 lemons, quartered lengthwise

2 bay leaves

12 kalamata olives (optional)

**1.** Preheat the oven to 375°F. Use some of the oil to grease a shallow baking dish just large enough to hold the fish and suitable for serving.

**2.** Heat the remaining oil in a large skillet over medium heat. Stir in the onion and garlic and cook gently for 3 to 4 minutes, until they are fragrant. Stir in the green and red pepper strips and then the tomatoes. Sprinkle with half the parsley and the oregano and season with salt and pepper to taste. Cover the pan and simmer the mixture for 10 minutes over low heat, stirring occasionally to prevent sticking.

**3.** Arrange the swordfish in the greased baking dish. Season with salt and pepper and squeeze on the juice of 2 lemon quarters. Add the bay leaves, and then pour on the tomato mixture. Cover the dish with a lid or foil.

**4.** Bake for 20 minutes. Remove the cover, add the olives, if desired, and bake 5 minutes longer.

**5.** Let the fish rest for 3 to 4 minutes, and then garnish with the remaining parsley and lemon quarters. Remove bay leaves before serving.

## ALAN KAPULER'S FAVORITE TOMATOES

Best known for developing the Peacevine cherry tomato and reintroducing the Brandywine, Alan says, "If I don't like it and I don't eat it, I won't grow it and I don't sell it."

Among the many varieties Alan does like to eat, grow, and sell are Ten Fingers of Naples, a paste tomato; early varieties Skorspelka and Stupice; Willamette, a midseason variety; and Palestinian Oxheart.

# Pan-Seared Tuna with Panzanella and Aioli

**SERVES 4**

Panzanella is an Italian salad of dry bread tossed with tomatoes and basil. It is one of the many Mediterranean dishes that team ripe juicy tomatoes with crusty bread. Here, in a recipe from Nora Pouillon, of Nora's and Asia Nora's in Washington, DC, the panzanella complements seared tuna, a dry fish perfectly partnered with the moist salad and the unctuous aioli — a garlicky mayonnaise from southern France. Aioli goes fantastically with juicy red tomatoes — try Mortgage Lifter or Ponderosa. If you are using paste tomatoes, use something with a good fresh flavor, such as Opalka or Amish Paste.

**Panzanella**

- 8 thick slices day-old baguette or country-style bread, cut into cubes
- 1½ pounds (about 8) ripe paste or heirloom tomatoes, cored
- ¼ cup sliced fresh basil
- ¼ cup extra-virgin olive oil
- 2 tablespoons good red wine vinegar
- 2 garlic cloves, peeled and finely minced
- sea salt and freshly ground black pepper
- 1 tablespoon lemon juice (optional)

**Aioli**

- 4 garlic cloves, peeled and smashed
- ½ teaspoon salt
- 1 egg yolk
- 1 teaspoon Dijon mustard (optional)
- ½ cup extra-virgin olive oil
- 2 teaspoons lemon juice
- freshly ground black pepper

**Tuna**

- 4 tuna steaks (4–6 ounces each)
- salt and freshly ground black pepper
- 1 tablespoon canola oil
- 2 cups arugula
- 2 tablespoons extra-virgin olive oil
- 2 teaspoons white or red wine vinegar or lemon juice

1. Preheat the oven to 400°F.

2. For the panzanella, spread the bread cubes in a single layer on a large baking sheet and toast for 5 minutes, until lightly colored.

**3.** Position a sieve over a bowl. Coarsely chop the tomatoes, place them in the sieve, and let them drain for a few minutes. Set the tomatoes aside in a separate bowl and reserve the tomato juices.

**4.** Add the bread to the tomato juices and leave it for about 3 minutes, until the bread has absorbed most of the liquid. Add the bread and basil to the tomatoes and toss well.

**5.** Whisk together the oil, vinegar, garlic, salt, and pepper in a small bowl to make a dressing. Pour over the salad and toss. Taste and add the lemon juice and additional seasoning if you think they will improve the salad. Set the panzanella aside.

**6.** For the aioli, place the garlic on a cutting board and sprinkle with the salt; mash them together using the side of a chef's knife or other wide blade.

**7.** Position a medium bowl on a wet paper towel to prevent slipping and add the garlic, egg yolk, and mustard, if desired; whisk until pale yellow. Add the oil, drop by drop, whisking continuously, until the sauce begins to thicken. Whisk in the remaining oil in a slow stream. Taste and add the lemon juice and pepper to taste. The aioli should be as thick as mayonnaise; if it is thicker, thin with a few drops of water.

**8.** For the tuna, season the steaks with salt and pepper. Heat the canola oil in a large skillet over high heat and sear the steaks for 2 to 3 minutes on each side, until medium rare. (If you don't like tuna that is rare in the middle, cook for a minute longer on each side.)

**9.** Toss the arugula with the olive oil and then with the vinegar.

**10.** To assemble the dish, spoon a serving of panzanella salad onto each dinner plate and top with a piece of tuna. Put a dollop of aioli onto the tuna and garnish the plate with the arugula.

NOTE: The aioli becomes thicker more quickly with the addition of mustard.

# Chicken Niçoise

SERVES 4

This favorite dish of the French Riviera captures the rich flavors of summer tomatoes and the fragrant herbs that grow on the nearby hills. Red tomatoes work very nicely in this dish, or try any black tomato for a deeper-colored sauce. There's plenty of delicious juice, so make sure you have bread for mopping it up.

**Sauce**

2 tablespoons extra-virgin olive oil

4 large garlic cloves, peeled and finely chopped

6 large basil leaves, torn

1 teaspoon fresh oregano

1 teaspoon fresh thyme

pinch of salt

6 anchovy fillets packed in oil, rinsed and coarsely chopped

3 cups chopped fresh or canned tomatoes (about 5 large fresh tomatoes)

½ cup dry white wine

1 bay leaf

2 tablespoons tomato paste

**Chicken**

1 (3-pound) chicken, cut into 8 serving pieces, or 4 skin-on, bone-in breasts and 4 skin-on, bone-in thighs

1 tablespoon chopped fresh oregano

1 tablespoon chopped fresh thyme

2 garlic cloves, peeled and cut into thin slivers

salt and freshly ground black pepper

2–3 tablespoons extra-virgin olive oil

12 niçoise or kalamata olives

1 (7-ounce) jar artichoke hearts, cut into several pieces (optional)

4 cups cooked rice

**1.** For the sauce, warm the oil in a large saucepan over low heat. Stir in the garlic, basil, oregano, and thyme. Sprinkle with salt. Cover the pan and let the mixture gently sweat for 4 to 5 minutes. Add the anchovies, tomatoes, wine, and bay leaf and bring to a simmer. Stir in the tomato paste and simmer for 10 minutes. Set aside while you cook the chicken.

**2.** For the chicken, wash and dry the pieces. Mix the oregano and thyme. Make 3 or 4 small cuts in each chicken piece and stick a sliver of garlic and a pinch of the herb mix into each of them. Sprinkle any remaining herbs on the skin and season with salt and pepper.

**3.** Preheat the oven to 400°F.

**4.** Heat 2 tablespoons of the oil in a large skillet over medium heat. Add the chicken in a single layer and cook for 6 to 7 minutes on each side, until the skin side is golden brown and the other side is whitish, not pink. Transfer the cooked pieces, skin side up, to a baking dish. Continue browning the chicken in a single layer, using the remaining 1 tablespoon oil, if needed.

**5.** Reheat the sauce to a simmer, and then pour it over the chicken. Dot with olives and the artichokes, if desired. Bake for 20 minutes, until the chicken is tender, basting occasionally. Test for doneness by inserting a knifepoint into the thickest pieces. The juice that emerges should be clear.

**6.** Serve hot over the rice.

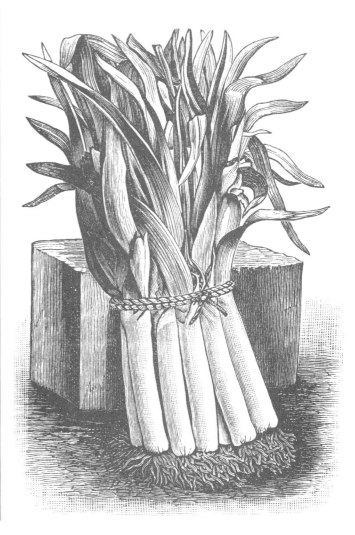

# Sautéed Chicken Breasts with Tomatoes and Summer Vegetables

**SERVES 4**

Chicken breasts sautéed with tomatoes and other garden vegetables make some of the quickest and most delicious summer meals. This version combines New World vegetables — peppers, corn, and beans, as well as tomatoes — with lime, chile, and cilantro to give the dish the flavors of Mexico.

⅓ cup lime juice (from 2–3 limes)

6–8 drops Tabasco

3 tablespoons extra-virgin olive oil

1 teaspoon fresh thyme or ¾ teaspoon dried

4 boneless, skinless chicken breast halves

20 green beans or wax beans, trimmed and halved

2 green bell peppers, seeded and cut into ½-inch strips

1 medium onion, coarsely chopped

8 large ripe plum or paste tomatoes, peeled, seeded, and cut lengthwise into quarters

kernels from 2 large ears of corn

1 garlic clove, peeled and minced

2 tablespoons chopped cilantro

1 teaspoon chili powder

salt and freshly ground black pepper

**1.** Mix the lime juice, Tabasco, 1 tablespoon of the oil, and the thyme in a shallow dish.

**2.** Cut each chicken breast half diagonally into 6 to 8 pieces, removing and discarding the silvery tendon as you cut. Toss the chicken in the juice mixture and let sit for 15 minutes, turning once or twice, while you prepare the vegetables.

**3.** Heat the remaining 2 tablespoons oil in a large skillet over high heat. Remove the chicken from the marinade with a slotted spoon and add it to the skillet, along with the beans, peppers, and onion. Sauté for 2 minutes, maintaining a brisk cooking pace to cook the vegetables quickly but without letting them brown.

**4.** Stir in the tomatoes, corn, and garlic. Season with cilantro, chili powder, salt, and pepper, and any remaining lime marinade. Bring the liquid to a boil and sauté for 2 minutes longer, until the chicken is cooked through. (To test, pierce with the point of a knife. The chicken is done when the juice runs clear.) Serve immediately.

# Easy Curried Chicken

### SERVES 4

Even those with timid palates should find this quick curry mild enough. I favor a hotter curry, so I generally add ½ to 1 teaspoon of dried crushed or chopped hot pepper. Serve the curry with rice and some Green Tomato Chutney (page 238).

8 bone-in chicken thighs or 4 chicken legs

   salt and freshly ground black pepper

2 tablespoons canola oil

1 large onion, chopped

4 garlic cloves, peeled and chopped

1 tablespoon peeled and chopped or grated fresh ginger

6 cardamom pods

2 bay leaves

1 cinnamon stick

2–3 teaspoons curry powder

6 medium tomatoes, peeled, seeded, and chopped, or 2 cups canned

¼ cup chopped cilantro or parsley

⅓ cup flaked almonds, toasted (see Note) (optional)

**1.** Cut excess fat from the chicken pieces. (You can skin them completely if you prefer, though in this recipe the skin adds extra color and succulence.) Season with salt and pepper.

**2.** In a large pan that will hold the chicken in a single layer, heat the oil over medium heat.

Stir in the onion, garlic, ginger, cardamom, bay leaves, cinnamon, and curry powder and cook, stirring constantly, for 1 minute. Add the chicken pieces skin side down and continue cooking for 3 minutes longer, until the skin of the chicken has taken color from the spices. Add the tomatoes. Cover the pan and simmer over low heat for 25 to 30 minutes, until the chicken is tender and the juices run clear when the meat is pierced with a knifepoint.

**3.** Scatter 2 tablespoons of the cilantro into the pan, forking it around a bit. Cook for 2 minutes longer.

**4.** Remove the cardamom and cinnamon and discard. Transfer the chicken and its sauce to a serving platter and sprinkle the remaining cilantro on top. If you are using the almonds, scatter them on top, too.

NOTE: To toast almonds, place them in a shallow dish and toast in a 300°F oven for 6 to 7 minutes, until golden and fragrant. Alternatively, toast in a microwave oven for 1 minute or until golden and fragrant.

# West African Stew

This stew is popular in Ghana and other West African countries. It is often served with small dishes of fried plantains, sliced cucumbers, chopped tomatoes, peppers, and other vegetables. Adjust the hot pepper to suit your taste. Serve with rice or polenta.

1 (3-pound) chicken, cut into 8–12 pieces, or 6 chicken legs, each cut in half

2 tablespoons ground ginger

salt

¼ cup peanut or canola oil

3 medium-large onions, chopped

2 garlic cloves, peeled and chopped

1 tablespoon peeled and chopped fresh ginger

1 serrano chile, seeded and finely chopped

1 teaspoon ground cumin

2 cups canned or fresh diced tomatoes

2 tablespoons tomato paste

2 cups hot chicken broth

1 large sweet potato, peeled and cut into ½-inch slices

⅔ cup smooth peanut butter

cayenne pepper (optional)

½ cup salted peanuts, coarsely chopped

¼ cup snipped chives or chopped fresh parsley

**1.** Trim any excess skin and fat from the chicken. Mix the ginger and 1 teaspoon of salt, and rub it into the chicken pieces.

**2.** Heat the oil in a large saucepan or stew pot, and brown the chicken, a few pieces at a time. Remove them to a plate and add the onions, garlic, fresh ginger, and any leftover ginger rub to the pan. Cook gently for 3 to 4 minutes, until the onion has softened slightly and the ginger and garlic are fragrant. Stir in the chile and cumin. Cook for 1 minute longer. Stir in the tomatoes, tomato paste, and chicken broth, then return the chicken pieces to the pan and add the sweet potato. Bring to a simmer and cook for 15 minutes.

**3.** Remove 1 cup of the liquid from the pan. Mix it with the peanut butter, and then stir the mixture back into the pan. Taste and add salt, if necessary. Season with cayenne, if desired. Simmer uncovered until the sauce thickens, about 20 minutes.

**4.** To serve, transfer the chicken and sauce to a large platter. Sprinkle the peanuts and chives over the chicken.

# Polenta Concia with Gorgonzola and Fresh Herbs

SERVES 4–6

Polenta is a favorite dish of northern Italy. This version with Gorgonzola, another delicious food from northern Italy, comes from owner-chef Massimo Capra of Mistura in Toronto, who explains that *concia* means "dressed" — in this case, with the Gorgonzola and the herbs. Polenta is often served with a tomato sauce. Capra serves it with a rich tomato sauce made with sausage, but any hearty tomato sauce will work here.

2 tablespoons extra-virgin olive oil

1 teaspoon salt

1 pound (3 cups) polenta (coarse yellow cornmeal)

8 ounces Gorgonzola cheese, crumbled

1 cup coarsely grated Parmigiano-Reggiano

4 tablespoons torn basil leaves, plus some sprigs for garnish

2 tablespoons snipped chives

2 tablespoons chopped fresh parsley

Ragù di Salsicce (page 28), heated

**1.** Grease a 10-inch casserole dish or other shallow baking dish. Bring 2 quarts of water to a rolling boil in a large deep pan. Add the oil and salt.

**2.** Place the polenta in a large measuring cup or pitcher. Hold it high above the water, and let about a quarter of the polenta rain slowly into the water, stirring constantly. When the first portion is stirred in, rain in another quarter, stirring as before. Continue this way until all of the polenta has been incorporated.

**3.** Reduce the heat to low and stir the polenta for 5 minutes. Place a heat-diffuser mat under the pan and a lid on top, and cook for 30 minutes longer, stirring often, until the polenta forms a very thick smooth porridgelike mass.

**4.** While the polenta is in the last few minutes of cooking, mix the Gorgonzola with the Parmigiano-Reggiano, basil, chives, and parsley. Fold about half of this mixture into the hot polenta.

**5.** Spoon the polenta into the prepared casserole dish and smooth the surface. With a wooden spoon or the edge of a palette knife, mark the polenta into square or lozenge shapes. Scatter the remaining cheese and herb mixture on top and add the basil sprigs as garnish. Serve immediately with Ragù di Salsicce dolloped on top.

# Gnocchi with Ricotta, Roasted German Stripe Tomatoes, Prosciutto, and Spinach

SERVES 4

Dan Smith, who created this deeply flavorful dish, is owner-chef of John Andrews Restaurant, which nestles in the Berkshires in South Egremont, Massachusetts. He notes that gnocchi can be made and refrigerated for up to 2 days before you need them; you can even freeze them for a few weeks without loss of flavor. He also points out that if you roast the tomatoes and prepare the gnocchi dough ahead of time, you can get the dish onto the table in only a few minutes.

## Roasted Tomatoes

2 pounds German Stripe tomatoes, peeled, seeded, and cut into 1-inch slices

¼ cup extra-virgin olive oil

2 garlic cloves, peeled and finely chopped

6 sprigs of fresh thyme, leaves only, or 1 teaspoon dried

salt and freshly ground black pepper

## Sauce

½ cup extra-virgin olive oil

2 garlic cloves, chopped

2 shallots, minced

roasted tomatoes (see above)

½– ¾ cup chicken stock

8–10 cups (10-ounce bag) fresh spinach, washed and coarse stems removed

6 thin slices prosciutto (about 3 ounces)

½ cup freshly grated Parmigiano-Reggiano

## Gnocchi

1 (15-ounce) container ricotta

1½ cups freshly grated Parmigiano-Reggiano

3 egg yolks

¼ cup snipped chives

3 tablespoons chopped flat-leaf parsley

about 1 cup all-purpose flour, plus more for dusting

1 teaspoon kosher salt plus more as needed

freshly ground black pepper

**1.** For the roasted tomatoes, preheat the oven to 300°F.

**2.** Place the tomatoes on a large baking sheet. Mix the oil with the garlic, thyme, and salt and pepper to taste. Pour this mixture over the tomatoes. Roast until the slices have shrunk to half their original size, about 1½ to 2 hours. Allow the tomatoes to cool. If you are making them ahead of time, refrigerate until you are ready to use them.

**3.** For the sauce, heat the olive oil in a large skillet over medium heat. Add the garlic and shallots and cook for 1 minute. Add the roasted tomatoes and stock and cook for a few minutes longer, until slightly softened. Stir in the spinach and cook until it has wilted, about 1 minute. Set the sauce aside to finish when the gnocchi is ready.

**4.** For the gnocchi, mix the ricotta, Parmigiano-Reggiano, egg yolks, chives, and parsley in a large mixing bowl. Stir in ½ cup of the flour. Test the mixture with your fingers. If it is sticky, mix in another ¼ cup flour and test again. Add flour as needed to make a mixture that barely coheres in a soft mass. Season it with 1 teaspoon of salt and pepper to taste and turn the dough onto a pastry board thoroughly dusted with flour.

**5.** Bring 4 quarts of water to a boil in a large pasta pot while you work on the gnocchi.

**6.** Knead the dough for 2 to 3 minutes, until it is smooth and without cracks. Break off a piece of dough about the size of a small walnut. Press it against the back of a fork and roll it, using your thumb, to form a gnocchi with ridges on one side and the indentation of your thumb on the other. Drop the test gnocchi into the boiling water. It will sink, then rise to the surface after about 2 minutes. It should be light in texture but hold together. If the gnocchi falls apart a little

during cooking, knead the dough for 1 to 2 minutes longer, and test again.

**7.** When the dough has achieved the correct light but firm texture, divide it into 4 pieces. Roll each piece into a sausagelike roll about 1 inch in diameter. Slice the rolls into ¾-inch pieces. Shape each piece as described above. Set the shaped gnocchi onto a floured board.

**8.** When all the gnocchi are prepared, drop them in batches into the boiling water. Do not crowd the pan, because the gnocchi need room to rise. As they reach the surface, lift them from the pan with a slotted spoon and place on a cloth or paper towel to drain.

**9.** When all the gnocchi are cooked, return the sauce to medium heat and bring it to a simmer. Add as many gnocchi to the sauce as you need, and toss gently. Cook for 1 to 2 minutes, just until the gnocchi and the sauce are both hot. Season to taste with salt and pepper.

**10.** Cut each slice of prosciutto into 2 or 3 large pieces and stir them into the pan. Sprinkle on the Parmigiano-Reggiano. Serve immediately. (Any cooked gnocchi can be stored covered with plastic wrap in the refrigerator.)

# Dan Smith
## JOHN ANDREWS RESTAURANT,
### *South Egremont, Massachusetts*

Dan Smith was brought up on his family farm in Iowa, surrounded by the simple beauty of America's agricultural heartland. His connection to food was immediate and its effect enduring. He went to school to earn a degree in agriculture in order to run the farm, moonlighting in restaurants to help cover school expenses. Dan realized his passion was not in growing food but in cooking it.

Today Dan is the owner-chef of John Andrews Restaurant, which opened in 1990. The restaurant is located in the Berkshire hills, not far from the New York border. The building is a nineteenth-century New England clapboard house consisting of two simple but beautiful dining rooms, one of which overlooks lovely perennial gardens.

Dan experiences cooking as an art and as an outlet for his own artistic nature. "It's an expression of how I feel about food and hopefully my clients are picking up on it . . . picking up on my beliefs." Dan's studio is his cramped kitchen, where he works his craft quietly behind the scenes. He has a small kitchen staff, and rarely is he not cooking himself. He shies away from public exposure. Dan is one of the least egotistical chefs I have ever met.

He has always been fascinated by the variety of food ingredients and is delighted by recent trends in local and organic agriculture. The appearance of a new supplier with new ingredients is always appealing. Dan believes one of his roles as a chef is to "help keep things sustainable, which makes the local area more viable and, of course, produces a better meal." His only regret about being a chef in New England is that the season of farm production is just too short.

Dan describes his cooking as "new American with northern Italian influences." One of his specialties is duck. Dishes include a Local Roast Muscovy Duck with Risotto Style Barley and Black Trumpet Mushrooms with Caramelized Shallots. Spend an evening at John Andrews. You may not see Dan, but you'll know he's there. It's worth the trip.

# Tagine of Beef with Tomatoes, Zucchini, and Olives

**SERVES 6**

In Morocco, a tagine is a one-dish meal that is traditionally eaten out of a communal dish. This version is simple to prepare and is a good way to enjoy seasonal vegetables. The recipe comes from Kitty Morse, who was born in Casablanca and is the author of nine cookbooks. Now resident in the United States, she leads an annual gastronomic tour to Morocco. The tour includes cooking demonstrations in her family home, a restored pasha's residence near Casablanca.

3 tablespoons extra-virgin olive oil

1 medium onion, diced

1½ pounds lean beef chuck, cut into 2-inch chunks

2 pounds tomatoes, peeled (optional) and coarsely cubed

20 sprigs cilantro, tied with cotton thread or string

2 teaspoons ground cumin

½ teaspoon freshly ground black pepper

3 medium zucchini, peeled, halved, and cut into 2-inch pieces

8 ounces Moroccan green or purple olives in brine (pitted preferred), drained and rinsed under running water

20 fresh parsley sprigs, minced, plus several for garnish

¾ teaspoon salt

½ cup beef broth, as needed

**1.** Preheat the oven to 400°F. In a medium Dutch oven or enameled casserole dish, heat the oil over medium-high heat. Cook the onion and beef, stirring occasionally, until the meat is lightly browned, 3 to 4 minutes.

**2.** Add the tomatoes, cilantro, cumin, and pepper. Cover tightly and bake for 50 to 60 minutes, until the meat is fairly tender. Remove from the oven and discard the cilantro.

**3.** Add the zucchini, olives, minced parsley, and salt to the beef and tomato mixture. If the dish is too dry, add the ½ cup of broth. Return the pan to the oven. Cover and bake for 35 minutes, until the zucchini is tender. Garnish with parsley and serve immediately with crusty bread.

# Deconstructed Cabbage Rolls with Tomato Sauce

**SERVES 4**

**M**y grandmother used to make cabbage rolls with great expertise. These deconstructed rolls were also inspired by similar recipes in community cookbooks. Cabbage rolls appear in many northern European cuisines, including Polish, Russian, and Jewish. Here the ingredients are layered, lasagna style, which removes the fiddly work of rolling the cabbage leaves around the stuffing, making this an easy — and nourishing — family supper.

4 cups fresh or canned diced tomatoes, with juice

2 tablespoons tomato paste

salt and freshly ground black pepper

8 cups (about 1½ pounds) sliced green cabbage, cut into 1-inch strips

1 tablespoon canola oil

1 medium onion, chopped

1–2 garlic cloves, peeled and minced

1 pound lean ground beef

1 teaspoon cumin seeds, crushed

¾ teaspoon ground cinnamon

Tabasco

1½ teaspoons dried oregano or 1 teaspoon fresh

¾ cup breadcrumbs made from day-old bread

**1.** Put the tomatoes in a medium saucepan and stir in 1 tablespoon of the tomato paste. Season with salt and pepper and simmer, stirring often, for 4 to 5 minutes, until the tomato chunks are bathed in a somewhat thick sauce rather than simply in the juice. Set aside.

**2.** Preheat the oven to 375°F and grease a shallow 10-inch square lidded baking dish or other casserole dish of similar capacity.

**3.** Bring a large pan of water to a boil. Add 1 teaspoon of salt and then the cabbage. Cover the pan and cook the cabbage for 7 minutes, until tender. Drain in a colander, pressing firmly to squeeze out excess water.

**4.** Meanwhile, heat the oil in a skillet over medium heat. Add the onion and garlic and sauté for 3 to 4 minutes, until slightly softened. Stir in the beef and sauté for 4 to 5 minutes, turning until all the meat is evenly browned.

Season with the cumin, cinnamon, a few drops of Tabasco, and salt to taste. Stir in the remaining tablespoon of tomato paste and about ½ cup of the prepared tomatoes. Continue cooking and stirring over medium heat for 3 to 4 minutes, until the ingredients are thoroughly mixed.

**5.** To assemble the dish, put half the cabbage into the baking dish and season with pepper. Spread the meat mixture on top and cover with the rest of the cabbage.

**6.** Return the remaining prepared tomatoes to the heat, stir in the oregano, and bring to a simmer. Spread the mixture over the top layer of cabbage. Cover the dish with the lid (or foil) and bake for 18 to 20 minutes, until heated through. Remove the lid, sprinkle on the breadcrumbs, and bake for 5 minutes longer, until lightly gold and crisp on top.

**7.** Let the casserole sit for 5 minutes, and then serve.

MORE MAIN DISHES

# Tomato-Rice Casserole with Poblanos, Beef, and Melted Cheese

#### SERVES 3-4

Full of the warm earthy flavors of Mexico, this casserole can be served as a main dish — especially good on a chilly evening. The recipe comes from Rick Bayless, owner of Chicago's Frontera Grill and Topolobampo restaurants and author of several cookbooks on Mexican cuisine.

1 pound (about 6 medium large) poblano chiles

1 pound ripe tomatoes (2–3 medium-large or 6–8 plum tomatoes)

1 tablespoon vegetable oil

1 large white onion, cut into ¼-inch slices

3 garlic cloves, peeled and finely chopped

½ teaspoon dried oregano

about 2 teaspoons salt

1 cup rice

1 cup grated Mexican Chihuahua or other melting cheese, such as Monterey Jack or sharp cheddar

1½ cups boneless cooked beef, cut into ½-inch strips

1. Put the chiles and tomatoes on a baking sheet, place it about 4 inches under a hot broiler, and broil until the chiles have blackened on all sides, about 5 minutes. Remove the chiles from the baking sheet and cool them under paper towels; peel, remove the stem and seeds, and rinse briefly to remove bits of skin. Slice into ¼-inch strips.

2. Meanwhile, leave the tomatoes until they, too, have blackened on both sides and the skins have burst, about 6 minutes each side. Cool the tomatoes, and then peel, collecting all the juice.

3. Warm the oil in a medium skillet over medium heat; add the onion and cook it for 5 minutes. Toss in the garlic and oregano and cook 1 minute longer; stir in the chiles, the tomatoes, including their juice, and 1 teaspoon of the salt. Cook for about 4 minutes, until slightly reduced.

4. Boil 3 quarts of water and the remaining teaspoon salt in a large pot. Add the rice. Simmer uncovered for about 15 minutes, until the grains are tender but not mushy or splayed. Pour into a strainer and cool.

**5.** Preheat the oven to 350°F and grease an 8-inch square pan or casserole or baking dish of similar capacity. Spread half the rice over the bottom of the pan. Spoon on half the chile-tomato mixture, spreading it to the edges. Sprinkle over it about half the cheese and the strips of beef. Cover with the remaining rice, then the remaining sauce, and top with the remaining cheese. Bake until bubbling and brown, 20 to 30 minutes. Let stand 10 minutes, and then serve.

## COMING SOON TO A DRUGSTORE NEAR YOU

Wild tomato plants yield a substance known as IBI-246, which has been tested for its ability to repel insects, including mosquitoes, ticks, fleas, ants, flies, and cockroaches. This substance is used in some cosmetics and will likely be showing up soon in bug repellents.

MAGNIFICENT TOMATO

# Lamb Provençal

SERVES 4

Herbes de Provence is a mixture of the herbs that grow on the parched hillsides of southern France: rosemary, thyme, savory, marjoram, and lavender are the common ingredients. These herbs, plus the southern vegetables — eggplant, zucchini, and, of course, ripe summery tomatoes — give this dish the flavors that typify Provence. Serve with rice.

1 medium eggplant (about 1 pound)

4 teaspoons sea salt

8 lamb loin chops (about 2 pounds total)

1 teaspoon herbes de Provence or a mixture of rosemary, thyme, and savory

about ¼ teaspoon freshly ground black pepper

2 tablespoons olive oil

1 medium onion, chopped

1 garlic clove, peeled and chopped

3 cups fresh or canned peeled, seeded, and coarsely chopped tomatoes

1 bay leaf

2 zucchini (4–5 inches each), cut into ½-inch slices

12 green or black olives, preferably pitted

1. Cut the eggplant lengthwise into 6 or 8 pieces, then slice them across to make ½-inch chunks. Put the chunks into a colander and sprinkle with 3 teaspoons of the salt. Leave for 60 minutes, then rinse and pat dry.

2. Meanwhile, sprinkle the lamb chops with ½ teaspoon of the remaining salt, the herbes de Provence, pepper, and 1 tablespoon of the oil. Let the chops rest for 45 to 60 minutes, turning once or twice.

3. Warm the remaining 1 tablespoon oil in a large skillet over medium heat; add the onion and garlic and cook for 3 minutes. Add the chops and cook each side for 3 to 4 minutes, until browned. Remove the chops from the pan and set aside.

4. Toss in the eggplant pieces and sauté for 3 minutes. Stir in the tomatoes and bay leaf and bring to a simmer. Return the chops to the pan, cover, and simmer for 20 minutes.

5. Sprinkle the zucchini slices with the remaining ½ teaspoon salt and let them stand in a colander while the chops are cooking. Rinse them in cold water, pat them dry, and add them to the chops, along with the olives. Cook for 5 minutes longer, or until the zucchini pieces are tender (but not soggy) and the olives are warm. Serve hot.

# Shahi Kofta Curry

**SERVES 4**

The recipe for these lamb dumplings in a tomato almond cream sauce comes from Raghavan Iyer, author of *660 Curries* and *The Turmeric Trail: Recipes and Memories from an Indian Childhood*. He calls it "a dish fit for a king" — king is *shahi* in Hindi — and recommends serving it with a mildly spiced Basmati rice pilaf.

1 pound ground lamb (see Note)

½ cup finely chopped red onion

¼ cup finely chopped fresh mint

2 tablespoons finely chopped fresh cilantro

1 tablespoon garam masala

1 tablespoon finely chopped garlic

1 teaspoon salt

2 tablespoons vegetable oil

1 teaspoon cumin seed

¼ cup ground blanched almonds

1½ cups tomato sauce

½ teaspoon ground cardamom

½ teaspoon cayenne pepper

½ cup heavy cream

**1.** Mix the lamb, onion, mint, cilantro, garam masala, garlic, and salt in a medium bowl. Divide the mixture into 12 equal parts and shape each part into a ball.

**2.** Heat the oil in a large skillet or Dutch oven over medium-high heat; add the cumin and sizzle for 10 seconds. Add the lamb dumplings and brown them for about 5 minutes, turning occasionally to ensure even browning. Remove the dumplings from the skillet.

**3.** Add the almonds to the skillet and stir-fry for 30 seconds, until golden. Stir in the tomato sauce, cardamom, and cayenne. Lower the heat and simmer, covered, stirring occasionally for 5 minutes, until a thin film of oil starts to form on top of the tomato sauce.

**4.** Add the dumplings and mix gently to coat with the sauce. Continue simmering, covered, stirring very gently occasionally. Cook for 15 minutes, until the lamb is cooked but still slightly pink in the center.

**5.** Fold in the cream; cook for 1 minute longer, just until the sauce has reheated.

NOTE: Ground turkey works as a substitute for the lamb, but the dish will not be as full-flavored.

# Lamb-Stuffed Green Chiles
## with Fresh Tomato Purée

SERVES 6

Here is a traditional Native American dish from the Southwest. The recipe comes from *Foods of the Southwest Indian Nations*, by Lois Ellen Frank, who writes, "What makes this dish so delicious is the fresh tomatoes in the purée, which I grow myself or buy at my local farmers' market when they are in season. You can use a variety of fresh tomatoes. I've made this tomato purée with fresh Roma tomatoes, Red Plum tomatoes, little Yellow Pear tomatoes, and Green and Red Zebra tomatoes, all of which taste wonderful." She also explains that the adobe bread called for in the recipe is a yeasted oven bread made in New Mexico by many of the Indian pueblos. If you cannot get it, she suggests using any day-old or oven-dried nonsourdough yeasted bread to make the crumbs by processing in a food processor or grating with a box grater.

**Stuffed Chiles**

12 firm green New Mexico mild or Anaheim chiles

1 tablespoon cooking oil

⅔ cup finely chopped wild or yellow onions

1½ pounds ground lamb

1 cup adobe breadcrumbs or other finely ground breadcrumbs

2 ripe tomatoes, diced

2 garlic cloves, peeled and minced

1 teaspoon salt

½ teaspoon white pepper

½ teaspoon dried thyme

2 bay leaves

1 tablespoon chopped fresh tarragon or 1 teaspoon dried

**Fresh Tomato Purée**

1 tablespoon extra-virgin olive oil

6 garlic cloves, peeled and minced

1¼ pounds (about 3 medium-large) tomatoes, coarsely chopped

sour cream (optional)

**1.** For the stuffed chiles, roast the chiles on a hot grill or by holding them with tongs directly over a gas flame. Roast them quickly, just until the skins are charred black, and then put them into a paper bag. Fold the top closed and leave the peppers for 5 to 10 minutes. Remove and peel the charred skins and remove the seeds, keeping the peppers whole. (Do not roast the peppers in an oven, because they may become too soft to stuff easily.) Set aside.

2. Heat the cooking oil in a large skillet over medium heat and sauté the onions for about 4 minutes, until translucent. Add the lamb and brown 15 minutes, stirring occasionally to prevent burning.

3. Drain off the excess fat and add the breadcrumbs, the diced tomatoes, garlic, salt, pepper, thyme, bay leaves, and tarragon. Lower the heat and simmer 15 minutes longer. Remove from the heat and cool.

4. Oil a large baking dish. Slice the chiles lengthwise, spread them open on a work surface, and generously stuff each chile with the lamb mixture. Place the stuffed chiles in the baking dish with the open side down and set aside.

5. For the tomato purée, heat the olive oil in a medium saucepan over medium-low heat. Add the garlic and sauté for 1 minute. Add the chopped tomatoes and cook 15 minutes longer, stirring occasionally to prevent burning, until the excess liquid evaporates. The sauce will reduce and thicken. At this point you can pour the sauce through a fine sieve to remove the skins or you can serve it as it is. Set aside.

6. Preheat the oven to 350°F.

7. Place the chiles in the oven and bake until hot, 5 to 10 minutes. For a spicier flavor, cook the chiles a bit longer. Serve immediately with the tomato purée. Garnish with sour cream, if desired.

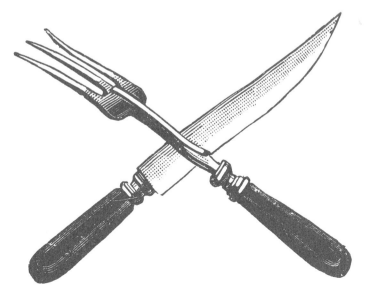

# Veal Parmigiana

### SERVES 4

Veal parmigiana is unknown in Italy. It is an Italian American dish, probably devised to use the veal more easily available in America than the eggplant in the traditional parmigiana.

4 veal scallops (about 5 ounces each)

salt and freshly ground back pepper

3 tablespoons all-purpose flour

1 egg beaten with 1 tablespoon water

1 cup dry breadcrumbs

⅔ cup grated Parmesan cheese

2 cups Marinara Sauce (page 19) or store-bought herb-flavored tomato sauce

2 tablespoons olive oil

1 tablespoon butter

8 ounces mozzarella, shredded or sliced

1. Place the veal on a board and beat it flat with a meat hammer or rolling pin. If you see any thin silvery strips of sinew, remove them so they won't shrink and distort the meat during cooking. Season the veal with salt and pepper.

2. Place the flour on one plate, the egg on another, and the breadcrumbs mixed with ⅓ cup of the Parmesan on a third. Dip the veal pieces in the flour, shaking to get rid of any residue, then in the egg, and finally in the breadcrumbs. Let them rest for 20 minutes so the crumbs can adhere.

3. Preheat the oven to 375°F and grease a shallow baking dish large enough to hold the veal in a single layer. Pour in a thin layer of tomato sauce.

4. Heat the oil and butter in a large skillet and briefly sauté the veal until golden — about 1 minute on each side. Place the pieces in the prepared dish and sprinkle them with the remaining Parmesan. Bring the remaining tomato sauce to a simmer, and then pour on just enough to cover the veal. Top with the mozzarella. Cover the dish with foil and bake for 8 to 10 minutes; remove the foil and bake 5 minutes longer. Let rest a few minutes, and then serve.

# Rabbit Cacciatora

SERVES 3–4

The Italian word *cacciatora* means "hunter style" and characterizes dishes that take their inspiration from dishes made from birds or small animals caught by hunters and mixed with flavorings of herbs, onions, tomatoes, and Italy's ubiquitous wine and olives. Here in America chicken generally replaces game, but in Italy rabbit remains a favorite. It is a truly delicious meat, mild and tasty, and it pairs well with red or black tomatoes. Serve with polenta or a wide cut of pasta such as tagliatelle or pappardelle dressed with a little Pesto Rosso (page 32).

1 rabbit, cut into 8 pieces (see Note)

   salt and freshly ground black pepper

4 parsley sprigs

2 sprigs rosemary, each about 2 inches long

2 garlic cloves, peeled and sliced

2 bay leaves

1¾ cups Italian red wine

2 tablespoons extra-virgin olive oil

1 medium-large onion, chopped

1 celery stalk, cut into ½-inch lengths

3 cups fresh or canned chopped tomatoes

2–3 teaspoons tomato paste

12 Italian black or kalamata olives

**1.** Put the rabbit pieces in a casserole dish or baking dish. Season with salt and pepper and tuck the parsley, rosemary, half the garlic slices, and the bay leaves among them. Pour on the wine and let sit for 2 hours (or up to 12 hours, if preferred), turning the pieces 2 or 3 times.

**2.** When you are ready to prepare the dish, remove the rabbit pieces from the marinade and wipe them dry. Reserve the marinade. Heat the oil in a casserole dish or large saucepan with a lid. Add the rabbit pieces and cook gently for 5 to 6 minutes, until lightly browned. Remove and add the onion, remaining garlic, and the celery and cook for 4 to 5 minutes, until slightly softened. Add the tomatoes and any juice. Strain in the marinade. Add the bay leaves and rosemary from the marinade. Cover the pan and simmer for 45 to 55 minutes, until the rabbit is tender.

**3.** Stir in the tomato paste a spoonful at a time, using only enough to thicken the sauce. Taste for seasoning and add more salt and pepper if necessary. Finally, add the olives and simmer 10 minutes longer. Serve hot.

NOTE: Chicken can be substituted for the rabbit. It will need only 15 to 20 minutes of simmering to reach tenderness in step 2.

 # Trio of Stuffed Tomatoes

SERVES 4

Almost any kind of tomato can be used for stuffing, but it is best to avoid overripe ones. The suggestion in these recipes is four large tomatoes, but a greater number of smaller tomatoes, Ping Pong–ball size and up, can be substituted. There are a number of hollow or stuffing tomatoes, for example, Yellow Stuffer and Red Stuffer. The water content of these tomatoes is much lower than that of slicing tomatoes, and they are less prone to fall apart, but they also have much less flavor. Three stuffing options are given below.

## Tomatoes

    8 slices whole wheat bread

    6 tablespoons butter

    1 teaspoon chopped fresh oregano or
        ½ teaspoon dried

    8 large ripe tomatoes

## Chicken and Corn Stuffing

    2 cups cooked chopped chicken

    1 cup fresh corn cut from the cob

    6 tablespoons finely chopped onion

    ½ cup dried seasoned breadcrumbs

    2 tablespoons snipped fresh tarragon or
        2 teaspoons dried

    2 teaspoons Worcestershire sauce

        salt and freshly ground black pepper

## Lamb and Pine Nut Stuffing

    ⅔ cup pine nuts

    2 tablespoons extra-virgin olive oil

    6 tablespoons finely chopped onion

    2 garlic cloves, peeled and chopped

    2 cups cooked chopped lamb

    1 cup fresh whole wheat breadcrumbs

    2 teaspoons herbes de Provence or rosemary

    2 teaspoons Worcestershire sauce

        salt and freshly ground black pepper

## Cheese and Olive Stuffing

    4 cups whole wheat breadcrumbs

    1 pound sharp cheddar cheese, grated (4 cups)

    ½ cup freshly grated Parmesan cheese

    2 teaspoons snipped chives

    16 pitted kalamata or other black cured olives,
        each cut into 3 or 4 pieces

    2 tablespoons Worcestershire sauce

        salt

1. Preheat the oven to 400°F and grease a shallow baking dish just large enough to hold the tomatoes in a single layer.

**2.** For the toast, cut 8 circles of whole wheat bread, using a cookie cutter. In a small bowl, mix 4 tablespoons of the butter with the oregano and spread on the circles. Set them on a small baking sheet until needed.

**3.** For the tomatoes, remove remnants of the stems. Sit each tomato on its stem end and slice a lid from the top; reserve the lids. Using a sharp knife and a teaspoon, remove the flesh and seeds to a sieve placed over a bowl. Turn the hollowed tomatoes upside down to drain for 15 to 20 minutes while you make the stuffing. (Some of the juice that drips into the bowl and some of the tomato flesh are used in the stuffings.)

**4.** For the chicken stuffing, mix the chicken, corn, onion, breadcrumbs, tarragon, and Worcestershire in a medium bowl. Season to taste with salt and pepper. Stir in about ⅓ cup of the chopped tomato flesh from the sieve and a little of the juice from the bowl, using just enough to make everything cohere.

**5.** For the lamb stuffing, preheat the oven to 300°F. Place the pine nuts in a dry skillet over medium heat and toast until golden, about 5 minutes, shaking the pan often and watching carefully to prevent scorching. Heat the oil in a medium skillet over low heat; add the onion and garlic, and sauté until barely softened, 3 to 4 minutes. Remove from the heat and stir in the pine nuts, lamb, breadcrumbs, herbes de Provence, and Worcestershire. Season with salt and pepper. Add about ⅓ cup of the tomato juice

and chopped flesh from the prepared tomatoes and mix until everything coheres.

**6.** For the cheese and olive stuffing, combine the breadcrumbs, cheddar, Parmesan, chives, olives, and Worcestershire in a medium bowl. Add a tablespoon of the juice from the prepared tomatoes and about ¼ cup of the chopped flesh. Use enough juice and tomato to make a cohesive mixture, and season to taste with salt.

**7.** Fill the prepared tomatoes with the stuffing, mounding a little above the top rim. Put a bit of the remaining butter on each. Place in the prepared baking dish. Cover with foil and bake for 10 minutes; remove the foil, place on the tomato lids, and bake 5 minutes longer. At the same time, put the baking sheet of bread circles to toast in the oven.

**8.** To serve, let the tomatoes rest for a couple of minutes, then set each one on a toast circle.

 # Rabbit Paella with Arugula
# and Heirloom Tomato

**SERVES 4**

David Garrido, former executive chef at Jeffrey's in Austin, Texas, developed this simple paella. Having grown up as the son of a Mexican diplomat, he has an international background that underpins his pairing of diverse tastes and textures for surprising affinities. Paella, the classic dish of southern Spain, often comes with multiple ingredients, including chicken, sausage, scallops, or shrimp. David says, "I love paella, but I like it the simple way." This recipe shows how good it can be.

1 pinch saffron threads (enough to cover a dime)

1 cup warm water

3 tablespoons extra-virgin olive oil

1 rabbit, cut into 8 serving pieces

salt and freshly ground black pepper

⅓ cup diced onion

3 garlic cloves, peeled and finely chopped

1 serrano chile, stemmed, seeded, and finely chopped

1 cup Texmati rice

1 cup white wine

1⅓ cups peeled, seeded, and coarsely chopped heirloom tomatoes

3 bay leaves

4 lemon wedges

1 bunch arugula, washed and dried

NOTE: Cutting rabbit is an art. It is very easy to miss the small rib bones. Cut carefully or buy precut pieces.

**1.** Preheat the oven to 350°F.

**2.** Put the saffron in a small bowl and cover with ½ cup of the water. Stir and set aside.

**3.** Heat the oil in a medium skillet over medium heat. Season the rabbit pieces with salt and pepper and cook for 6 to 8 minutes, until all sides are golden brown. Remove the rabbit pieces to a dish; cover with foil and place in the oven for a few minutes while you deal with the rice and flavorings.

**4.** Add the onion, garlic, and chile to the oil in the skillet and cook for 3 to 4 minutes, until the onion is translucent. Stir in the rice and sauté for 2 minutes, until it begins to turn golden brown.

Add the wine and cook for 4 to 6 minutes, until it is almost completely absorbed.

**5.** Stir in 1 cup of the chopped tomato, the saffron and its soaking liquid, the remaining ½ cup water, the bay leaves, and 1 teaspoon of salt. Remove the rabbit pieces from the oven and nestle them in a single layer in the rice. When the mixture reaches a simmer, lower the heat as much as possible and continue cooking for 15 to 18 minutes or until the rice is tender and the liquid absorbed. Add the remaining tomatoes during the final 2 to 3 minutes of cooking time so that they warm through.

**6.** Transfer the paella to a warmed serving platter and garnish with the lemon wedges and arugula. Serve immediately.

# WHAT'S LOVE GOT TO DO WITH IT?

Beginning in the sixteenth century, some herbalists suggested that tomatoes might be an aphrodisiac. This notion seems to be derived from the French word *pommes d'amour,* rather than any known properties of the vegetable. The Italian word is similar, *pomodoro,* but means something entirely different — apple of gold or yellow. This name was first used in a translation of Dioscorides by Matthiolus in 1554, when he discussed an Old World plant, eggplant, in context with the tomato. Interestingly, Italy is the only country in the world that still calls tomatoes by this name, using one that is essentially incorrect. The idea that tomatoes were exclusively yellow and thus formed the ancient type first introduced to Europe is likely wrong but has been repeated throughout the history of tomatoes. It is possible that yellow tomatoes were introduced early on in Europe, as there were certainly yellow tomatoes in Mexico, but generally tomatoes were in hues of red.

Historian Rudolf Grewe theorizes that the confusion of the names of tomatoes arose because of their close association with eggplant. They are in the same plant family, plus the tomato was described by the early herbalists as a kind of eggplant, and suggestions for cooking them were identical to those for the cooking of eggplant. The eggplant was known long before the tomato, even though it would have been quite rare in northern Europe, being a plant of southern climes and originating farther east. The eggplant was called *pomme des Mours,* or apple of the Moors, in France; in Italy, *pomo del Moro,* as it was extensively used in Arab cuisine. Some of the rounder types of eggplants certainly look and feel like apples. The Italian *pomo* not only means apple but can refer to any applelike fruit. It is easy to see how this could have been mistakenly turned into the "apple of gold" or "love apple" in a time when many of the writers had never seen a tomato nor an eggplant and routinely plagiarized from one another.

MORE MAIN DISHES

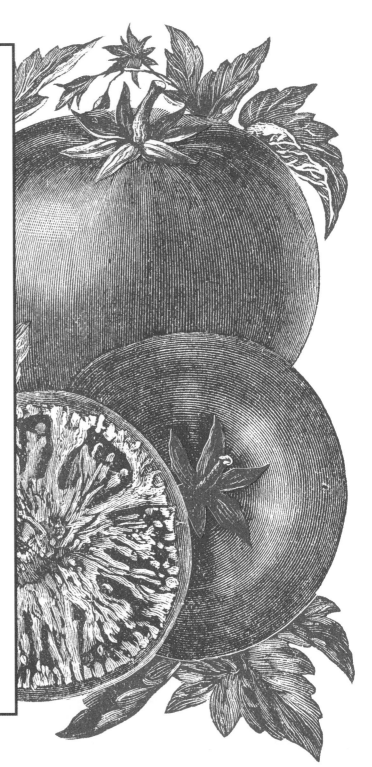

## Kent Whealy's
# Top 10 Tomatoes

Kent Whealy is the director and founder of the Seed Savers Exchange in Decorah, Iowa.

### German Pink
One of the two varieties that got me to start Seed Savers

### Brandywine (Sudduth's Strain)
Incredibly rich, delightfully intense flavor

### Cherokee Purple
Extremely sweet, a bit smoky, rivals Brandywine

### Green Zebra
Sweet zingy flavor

### Black from Tula
Rich, full flavor, great for slicing

### Hillbilly Potato Leaf
Gorgeous slicing tomato from Ohio, yellow streaked with red

### Plum Lemon
I got this from an elderly seedsman at Moscow's Bird Market.

### Riesentraube
Clusters of 20 to 40 round fruits; excellent

### Speckled Roman
Cross between Antique Roman and Banana Legs; meaty and productive

### Tommy Toe
Big yields of apricot-size red fruits; superb flavor

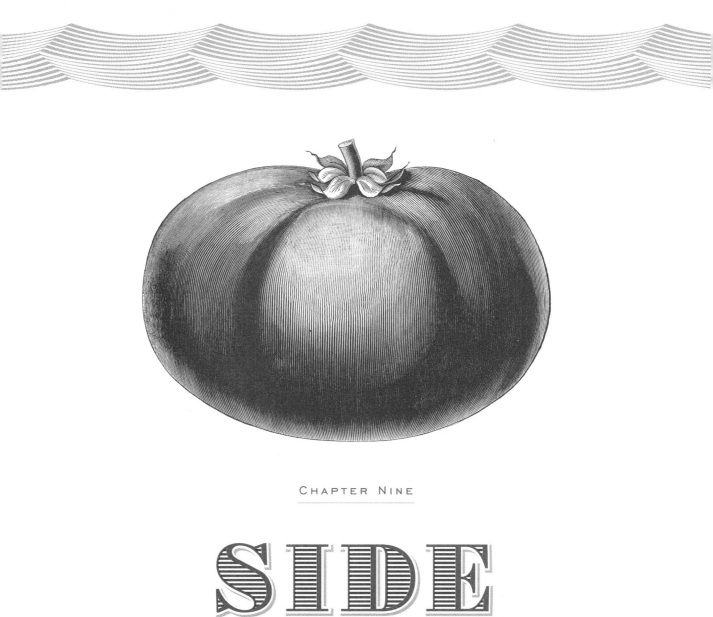

CHAPTER NINE

# SIDE DISHES

# Fried Green Tomatoes

Although green tomatoes are not fully ripe, they are not harshly sour; indeed, they shine as a vegetable and deserve more attention. The first recipe for fried green tomatoes was published in New York City in 1870. Various versions followed in the late nineteenth and early twentieth centuries. Whether or not this is a particularly traditional Southern dish is debatable. Without a doubt, interest in fried green tomatoes revived with the movie based on Fannie Flagg's book. If you'd like to make a vegetarian version, omit the bacon and fry the tomatoes in butter or extra-virgin olive oil.

---

1 pound (4 medium) green (unripe) tomatoes

salt and freshly ground black pepper

⅓ cup milk

½ cup all-purpose flour

⅔ cup yellow cornmeal

4 slices bacon

3–4 parsley sprigs

---

1. Wash and remove the stem ends of the tomatoes. Slice them ¼ inch thick and let the slices rest for 10 minutes. Pat dry and season lightly with salt and pepper.

2. Pour the milk into a shallow dish. On its left, put the flour into another shallow dish, and on its right, put the cornmeal into a third shallow dish. Drop the tomato slices first into the milk, turning to coat both sides, then into the flour, again turning to coat both sides; then dip both sides again into the milk, and finally let them sit for about 30 seconds, first one side, then the other, in the cornmeal. Remove the prepared tomato slices to a cutting board. When all the slices are ready, scatter any leftover cornmeal over them, cover with a cloth, and let rest for 10 to 15 minutes.

3. When ready to cook, fry the bacon in a large skillet over medium heat until the fat is rendered and the bacon is crisp. Remove the bacon to paper towels, leaving the fat in the pan.

4. Add the tomato slices to the hot bacon fat. Cook gently for 4 to 5 minutes per side, turning when each side is golden. Reduce the heat, if necessary, to prevent them from browning. Drain on paper towels to remove excess fat.

5. To serve, place the tomato slices on a warmed plate. Garnish with the reserved bacon, crumbled if you like, and parsley sprigs.

# Broiled Tomatoes

SERVES 4

Serve this easy and tasty dish as a side with grilled or broiled chicken or other meat dishes. It is also a great choice with eggs for Sunday brunch. The topping of toasted crumbs contrasts delightfully with the melting tomatoes.

4 medium-large ripe but firm tomatoes

salt

5 tablespoons butter, at room temperature

4 tablespoons finely chopped fresh parsley

2 medium garlic cloves, peeled and finely chopped

freshly ground black pepper

⅓ cup breadcrumbs made from day-old bread

1. Cut the tomatoes in half horizontally. Lightly sprinkle the cut surfaces with salt and turn them cut side down on a double thickness of paper towels to drain some of the moisture. Leave them for 10 to 15 minutes.

2. Preheat the broiler. With a little butter, grease a shallow pan just large enough to hold the tomato halves in a single layer.

3. Mash the remaining butter in a small bowl with the parsley and garlic. Place the tomatoes in the prepared pan, cut side up. Spread the surfaces with the butter, pushing some into the seed cavities.

4. Place the pan of tomatoes under the broiler and broil for 5 to 8 minutes, until the tomatoes are very hot and the surface looks a little shriveled.

5. Remove from under the broiler and grind pepper on top of the tomatoes. Scatter on the breadcrumbs. Replace under the broiler and broil for a few more minutes, until the crumbs are golden. Watch carefully during this time to make sure the topping does not burn.

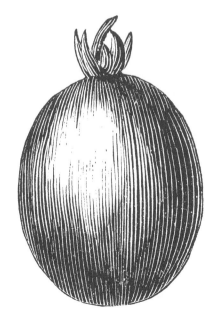

# Heirloom Tomato and Toasted Garlic Gratin

### SERVES 4

An homage to the delights of ripe heirloom tomatoes, this gratin comes from chef Michel Nischan, an energetic advocate of organic and in-season vegetables. Here he enhances sliced tomatoes by first draining away some of their juice, then browning them with garlic and Pecorino Romano cheese. Finally, he stacks the fragrant slices into an elegant tower for serving. Michel specifies Marvel Striped tomatoes, a large bicolor variety that originated in Mexico. Any bicolor will work well, including German Stripe, Pineapple, or Regina's. Or you can mix and match black, yellow, orange, and red tomatoes.

4 large tomatoes, preferably Marvel Striped

sea salt

1 cup extra-virgin olive oil

3 plump garlic cloves, peeled

1–2 tablespoons fresh oregano, plus sprigs for garnish

½ cup freshly grated Pecorino Romano cheese

1. Cut the tomatoes into ¼-inch slices and sprinkle lightly with salt. Let the tomato slices stand on paper towels for 1 hour. The salt will draw out any excess water and concentrate the tomato flavor.

2. Heat the oil in a small saucepan over high heat until it just begins to ripple. Slice the garlic, using a French or Japanese mandoline or a vegetable peeler. Cook for 1 minute, or until the garlic slices turn light golden brown. Transfer the garlic slices from the oil to a paper towel and cool. (Reserve the oil, now garlic-flavored, for frying croutons or sautéing vegetables.)

3. Preheat the broiler. Use a slotted spatula to transfer the tomato slices to a baking sheet. Sprinkle the tomato slices evenly with the garlic and oregano, and then sprinkle cheese over each slice. Place the cookie sheet 6 inches under a hot broiler and cook until the cheese melts and slightly browns.

4. Remove the baking sheet from the broiler and assemble the tomato slices atop each other. Garnish with an oregano sprig and serve.

# Scalloped Tomatoes

### SERVES 4

Scalloped tomatoes are especially good made with juicy late-summer tomatoes and breadcrumbs from flavorful whole wheat bread.

- 3 tablespoons butter
- 3–4 cups breadcrumbs made from day-old whole wheat bread
- 2 pounds (or more as needed to fill your dish) slicing tomatoes, peeled and cut into ½-inch slices
- salt and freshly ground black pepper

1. Preheat the oven to 350°F. Lightly grease an 8-inch square pan or baking dish with a little of the butter. Cut the remaining butter into small pieces.

2. Spread about one-third of the crumbs over the bottom of the pan, making sure to completely cover it. Cover the crumbs with a layer of tomato slices, and season with salt and pepper. Scatter enough crumbs on top to cover the tomatoes, and then add another layer of tomato slices. Season with salt and pepper. Dot with butter. Cover with the remaining crumbs.

3. Bake for 15 to 20 minutes, until the tomatoes are cooked and the top crumbs are crispy.

# Spicy Stewed Tomatoes

### SERVES 4

There are hundreds of variations on stewed tomatoes. This one is mine. Serve it as a side dish with beans and rice, meat, or fish. It is also delicious as a pasta sauce.

- 2 tablespoons extra-virgin olive oil or canola oil
- 1 large mild onion, such as a Spanish onion or sweet Vidalia onion, peeled, halved, and thinly sliced
- 1 pound (about 3 medium) ripe tomatoes, peeled, seeded, and coarsely chopped
- 1 small green chile, such as jalapeño or serrano, seeded and finely chopped
- 1 tablespoon sugar
- salt and freshly ground black pepper

1. Heat the oil in a large saucepan over medium heat and stir in the onion. Cook for 5 to 6 minutes, until the onion is soft and just slightly browned.

2. Stir in the tomatoes, chile, sugar, and salt and pepper to taste. Cover and cook over low heat, stirring occasionally to prevent sticking, for 20 minutes, until everything is tender.

3. Check the seasoning and add salt and pepper as needed. Serve hot.

# Ratatouille

SERVES 12–15

When tomatoes are in season, so are eggplants and zucchini, which is what makes this Mediterranean dish so perfect for gardeners. This particular recipe, from Carol W. Costenbader's *Big Book of Preserving the Harvest,* was developed to serve immediately or go into the freezer to enjoy later, when summer is a distant memory.

6 tablespoons extra-virgin olive oil

4 small zucchini, sliced

2 yellow onions, sliced

2 green bell peppers, seeded and chopped

3 garlic cloves, peeled and minced

3 medium tomatoes, peeled, seeded, and chopped

3 small eggplants, cubed

salt

2 tablespoons chopped fresh parsley

1 tablespoon chopped fresh basil

1 teaspoon dried oregano

1. Heat 4 tablespoons of the oil in a large skillet over medium-high heat. Add the zucchini, onions, peppers, and garlic and sauté until soft, about 5 minutes. Add the tomatoes and heat thoroughly to help evaporate the liquid. Transfer the mixture to a 3-quart casserole dish.

2. Meanwhile, "sweat" the eggplants by tossing the cubes with ½ teaspoon of salt in a large bowl. Let rest for 30 minutes. Rinse briefly and then pat the cubes dry.

3. Sauté the eggplant with the remaining 2 tablespoons oil in the skillet over medium-high heat until well browned and tender, about 5 minutes.

4. Add the eggplant to the onion mixture and stir well. Add the parsley, basil, and oregano and stir to distribute evenly. Let cool. Taste and adjust the seasoning.

5. Serve reheated or at room temperature. Or divide into two portions and store in plastic freezer bags in the freezer for up to 3 months.

# Potatoes Pizzaiola

**SERVES 4**

The name of this Italian dish means "pizza-style potatoes," and with tomatoes, onions, and oregano in the ingredients list, it's easy to see why. It accompanies steaks and chops wonderfully and is a perfect partner to other vegetable dishes. It's also good just on its own.

¼ cup extra-virgin olive oil

1 teaspoon fresh oregano or 1½ teaspoons dried

1½ pounds Yukon Gold potatoes, peeled and cut into ¼-inch slices

2 medium onions, cut into ¼-inch slices

sea salt and freshly ground black pepper

3 cups fresh or canned peeled, seeded, and diced tomatoes

**1.** Preheat the oven to 375°F and use a little oil to grease a 9- by 13-inch baking dish.

**2.** Mix the remaining oil with the oregano in a large bowl. If the potato slices are wet, pat them dry with paper towels, then toss them with the oil in the bowl. Arrange alternating rows of potato slices and onion slices in the prepared baking dish. (Don't worry if the rows are not perfectly straight.) Drizzle any oil remaining in the bowl over the potatoes and onions. Season generously with salt and pepper.

**3.** Scatter the tomatoes and their juices on top. Sprinkle lightly with salt. Cover the pan with foil and bake for 50 to 60 minutes, until the potatoes and onions feel tender when pierced with a knifepoint.

**4.** Let rest for 5 minutes before serving.

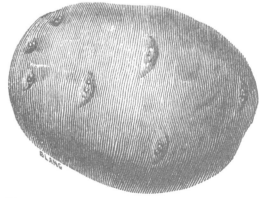

**PRINCE EDWARD ISLAND ROSE**

# A TOMATO A DAY KEEPS THE DOCTOR AWAY

Tomatoes contain a significant amount of vitamin C. A small tomato, weighing about 3 ounces, supplies 23 to 30 milligrams of vitamin C or from a third to half of the recommended daily requirement. Vitamin C can thin blood, protects it against oxidation, and lowers cholesterol and blood pressure.

This same tomato can supply 15 to 20 percent of the recommended vitamin A, plus 200 milligrams of potassium. Potassium is useful in regulating blood pressure and thus reducing the likelihood of stroke. A potassium supplement of 1,000 milligrams can reduce the incidence of stroke in men by about 60 percent. Or you can eat a pound of tomatoes a day.

Significant amounts of lycopene are present in tomatoes. Lycopene is a carotenoid, one of the phytochemicals that are the nutritionally beneficial active compounds present in fruits and vegetables. Carotenoids give the red color we typically associate with tomatoes. The redder the tomato, the more lycopene it contains.

Lycopene is a potent antioxidant. Antioxidants are believed to play a significant role in the prevention of cancer, and various studies indicate that it may also play a positive role in reducing the risk of heart disease and boosting immune function.

The landmark article that put lycopene on the map was a report published in the *Journal of the National Cancer Institute* by Harvard researchers in 1995. This study found that the consumption of tomatoes, tomato sauce, tomato juice, and pizza was associated with a lower risk of prostate cancer. Curiously, lycopene is actually present in higher amounts in most processed tomato products than in fresh tomatoes and can be more readily absorbed by the body.

While some of the medical claims made for tomatoes in the nineteenth century seem wild and exaggerated, we now know that tomatoes really do have healing properties.

 # Tomato and Potato Casserole

### SERVES 4

In this recipe, the exact amounts of ingredients depend on the size of dish you are using, so consider the quantities below to be just suggestions. The casserole can be served as either a side dish or a simple vegetarian main dish, and it's one that kids will like.

2 pounds potatoes, peeled

salt and freshly ground black pepper

2 teaspoons dry mustard

⅓ cup milk

8 ounces extra-sharp cheddar cheese, grated (2 cups)

3 cups chopped fresh or canned tomatoes

1–2 teaspoons tomato paste as needed

¼ cup chopped basil or parsley leaves

10 cherry tomatoes, halved, or 1 or 2 slicing tomatoes, sliced

**1.** Put the potatoes in a large pan of cold water, add about ½ teaspoon of salt (or to taste), bring to a boil, and cook for 20 to 25 minutes, until soft. Drain the potatoes and sprinkle with pepper to taste.

**2.** Mix the mustard with the milk and pour it over the potatoes; roughly mash them. Reserve 2 tablespoons of the cheddar; add the remainder to the potatoes and mash until smooth. Taste and add salt and pepper as needed.

**3.** Preheat the oven to 375°F and grease an 8-inch round baking dish or something similar.

**4.** If you are using canned tomatoes, drain them and reserve the liquid. Combine the tomatoes with enough of the liquid and a little tomato paste to make a thick, saucy mass. If using fresh tomatoes, simmer them for a few minutes to release their juice, and then add tomato paste only if needed.

**5.** Stir the basil into the tomatoes and pour the mixture into the prepared dish. Top with the potato mixture. Arrange the cherry tomatoes attractively around the edge of the dish. Run a fork over the potatoes to rough them up, and then scatter on the reserved cheddar.

**6.** Bake in the center of the oven for 15 to 20 minutes, until heated through. If the top browns too much before the casserole is hot, cover the dish with foil and lower the heat to 350°F. Serve hot.

 # Greek Beans with Tomatoes

This is a favorite dish in Greece, where it is often served as one of the small dishes that precede a meal; similar versions exist in Italy. The generous amount of olive oil used in cooking seals the surface of the beans and preserves their flavor so leftovers still taste good the next day. Ideally the green beans should have just been picked. If you grow your own, try planting Black Valentine beans, an heirloom variety with lots of flavor and no strings. Any type or color of tomato can be used in this dish, but I like using red or black ones, both for their flavor and for contrast with the beans.

⅓ cup extra-virgin olive oil

2 medium onions, halved and cut into ⅓-inch slices

1–2 garlic cloves, peeled and finely chopped

salt and freshly ground black pepper

1 pound green beans, trimmed

1 large potato, peeled and cut into ½-inch slices

2 cups fresh or canned peeled and diced tomatoes, with juice

⅓ cup water, if needed

3 tablespoons coarsely chopped fresh parsley

**1.** Heat the oil in a medium saucepan over low heat. Stir in the onions and garlic, season lightly with salt, cover the pan, and let the onions and garlic sweat over low heat for 5 to 6 minutes, until tender. Stir once or twice to prevent sticking. Stir in the green beans, cover the pan, and cook for 5 minutes longer, stirring once or twice.

**2.** Add the potato slices and tomatoes, including about ½ cup of juice if you are using canned tomatoes. If you are using fresh tomatoes, add ⅓ cup of water. Add half the parsley and season again with salt and pepper. Cover the pan and cook for 15 minutes, and then uncover and cook 15 minutes longer, until all the vegetables are tender and a lot of the liquid has evaporated. Stir from time to time to prevent sticking.

**3.** Stir in the remaining parsley, and then spoon the mixture onto a serving platter. Serve warm or at room temperature.

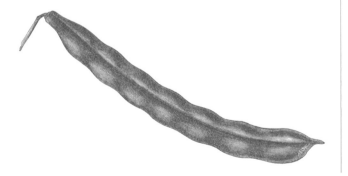

THE CARDINAL

## CR Lawn's
# Top 10 Tomatoes

CR founded Fedco Seeds more than 25 years ago in Maine. It is a small seed company featuring a variety of seeds, including many heirlooms.

### Brandywine
Sets the standard for its rich old-timey tomato flavor

### Aunt Ruby's German Green
Rich and tart, sweet and spicy; the best green tomato

### Sun Gold
A cherry that perfectly blends rich sweetness with a hint of acid tartness

### Cherokee Purple
Brick-red flesh with smoky, juicy, winy flavor

### Cosmonaut Volkov
Full-bodied sweet, rich, juicy; the best early tomato

### Pineapple
Marbled bicolor with silky smooth texture, complex fruity taste

### Black Krim
Iridescent purple; smoky flavor like a good single-malt Scotch

### Lillian's Yellow Heirloom
Superb creamy consistency, complex meaty flesh

### Orange Banana
Makes an ambrosial sauce with a vivid fruity complexity

### Mark Twain
Juicy, luscious, with deep red interior color

# Corn Maque Chou

SERVES 4–6

Chef Greg Sonnier served this classic Cajun corn and tomato stew at Gabrielle in New Orleans. What will really make this dish is using both heirloom tomatoes and heirloom corn. Heirloom corn is virtually impossible to find commercially grown, because the old varieties cannot compete with the sweetness of the new hybrids. But the old varieties have incredibly good corn flavor. If you have access to heirloom corn, just increase the amount of sugar called for in the recipe. Golden Bantam and Black Sweet (Black Mexican) are two corn varieties still available from heirloom seed companies.

¼ cup extra-virgin olive oil

6 whole garlic cloves, peeled

1½ cups chopped onion

1 red bell pepper, seeded and cut into ½-inch pieces

kernels from 3 ears of corn

4 Roma or other plum tomatoes, peeled and coarsely chopped

1 (6-ounce) can evaporated milk

¼ cup torn basil

2 teaspoons fresh thyme

2 teaspoons sugar

salt and freshly ground black pepper

1. Heat the oil in a large skillet and cook the garlic in it for 3 to 4 minutes, until lightly golden. Remove the garlic.

2. Add half the onion to the oil and sauté until golden brown, and then stir in the remaining onion and the red pepper. Continue cooking until the onions are tender.

3. Stir in the corn (including the corn milk — see Note), the tomatoes, evaporated milk, basil, and thyme. Simmer, uncovered, for 10 minutes, until the vegetables are tender and the mixture has thickened.

4. Season the mixture with the sugar and salt and pepper to taste. Serve hot.

NOTE: To remove the corn milk from the cobs, run the back of the knife blade along the cob after you have cut off the kernels.

# Zucchini and Tomatoes with Cream

### SERVES 4

A delicious and refreshing combination of two of the most prolific summer vegetables from Diana Kennedy's *The Cuisines of Mexico*. For the most authentic flavor, try growing one of the old vining zucchinis, such as Costata Romanesca. Vining zucchini take up more garden space than the modern bush types, but the flavor is hands-down better.

1½ pounds (about 4 medium) zucchini, trimmed and diced

¾ pound (2–3 medium) tomatoes, peeled and seeded

6 peppercorns

4 sprigs cilantro

2 mint sprigs

½-inch cinnamon stick

4 whole cloves

2 serrano chiles

½ cup light cream

salt and freshly ground black pepper

**1.** Put the zucchini and tomatoes in a large pan with the peppercorns, cilantro, mint, cinnamon, cloves, chiles, cream, and salt and pepper to taste. Cover the pan and cook the mixture over low heat, scraping the bottom of the pan from time to time to prevent burning.

**2.** If the vegetables are dry, add a little water. If you have juicy summer tomatoes, and the mixture is too thin, remove the lid, raise the heat, and cook to evaporate the excess. After 20 to 30 minutes, the vegetables will be tender and the sauce thick.

 # Sun-Dried Tomato and Saffron Pilaf

SERVES 4

**G**ood at any time, this is especially nice in winter when the intense flavor of sun-dried tomatoes and the sunny colors of the dish recall summer.

1 cup basmati or other long-grain rice

large pinch saffron (enough to cover a dime)

1⅔ cups warm water

⅓ cup golden raisins

1 tablespoon butter

2 tablespoons chopped shallot

1 small garlic clove, peeled and finely chopped

12 sun-dried tomatoes, snipped into small pieces

¾ teaspoon salt

1 small bay leaf

**1.** Place the rice in a sieve and run cold water over it for a minute. Transfer to a medium bowl and cover with plenty of cold water. Let stand for at least 30 minutes, or up to 60 minutes, changing the water once or twice. When the water looks clear, strain the rice through a sieve.

**2.** While the rice is soaking, combine the saffron with ⅓ cup of the warm water. In a separate small bowl, soak the raisins in warm water to cover.

**3.** For the pilaf, melt the butter in a medium pan over low heat. Stir in the shallot and garlic and cook to soften for 2 to 3 minutes. Stir in the drained rice. When the rice is glistening with the butter, add the saffron and its water, plus 1⅓ cups additional water. Stir in the tomatoes and salt and add the bay leaf. Simmer for 10 minutes, until most of the liquid has been absorbed and craters appear on the surface of the rice.

**4.** Drain the raisins. Using a fork, gently stir them into the rice. Remove the bay leaf. Take a clean cloth towel and place it over the pan. Hold it in place with the lid. Remove from the heat but keep in a warm spot for 15 to 20 minutes, until the rice is fluffy.

# THE TOMATO IN EUROPE

Precisely how and when tomatoes arrived in Europe is not known, but it seems highly likely they went first to Spain. The Spanish were colonizing Mexico and taking samples of all kinds of New World products back to Spain through the port of Seville. The linguistic evidence for tomatoes' direct arrival from Mexico to Spain is strong, since the Spanish immediately began calling them *tomate* directly from the Aztec word *tomatl* whereas other countries such as France didn't use *tomate* for a couple of centuries, and Italy never adopted it. By the middle of the fifteenth century, tomatoes had already arrived in Italy and the Netherlands.

The first published reference to tomatoes in Europe was by Matthiolus, an Italian, in his Italian translation and commentaries on Dioscorides, the ancient Greek herbalist, in his *Della historia e materia medicinale,* published in 1544. He mentions the tomato in association with eggplant without directly naming it, referring to it as a sort of mandrake, "segmented, green at first and when ripe a golden color, which is eaten in the same manner as eggplant, fried in oil with salt and pepper." Mandrake itself is a fairly poisonous plant that had pervasive negative associations as a plant of witches, setting the stage for the long-held belief that tomatoes are bad for you.

John Gerard, an Englishman, in his *Herbal* of 1597, pictures the tomato with segmented fruit and wrote that "in Spaine and those hot regions they used to eat the apples [tomatoes] prepared and boil'd with pepper, salt, and oil: but they yield very little nourishment to the body and the same naught and corrupt. Likewise they do eat apples with oil, vinegar, and pepper mixed together for sauce to their meat, even as we in these cold countries do mustard." He said he received seeds of tomatoes from Spain, Italy, and other hot countries.

Gregorio de los Ríos, a Spanish priest, wrote a gardening book in 1592 that says there are two or three types of tomatoes that bear segmented fruits that turn red and "it is said they are good for sauces," but apparently he had not tried them for that purpose.

Herbalists continued to state that tomatoes were not good for you well into the nineteenth century. But clearly there are enough references to indicate that they were being eaten in some places, at least locally in Spain. In 1745, Altamiras published a cookbook with 13 recipes for everyday use of tomatoes, including with fowl, fish (cod), pumpkin, and rice in combination with garlic, onions, and herbs.

# Beefsteak Tomato Gratin

SERVES 4

Baking intensifies the flavor of these thickly sliced tomatoes, while garlic, parsley, and thyme bring the aromas of the summer herb garden. Serve this as a side dish with meat or fish, or let its flavors take center stage by offering it as a first course. Brandywine, Ponderosa, and Winsall are good varieties for this dish, but any beefsteak will do.

4 large ripe beefsteak or other large tomatoes

sea salt and freshly ground black pepper

¼ cup chopped Italian parsley

2 teaspoons fresh thyme

3 large garlic cloves, peeled and minced

3 tablespoons extra-virgin olive oil

3 tablespoons fresh coarse breadcrumbs

1 tablespoon finely grated Parmesan cheese

1. Preheat the oven to 450°F. Core the tomatoes. Cut each one horizontally into thick slices.

2. Arrange a layer of tomatoes in an 8-inch square baking dish. Season with salt and pepper and sprinkle on half the parsley, thyme, and garlic. Drizzle with 1 tablespoon of the oil.

3. Top with the remaining tomato slices, seasoning them as before with salt, pepper, and the remaining parsley, thyme, garlic, and 1 tablespoon of the oil.

4. Bake for 35 to 40 minutes, until soft and a little browned, basting occasionally with the juices. Sprinkle with the breadcrumbs and Parmesan, and then drizzle on the remaining 1 tablespoon oil. Bake 8 to 10 minutes longer, until the crumbs are toasty. Cool briefly before serving.

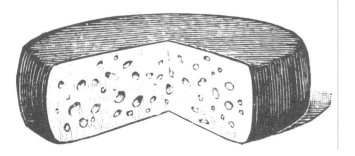

CHAPTER TEN

# DESSERTS

# Tomato Jam Tart

SERVES 6

Roberto Donna, owner-chef of Galileo in Washington, DC, created this recipe for a traditional Italian-style tart. He fills it with his Tomato and Citrus Marmalade on page 245, a rich confection of tomatoes with oranges and lemons. You could also use the Tomato and Lemon Jam on page 242 or the Yellow Tomato and Pineapple Jam on page 244 as the filling. Serve with a vanilla-flavored sauce such as crème anglaise.

2¼ cups all-purpose flour

5 teaspoons sugar

¼ teaspoon salt

9 tablespoons (5 ounces) cold butter, cut into ¼-inch pieces

½ cup ice water, or more as needed

1¼ cups Tomato and Citrus Marmalade (page 245)

1 tablespoon cream or half-and-half or milk

1. Mix the flour, 3 teaspoons of the sugar, and the salt in a large mixing bowl. Add the butter to the bowl and mix lightly.

2. When all the bits of butter are coated with the flour mixture, add ½ cup of ice water all at once. Toss quickly to coat all the particles. Add more water, a tablespoon at a time, if the mixture is too dry to come together as a dough, but be careful not to overmix. Form into a disk, pressing lightly, wrap in plastic wrap, and refrigerate for 1 hour. (You can leave it longer if more convenient.)

3. When the dough has chilled and you are ready to proceed, preheat the oven to 425°F and grease a baking sheet or line it with parchment paper.

4. Roll the pastry dough into a circle approximately 12 inches in diameter. Place it on the prepared baking sheet. Spread the jam in the center, leaving a 1½-inch border. Fold the border to make a rim for the tart. Return the tart to the refrigerator to chill for 20 to 30 minutes.

5. Before putting the tart into the oven, brush the rim with the cream and lightly sprinkle with the remaining 2 teaspoons sugar. Bake for 15 minutes, and then lower the heat to 350°F and bake 5 minutes longer, until the filling bubbles in the center.

6. Place on a wire rack to cool to room temperature before serving.

THE CARDINAL

## Lawrence Davis-Hollander's
# Top 10 Tomatoes

The tomatoes are not ranked in any particular order. My favorites are all slicing tomatoes, but they can be used in all sorts of dishes.

### Livingston's Beauty
I have to include a few of Livingston's varieties — they have that great old tomato taste.

### Brandywine (Pink)
Big, bold, meaty; the Burgundy wine of tomatoes — robust and rounded

### Aunt Ruby's German Green
Spicy and tasty; the best-tasting green

### Lambert's General Grant
Otherwise known as Dr. Neal; rich and meaty

### Magnus
Another Livingston creation; uniform, pink, and delicious

### Winsall (Wins All)
Bred from Ponderosa; therefore, pink, meaty, and tasty

### Indian Moon
The best-tasting orange; lots of tangy flavor

### Eva Purple Ball
Consistent, uniform, tasty tennis balls of purple-pink color

### Cardinal
A classic red; great acid-sweet taste

### Ponderosa Pink
More old-time meaty tomato taste

 # Candied-Tomato Tart with Five-Spiced Hazelnut Crust

SERVES 6–8

This tart was once on the menu at one of the Boston area's most beloved restaurants, Blue Ginger in Wellesley, Massachusetts. The candied tomatoes are a revelation, with a flavor reminiscent of tropical fruit. The crust is both spicy and flaky. This is a fabulous dessert, one of my favorites, and well worth the effort.

**Candied Tomatoes**

3 cups water

4 cups sugar

1 cup light corn syrup

3 pints heirloom pear tomatoes

**Candied Tomato Tart**

½ cup (1 stick) butter, at room temperature

⅓ cup granulated sugar

1 medium egg, beaten, at room temperature

1 teaspoon vanilla extract

1¼ cups cake flour

¾ cup hazelnut flour or finely ground hazelnuts

½ teaspoon ground cinnamon

½ teaspoon ground five-spice powder

¼–½ cup orange marmalade or apricot jam

½ cup lightly toasted sliced almonds

2 tablespoons confectioners' sugar

1. On day one, combine the water, sugar, and corn syrup in a large saucepan. Heat until the sugar is dissolved. Once the syrup reaches a low simmer, add the tomatoes. Turn off the heat and let the tomatoes sit in the pan overnight. Cover the pan halfway with plastic wrap or a lid, but do not cover completely; some evaporation must occur.

2. On day two, return the syrup and the tomatoes to a simmer. Once again turn off the heat and let the tomatoes sit in the pan overnight, partially covered.

3. On day three, taste the tomatoes, and if they do not seem sweet, tender, and slightly translucent, repeat the process. Continue each day until the tomatoes are candied to your liking.

4. For the tart, cream the butter and granulated sugar in a large mixing bowl until the mixture is very pale. Mix in the egg and vanilla. Scrape the bowl and continue mixing until combined.

**5.** In a separate bowl, combine the cake flour, hazelnut flour, cinnamon, and five-spice powder. Add it one-third at a time to the creamed mixture, mixing well after each addition.

**6.** Put the dough into a 2-quart plastic bag and press it to form a 1-inch thick disk. Chill well for at least 1 hour or overnight, if you prefer.

**7.** Grease a 9-inch tart pan. Spread a sheet of plastic wrap on your counter or pastry board and place the chilled dough on it. Cover with another piece of plastic wrap of the same size. Roll the dough ¼ inch thick. Remove the top piece of plastic wrap. Invert the prepared pan over the pastry. Run a spatula under the bottom piece of plastic wrap to loosen it, and then quickly invert the pastry and the pan. The pastry will now lie across the pan and you can easily tuck it into place and discard the plastic wrap. Trim off excess pastry from the edges and save it for decorating the tart.

**8.** Preheat the oven to 350°F while you fill the tart. Spread the marmalade on the pastry and brush a little on the top edges. Sprinkle on the almonds. Add the candied tomatoes. Roll out the scraps of dough, placing them between two sheets of plastic wrap if they seem sticky. Cut into strips and arrange a lattice or starburst pattern on the tart.

**9.** Bake for 20 to 30 minutes, until the crust is golden.

**10.** Cool on a wire rack. Before serving, put the confectioners' sugar into a sieve and shake it over the tart.

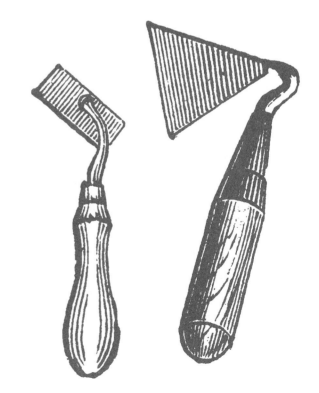

# Tomato Custard Pie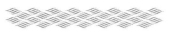

### SERVES 6–8

I've never met a custard pie I didn't like, and this pie is really quite good and easy to make. Recipes for tomato custards and tomato custard pies were common in the nineteenth and early twentieth centuries, and though they sound odd today, they are related to pumpkin custard pies and taste surprisingly similar. A scattering of raspberries enhances the coral-colored filling in this pie. A dollop of whipped cream or vanilla ice cream is the perfect accompaniment.

**Pastry**

1¼ cups all-purpose flour

¼ cup cake flour

1 tablespoon sugar

½ teaspoon salt

⅓ cup shortening

1 tablespoon cold butter

about ¼ cup chilled water, or more as needed

**Filling**

2 eggs

2 cups Canned Tomato Purée (page 234)

2 tablespoons lemon juice

1 cup brown sugar or natural cane sugar

½ cup milk or soy milk

1 tablespoon ground ginger

½ teaspoon ground cinnamon

1. Preheat the oven to 400°F.

2. For the pastry, stir the all-purpose flour, cake flour, sugar, and salt together in a large bowl. Add the shortening and butter in pieces. Rub them in with your fingers, working quickly and lightly until the mixture is very coarse crumbs. Make a well in the center and pour in the water. Pull the mixture together into a dough. If it is too dry, add more chilled water, 1 teaspoon at a time.

3. Let the dough rest in the refrigerator for 30 minutes, then flour a counter or a pastry board and grease a 9-inch pie plate. Roll out the dough and fit it into the pie plate. Prick the bottom all over with a fork. Fit aluminum foil on top of the crust, and then scatter with rice, dried beans, or pie weights. Bake for 12 minutes. Remove the foil and weights and return the pie shell to the oven for 2 to 3 minutes longer to dry the surface. Increase the oven temperature to 425°F.

**4.** For the filling, beat the eggs in a medium bowl. Beat in the tomato purée and lemon juice. Add the sugar, milk, ginger, and cinnamon and beat until thoroughly mixed. Pour into the pie shell.

**5.** Bake for 15 minutes. Reduce the oven to 350°F and bake 30 minutes longer, until a knife-point inserted into the center comes out clean.

**6.** Cool the pie on a wire rack. Serve at room temperature, or chill in the refrigerator if you are not serving immediately.

# EARLY TOMATO "RECEIPTS"

The first tomato recipe in English was of Spanish origin and was published in a supplement to 1758's *The Art of Cookery* by Hannah Glasse, one of the most influential English cookbooks of the period. The book was printed in Philadelphia in 1792, and in 1798 as *The New Art of Cookery* by Richard Briggs. In 1804, Alexander Hunter published *Receipts on Modern Cookery* and included two recipes for a type of tomato sauce for bottling that included garlic, salt, ginger, chili vinegar, and cayenne. Three years later, the same recipe appeared in English author Maria Eliza Rundell's *A New System of Domestic Cookery*, published in America in 1814. Within a few years, recipes appeared in many American cookbooks.

Mary Randolph in her *Virginia Housewife* had 17 of her own tomato recipes, while N. K. M. Lee compiled 12 from various sources in 1832. Eliza Leslie's *Directions for Cookery*, published in 1837, had 13 recipes, and more were added in subsequent editions. To keep tomatoes, she wrote, "take fine ripe tomatas, and wipe them dry, taking care not to break the skin. Put them in a stone jar with cold vinegar, adding a small thin muslin bag filled with mace, whole cloves, and whole peppers. . . . Tomatas pickled in this manner keep perfectly well and retain their color."

By the 1840s, cookbooks promoted tomatoes as pickles, preserves both sweet and savory, and sauces. They were baked, stewed, broiled, stuffed, scalloped, made into vinegar or wine, put into pies, cooked with eggs, served as a fresh salad, and, of course, made into ketchup.

# Tomato Sorbet

SERVES 8

If you have never eaten a tomato sorbet, you must do it at least once in your life. I've enjoyed this particular sorbet many times, and what is most outstanding about this version is its unadorned tomato flavor. The recipe comes from Shirl Gard, the pastry chef at the Old Inn on the Green in New Marlborough, Massachusetts. She notes that the best tomatoes for sorbet are heirlooms with lots of acid balance. "Indian Moon, Aunt Ruby's German Green, Quedlinburger Frue Liebe, and Paragon have yielded excellent results, " she says. "For more complexity, add additional varieties such as Brandywine, but don't mix too many colors. If you want to make sorbet using a green tomato variety, don't poach the tomatoes, because they lose their pretty color in cooking. Simply purée them in a blender and strain, then proceed as if using poached tomatoes." Shirl does not recommend using unripe green tomatoes and suggests making the sorbet in August or September, when local tomatoes are at their ripest and tastiest. You can serve this as a refresher between courses, instead of as a dessert, in which case it makes enough to serve 12.

2 pounds very ripe unpeeled fresh tomatoes, cored and cut into chunks

1¼ cups cold water

1 teaspoon powdered unflavored gelatin

1 cup sugar

¼ cup light corn syrup

2 tablespoons lemon juice

⅛ teaspoon salt

1. Poach the tomatoes: Place the tomato chunks in a bowl of stainless steel or heatproof glass or ceramic. Cover tightly with plastic wrap and set over a large saucepan one-quarter full of water. Bring to a simmer and let the tomatoes poach for 60 minutes. Remove from heat and let cool in the bowl with the plastic wrap still intact.

2. When cool, purée the tomatoes in a blender and strain through a fine-mesh strainer. Do not purée so finely that the strainer does not catch the seeds and tomato peels. Measure 2 cups of the purée and chill until you want to proceed with the recipe.

**3.** For the sorbet syrup, pour the cold water into a medium saucepan. Sprinkle the gelatin in a thin layer over the surface of the water. Let soften for 10 minutes. Add the sugar and corn syrup to the pan and bring to a boil, whisking constantly. Cool the syrup in an ice bath for 3 hours.

**4.** Combine the chilled tomato purée, sorbet syrup, lemon juice, and salt in a mixing bowl. Blend with a hand blender until completely smooth.

**5.** Spin the sorbet in an ice-cream maker following the manufacturer's instructions. Alternatively, if you don't have an ice-cream maker, pour the sorbet into a bowl or pan and freeze for 1 hour, until the edges are crystallized but the center is still semiliquid. Transfer the sorbet to a food processor or blender and process for 1 minute to break up the crystals. Return the sorbet to the freezer for 1 hour longer, and then blend again. Do this a third time, and then leave the sorbet to freeze completely.

## EAST COAST TOMATOES

In 1804 Dr. James Mease stated that tomato cultivation was growing rapidly in Pennsylvania. Eight years later he is credited with producing the first American tomato ketchup recipe. The *Lancaster Journal* in 1822 said that pies made out of tomatoes were excellent. While the spread of tomatoes throughout the region was relatively fast, many people still believed that they were poisonous, and certainly not everyone was growing them, let alone consuming them.

Tomato seeds were sold commercially in Philadelphia by 1800 by seedsman Bernard M'Nahon; in 1807, in New York by Grant Thorburn; in Baltimore, by 1810; though not in Boston until about 1827. Gradually, from the early 1820s to 1830s, tomatoes and their seeds became more and more available throughout the country. Recipes began to appear in many cookbooks, newspapers, and farm journals. Information was printed about growing them and saving seeds.

 # Green Tomato Chocolate Cake

**SERVES 12**

Among certain thrifty gardeners, there is a tradition of using up excess vegetables in cake. You cannot taste the vegetables, but they do add moistness. This recipe for Green Tomato Chocolate Cake is adapted from *Garden Way's Red and Green Tomato Cookbook*, by Janet Ballantyne.

⅔ cup (10⅔ tablespoons) butter, at room temperature

1¾ cups sugar

4 ounces unsweetened chocolate, melted

2 eggs

1 teaspoon vanilla extract

2½ cups sifted unbleached flour

½ cup unsweetened cocoa powder

2 teaspoons baking powder

2 teaspoons baking soda

¼ teaspoon salt

1 cup beer

1 cup puréed green tomatoes

¼-½ cup water, if needed

frosting (optional)

1. Preheat the oven to 350°F. Grease a 9- by 13-inch baking pan.

2. Cream together the butter and sugar in a large bowl. Stir in the chocolate, then the eggs, one at a time. Add the vanilla.

3. Sift the flour, cocoa, baking powder, baking soda, and salt into a medium bowl.

4. Add the flour mixture to the butter mixture alternately with the beer and tomatoes. If the batter appears stiff, add the water. (The moisture content of the tomatoes varies.)

5. Turn the batter into the prepared baking pan. Bake for 35 minutes, until a tester inserted into the center comes out clean.

6. Cool on a wire rack. Ice with your favorite frosting when cooled, if desired, or serve plain. This is a very rich, moist cake.

# CHAPTER ELEVEN

# PRESERVING

## *the Harvest*

THE VOLUNTEER

COPYRIGHTED 1887

ating fresh tomatoes from late fall through spring is anathema to me. Off-season tomatoes taste nothing like those real tomatoes of the summer. Many people are happy with pretending; I'm not.

If you preserve some of the tomatoes you or your local farmer grows, then you can enjoy a small portion of that rich summer warmth all year long. All tomatoes that are cooked down concentrate their flavors. What a pleasure, what a reward to open a jar of your own sauce when the snow is on the ground.

Tomatoes are among the easiest and most satisfying vegetables to preserve. Ripe tomatoes lend themselves to freezing and canning as whole tomatoes or purée. You can also make them into sauces, salsas, and ketchups for freezing or canning. Drying is another option. Green (unripe) tomatoes can be pickled or made into relishes. Finally, there is cold storage — not a long-term solution, but it can extend your harvest for about a month with little work involved.

## Freezing Tomatoes

If you have the freezer space, there is nothing easier than freezing your excess tomatoes. The only problem is their high water content — but you can deal with that before or after freezing.

The fastest method is to freeze the tomatoes whole. Just wash them and dry thoroughly. Remove the cores and place the tomatoes on a cookie sheet. Freeze until solid, then bag the tomatoes in ziplock bags and remove as needed. Thaw the tomatoes in a nonreactive metal sieve set over a bowl. As the tomatoes thaw, the skins should slip off easily and the tomatoes will release water. Save the water and use as much as needed for the dish you are making.

If you prefer, you can peel the tomatoes before freezing. Plunge them into boiling water for 30 to 60 seconds, and then slip off the skins. Freeze the tomatoes in plastic containers. Thaw them in a sieve, as above, or add them still frozen to sauces and soups and just cook off the excess water.

Alternatively, you can freeze your homemade salsas or soups. If you freeze an uncooked sauce, such as salsa, let it thaw in a sieve set over a bowl and add back just enough of the thawed juices to achieve a good consistency. Handled this way, a pint of your garden salsa out of the freezer will be far superior to anything you can make with "fresh" supermarket vegetables.

For cooked sauces, wash, core, and quarter the tomatoes. Simmer, covered, in a heavy saucepan until soft, then remove the lid. Add seasonings as desired. For stewed tomatoes, simmer for 15 to 30 minutes. To make a sauce, continue to simmer until the tomatoes are cooked down to a pleasing consistency, for 2 to 6 hours, depending on how big a batch you are working with. Stir frequently and don't allow the mixture to scorch. You can use a slow cooker or the oven preheated to 350°F

to reduce the chances of scorching. Cooking in the oven will take 1–3 hours, depending on the quantity and the juiciness of the tomatoes. A cooked tomato sauce, such as the Marinara Sauce on page 19 or the Tomato and Meat Sauce for Pasta on page 27 also can be frozen.

## Drying Tomatoes

Any type of tomato can be dried; typically, paste or plum tomatoes are used. I've had best results with small to medium paste tomatoes, those that can be cut in half lengthwise and will dry in the oven within 24 hours. There are some very large meaty paste tomatoes that exceed a pound in weight. These don't work as well. Black Pear, Black Plum, Yellow Plum, King Humbert, Red Pear, Yellow Pear, Purple Pear, Opalka, and many others make great dried tomatoes. Romas are pleasant but not as good.

You don't have to have a dehydrator or the perfect climate to make dried tomatoes — the oven works just fine.

To prepare the tomatoes for drying, wash and dry them, cut them in half, and scoop out the seeds and cores. Pat the interiors dry with paper towels.

After the tomatoes are dried, they should be pasteurized to ensure the insect eggs and spoilage organisms are destroyed. You can pasteurize in the oven or in the freezer. In the oven, arrange the dried tomatoes in one layer on shallow trays and bake for 10 to 15 minutes in a preheated 175°F oven. Let cool, then transfer to storage containers. To use the freezer, place the tomatoes into freezer bags and leave at 0°F for 2 to 4 days. Stand-alone freezers generally keep foods at 0°F; the freezer compartment of a refrigerator is not cold enough.

## Oven Drying

**1.** Prepare the tomatoes as described on page 229. Preheat the oven to 150°F. If there are wide gaps between the bars of your oven racks that might allow the tomatoes to fall through, cover the racks with clean sheeting, cheesecloth, or thin kitchen towels. Arrange the tomatoes on them so they are not touching. Do not attempt to dry more than two racks of tomatoes at a time, as this will vastly increase the drying time. Place the racks in the oven. Close the door and bake for 30 minutes.

**2.** Leaving the oven on, open the oven door to let out the moisture. Leave it propped open with a wooden spoon or something similar that will allow it to rest ajar. Dry for 6 to 8 hours longer, until the tomatoes are pliable and slightly leathery.

**3.** Condition the tomatoes by transferring them to a dry ceramic or glass (not aluminum) container and leaving it uncovered in a dry and airy place for 10 days. Stir the tomatoes at least once a day.

**4.** Pasteurize the tomatoes as described above.

**5.** Store in an airtight container at room temperature and use as needed.

## Sun Drying

The perfect climate required for sun-drying is about 100°F with humidity below 60 percent. The equipment you will need for this is a frame that holds clean sheeting, cheesecloth, or plastic screening. Don't use screening with galvanized wire, which will impart an off flavor to the tomatoes.

**1.** Prepare the tomatoes as described on page 229. Arrange them on the cloth in a single layer. Place the frames in the direct sun so that air can circulate on all sides. Cover the food with a second sheet or cheesecloth to protect from birds and insects.

**2.** Leave to dry for 1 to 2 days, bringing the tomatoes in at night to prevent dew from collecting on them. The tomatoes are dried when they are pliable and slightly leathery.

**3.** Condition the tomatoes by transferring them to a dry ceramic or glass (not aluminum) container and leaving it uncovered in a dry and airy place for 10 days. Stir the tomatoes at least once a day.

**4.** Pasteurize the tomatoes as described above.

**5.** Store in an airtight container at room temperature and use as needed.

## Dehydrator Drying

If you have a food dehydrator, prepare the tomatoes as described on page 229, set the timer according to the manufacturer's directions, turn on the dehydrator, and go. Tomatoes will be dried in 6 to 8 hours. Most dehydrators are sold through the mail, so comparison shopping via the Internet is recommended. Look for a model with plastic screens and one that is easily moved and stored.

## Cold Storage of Green Tomatoes

Harvest green tomatoes before the first frost, with the stems attached. Wash and dry thoroughly. Discard any with bruises. Put the green tomatoes into shallow cartons packed with straw, leaves, or shredded paper. Keep in a cool place where the temperature ranges between 55 and 70°F — often a back porch or an unheated attic provides the best conditions. Check the tomatoes every few days and remove them as they ripen.

## Canning Tomatoes and Other Tomato Preserves

Tomatoes are among the easiest vegetables to can, because their natural acid helps deter spoilage. However, the amount of acid varies from variety to variety, so make sure there is sufficient acid in the form of lemon juice, citric acid, or vinegar.

You can process tomatoes whole, diced, or made into juice or sauces of many kinds. The rewards are great. In winter, when fresh tomatoes are expensive and generally tasteless, you will have your own flavorful supply.

### Canning Equipment

Most supermarkets and hardware stores stock canning equipment, especially in late summer. Apart from ladles, funnels, and sieves, which you may already own, you need the following canning equipment:

- A boiling-water-bath canner with a wire rack to hold the jars.
- Canning jars in quart, pint, and half-pint sizes. Canning jars are made from glass tempered to withstand high heat during processing. They can be reused year after year if undamaged. Do not use jars in which you bought commercially prepared sauce or jam, because the glass may not be strong enough.
- Two-piece lids comprising a flat disk called a dome lid that sits on top of the jar and a screw ring to hold it in place. The lid cannot be reused, but undamaged screw rings can be used again.
- A jar lifter so you can handle hot jars.

### Boiling-Water-Bath Canning

Canning preserves food by processing it at high temperatures for long enough to kill bacteria, molds, and other organisms that cause spoilage. During processing, air is forced out of the jars, leaving a vacuum sealed by the lid. As long as the jars remain airtight, the vacuum protects the food inside from harmful organisms.

Because the acidity of the tomatoes varies, safe canning requires that the tomatoes be acidified. In the case of many preserves, the acid is part of the recipe — as in the case of ketchup, which contains vinegar. Otherwise, acidify the tomatoes by adding 2 tablespoons of bottled lemon juice or ½ teaspoon of citric acid to each quart jar.

For safe canning, follow these directions, based on USDA recommendations:

1. Prepare the tomatoes or the sauce or other preserve according to the recipe.

2. Prepare the lids and rings by putting them into a pan of water and bringing it to a boil. Boil them for 10 minutes. Do not remove them until you are ready to put them onto the jars.

3. Prepare the jars. You do not have to sterilize those used for food processed in a boiling-water bath for more than 10 minutes. Simply wash them in soapy water or a dishwasher, then rinse thoroughly to remove all traces of soap. For boiling-water-bath processing times of less than 10 minutes, sterilize the prewashed jars by submerging them in a canner filled with hot (not boiling) water, making sure the water rises 1 inch above the jar top. At sea level, boil the jars for 10 minutes; at higher elevations, boil for 1 minute longer for every 1,000 feet.

4. Add lemon juice or other acid to the jars as suggested in your recipe. Fill them with the prepared tomatoes or other product, leaving ½ inch headspace or the headspace indicated in your recipe. Wipe away any drips on rim, because they can spoil the seal. If bubbles appear as you fill the jars, run a clean spatula or knife inside the jar to release them. Do not stir, as it may create more bubbles.

5. Place the lids on top and secure with a metal ring, tightening it so it grips. (You do not need to exert extra pressure to make it extremely tight.) Load the jars into the rack.

6. Fill the canner half full with water and preheat to 180°F. Lift the rack by its handles and set it in the canner.

7. Add more boiling water if necessary to bring the water level to 1 inch above the jars.

8. Raise the heat as high as possible and wait until the water is boiling vigorously. Cover the canner with the lid. Lower the heat to maintain a moderate boil. As soon as you have covered the canner, set a timer for the recommended processing time. If you live at a high elevation, increase the processing time as necessary.

9. Have more boiling water on hand so you can add it to the canner should evaporation make the water fall below the recommended level. Arrange folded towels on a counter where you can place the processed jars for cooling.

10. When the jars have boiled for the recommended time, remove them from the canner, using a jar lifter. Set them on the towels, placing them at least 1 inch apart.

11. Let the jars cool for 12 hours, then test to establish that you have a good seal. Look at the center of the lid; it should be slightly concave. Press the center hard with your thumbs; if it does not move downward, or "give," it is sealed. You can also tap the lid with the rounded bowl of a teaspoon. If it is correctly sealed, it will ring clearly; if not it will sound dull. If the seal is faulty, the tomatoes or preserves inside the jars are not spoiled, but they cannot be kept for long periods. Store them in the refrigerator and use within 1 week.

# Canned Tomatoes

MAKES 7 QUARTS

While freezing tomatoes is comparatively fast, only canning results in a kitchen-ready product. Wash the tomatoes carefully and remove every blemish, hint of rot, green or white spot, and blossom end. It's best to use good-size paste tomatoes such as Black Pear, King Humbert, Opalka, or other "carrot" types. Medium-size slicers such as Stone or Paragon are classic canners, as are Eva Purple Ball and Redfield Beauty.

about 21 pounds tomatoes, peeled

14 tablespoons bottled lemon juice or 3½ teaspoons citric acid

7 teaspoons salt (optional)

1. Wash the canning jars and the lids as instructed on page 232.

2. Prepare the canner by filling it half full of water and placing it over a moderate heat to warm to 180°F.

3. Leave the peeled tomatoes whole or halve or quarter them if you prefer. Put them in a large pan and cover with water. Bring to a boil and simmer for 2 to 5 minutes.

4. To each clean jar, add 2 tablespoons of bottled lemon juice or ½ teaspoon of citric acid. Also add a teaspoon of salt, if desired.

5. Fill each jar with the hot tomatoes, leaving ½ inch headspace. Add boiling water, generally 1 to 1½ cups per quart, to cover the tomatoes. Cap and seal.

6. Process in a boiling-water bath for 45 minutes. Adjust for altitude , if necessary. (For altitudes of 1,001 to 3,000 feet, 50 minutes; 3,001 to 6,000 feet, 55 minutes; above 6,000 feet, 60 minutes.)

7. Cool and test for a seal as on page 232. Store properly sealed jars in a closet or on shelves in a dark place for up to 6 months. Store improperly sealed jars in the refrigerator and use within 1 week.

 # Canned Tomato Purée

MAKES 7 QUARTS

**W**ash the tomatoes carefully and remove every blemish, hint of rot, green or white spot, and blossom end.

about 35 pounds plum or other medium tomatoes, peeled

14 tablespoons bottled lemon juice or 3½ teaspoons citric acid

7 teaspoons salt (optional)

1. Wash the canning jars and the lids as instructed on page 232.

2. Prepare the canner by filling it half full of water and placing it over a moderate heat to warm to 180°F.

3. Leave the tomatoes whole or halve or quarter them if you prefer. Put them in a large pan and simmer over medium heat, stirring occasionally, until the tomatoes give up their juice and are very soft, about 30 minutes.

4. Pass through a food mill set with the finest blade to remove the tomato seeds and other coarse material.

5. Return the purée to the pan and simmer over medium heat for 1 to 2 hours, until it reaches a desired consistency.

6. To each clean jar, add 2 tablespoons of lemon juice or ½ teaspoon of citric acid. Also add 1 teaspoon of salt, if desired.

7. Fill each jar with the hot purée, leaving ½ inch headspace. Cap and seal.

8. Process in a boiling-water bath for 40 minutes. Adjust for altitude, if necessary. (For altitudes of 1,001 to 3,000 feet, 45 minutes; 3,001 to 6,000 feet, 50 minutes; above 6,000 feet, 55 minutes.)

9. Cool and test for a seal as on page 232. Store properly sealed jars in a closet or on shelves in a dark place for up to 6 months. Store improperly sealed jars in the refrigerator and use within 1 week.

 # Tomato Juice

MAKES ABOUT 7 QUARTS

This recipe makes a basic tomato juice. There is also a recipe for a Spicy Tomato Cocktail on page 66, if you prefer. Slicing tomatoes are the juiciest and thus are best used for making tomato juice. Wash the tomatoes carefully and remove every blemish, hint of rot, green or white spot, and blossom end. The juice may separate as it stands in the jars. Before serving, shake well.

23 pounds very ripe tomatoes, coarsely chopped

salt

sugar

14 tablespoons bottled lemon juice or 3½ teaspoons citric acid

1. Wash the canning jars and the lids as instructed on page 232.

2. Prepare the canner by filling it half full of water and putting it over moderate heat to warm to 180°F.

3. Put the tomatoes into a large pan over medium heat and simmer, stirring occasionally, until the tomatoes give up their juice and are very soft, about 30 minutes.

4. Pass through a food mill set with the finest blade to remove the tomato seeds and other coarse material.

5. Return the juice to the pan and bring to a boil. Taste and add salt and sugar to adjust the flavor.

6. To each clean jar, add 2 tablespoons of bottled lemon juice or ½ teaspoon of citric acid. Fill each jar with the hot tomato juice, leaving ½ inch headspace. Cap and seal.

7. Process in a boiling-water bath for 40 minutes. Adjust for altitude , if necessary. (For altitudes of 1,001 to 3,000 feet, 45 minutes; 3,001 to 6,000 feet, 50 minutes; above 6,000 feet, 55 minutes.)

8. Cool and test for a seal as on page 232. Store properly sealed jars in a closet or on shelves in a dark place for up to 6 months. Store improperly sealed jars in the refrigerator and use within 1 week.

# Tomato Ketchup

MAKES ABOUT 4 PINTS

Making ketchup at home is not difficult, and you have the advantage of being able to adjust the amount of salt, sugar, and spices to your liking. This ketchup is not particularly sweet, compared with the commercial product; you may want to increase the sugar to taste. Any type of tomato can be used to make ketchup, but the plum/paste varieties require the least cooking.

The extra step of straining the tomatoes twice produces a bright red ketchup that is not darkened by the spices. If you want to use juicy slicing tomatoes in this recipe, increase the simmering time to evaporate the excess liquid.

24 pounds plum tomatoes, washed and cut into quarters

2 tablespoons salt

4 large onions, coarsely chopped

12 garlic cloves, peeled and sliced

4-inch piece fresh ginger, peeled and sliced

2 tablespoons black peppercorns

1 teaspoon cayenne pepper

8 bay leaves

4 teaspoons allspice berries

16 cloves

2 cups cider vinegar

3 cups sugar, plus more as needed

1. Put the tomatoes in a large pan and sprinkle with the salt. Cook gently over low heat for 30 minutes, until the tomatoes are very soft. Strain them through a large sieve, in batches if necessary. Return the juices that pass through the sieve to a saucepan. Set aside the pulp and skins.

2. Add the onions, garlic, ginger, peppercorns, cayenne, bay leaves, allspice, cloves, and vinegar to the juice. Bring to a boil and let it bubble over medium-high heat for 30 minutes, by which time some of the liquid will have evaporated. Strain through a sieve into a clean saucepan. Discard the spices.

3. While the liquid and spices are boiling, strain the reserved pulp and skins through a food mill or a sieve to remove the seeds and skins.

**4.** Wash the canning jars and the lids as instructed on page 232. Prepare the canner by filling it half full of water and placing it over moderate heat to warm to 180°F.

**5.** Combine the strained pulp with the strained liquid. Stir in the sugar over low heat. When it has dissolved, taste the mixture and add more salt or cayenne or sugar to taste. Raise the heat to medium-high and boil, stirring to prevent sticking, for 45 to 60 minutes, until the mixture is as thick as commercially made ketchup. To test its consistency, drop a teaspoonful onto a plate. Leave it for 3 to 4 minutes. The dollop should remain mounded, not lie flat, and juice should not seep from the edge. Cook for a few minutes longer if necessary.

**6.** Pour into the jars, leaving ⅛ inch headspace. Cap and seal.

**7.** Process in a boiling-water bath for 15 minutes. Adjust for altitude, if necessary. (For altitudes of 1,001 to 6,000 feet, 20 minutes; above 6,000 feet, 25 minutes.)

**8.** Cool and test for a seal as on page 232. Store properly sealed jars in a closet or on shelves in a shady or dark place. If the seal is faulty, store the jars in the refrigerator and use within 1 month.

## FROM KETSIAP TO KETCHUP

Today "ketchup" invariably means tomato ketchup, but in the eighteenth century, ketchups were made from mushrooms, walnuts, anchovies, and other ingredients. They survived well into the nineteenth century, when tomato ketchup soared in popularity and finally pushed others to the sidelines. The cooks who made the early ketchups aimed to reproduce the spiced fish sauces called ketsiap. Brought from the Far East and South East Asia by Dutch traders, ketsiap was admired for its salty, spicy flavor and because it kept indefinitely. Tomato ketchup as we know it has vibrant flavors but otherwise little in common with the sauce that inspired it, though the word "ketchup" and the variant spelling "catsup" may derive from the Chinese ketsiap.

 # Green Tomato Chutney

MAKES ABOUT 4 PINTS

This chutney is popular in both England and New England, where cooler summers ensure that tomato growers always have a generous supply of green (unripe) tomatoes at the end of the season. Cheese and chutney sandwiches made with cheddar or Cheshire cheese and a fruity chutney such as this are an English favorite. This chutney is also good with meats and with Indian food.

3 pounds (about 12 medium) green (unripe) tomatoes, thinly sliced

3 tablespoons salt, plus extra for seasoning, if necessary

1 pound (3–4 medium) apples, peeled, cored, and quartered

1 pound (2 large) onions, coarsely chopped

1 cup (3–4 stalks) celery, sliced into ¼-inch pieces

3 garlic cloves, peeled and chopped

1 tablespoon grated fresh ginger

2 teaspoons ground coriander

1 teaspoon ground allspice

¼–½ teaspoon cayenne pepper

2 bay leaves

1½ cups cider vinegar

1 cup raisins

1 pound dark brown sugar

1. Layer the tomatoes in a colander, sprinkling each layer with salt. Let stand in a sink so that liquid can drain from the tomatoes for 1 to 2 hours. Rinse with cold water and pat dry with paper towels.

2. Combine the tomatoes, apples, onions, celery, garlic, ginger, coriander, allspice, cayenne (to taste), bay leaves, and vinegar in a large pan; cover and bring to a simmer over moderate heat. Cook for 10 minutes, and then add the raisins. Cook for 15 minutes longer, until the tomatoes are soft and the apples mushy, stirring from time to time.

3. While the chutney cooks, wash the canning jars and the lids as instructed on page 232. Prepare the canner by filling it half full of water and placing it over moderate heat to warm to 180°F.

4. When the tomatoes are soft, stir in the sugar. When it has dissolved, raise the heat and boil rapidly, uncovered, until the chutney is as thick as jam — 15 to 20 minutes; stir frequently. Spoon a little onto a plate, let it cool, and then taste it. Over the heat, stir in more salt if you think it needs it.

**5.** Pour the chutney into the jars, leaving ¼ inch headspace. Cap and seal.

**6.** Process in a boiling-water bath for 10 minutes. Adjust for altitude, if necessary. (For altitudes of 1,001 to 6,000 feet, 15 minutes; above 6,000 feet, 20 minutes.)

**7.** Cool and test for a seal as on page 232. Store properly sealed jars in a closet or on shelves in a shady or dark place. If the seal is faulty, store the jars in the refrigerator and use within 2 months. If you plan to eat the chutney within 2 weeks, you need not can it; simply store it in the refrigerator.

## THE TOMATO IN ENGLAND

England slowly adopted the tomato. Philip Miller wrote in 1752 that in "soups they are much used in England," though some people believed them "not wholesome from their great Moisture and Coldness" and that the "nourishment they afford must be bad." Around the same time, John Hill said the tomato was eaten by lots of people and was eaten raw or stewed by English Jews. A tomato recipe appears in a 1758 supplement to Hannah Glasse's *The Art of Cookery*. By the 1780s, tomatoes were becoming established in the English kitchen and were widespread before the turn of the century. In the early part of the nineteenth century, tomatoes began appearing in more British recipes. William Kitchiner gave us a recipe for tomato ketchup in 1816 that first used anchovies in the ingredients and in the following year had eliminated them and added malt vinegar.

# Tomato, Orange, and Ginger Chutney

MAKES 4–5 HALF-PINTS

Teaming tomatoes with oranges makes a great flavor combination — and yellow, orange, and bicolor tomatoes teamed with oranges make it especially beautiful. Try using Golden Peach, Limmony, Yellow Brandywine, or German Stripe — all excellent varieties. This sweet-sour chutney, really much like a marmalade, disappears from my kitchen rapidly. The chutney is a wonderful foil for rich meat dishes, chicken, and duck. I like it on toast.

2 pounds (5–6 large) firm tomatoes

2 medium navel or other seedless oranges

1 large onion, peeled

1½ cups cider vinegar

1 garlic clove, peeled and finely chopped

¼ teaspoon Tabasco (optional)

3 cups sugar

3 tablespoons ground coriander

1 tablespoon ground ginger

salt

1. Wash the tomatoes and oranges and trim off the coarse stem ends and any blemishes on the orange peel. Cut the tomatoes, oranges, and onion into big chunks and process in a food processor until you have a uniform mixture. Alternatively, chop them by hand.

2. Combine the tomato mixture with the vinegar and garlic in a large pan. Add the Tabasco, if you want a little fieriness. Simmer until the orange peel is soft, 20 to 25 minutes.

3. While the chutney cooks, wash half-pint canning jars and lids as instructed on page 232. Prepare the canner by filling it half full of water and placing it over moderate heat to warm to 180°F.

4. When the orange peel is soft, stir the sugar into the chutney over low heat. Stir in the coriander, ginger, and 1 teaspoon of salt. Increase the heat and cook briskly, stirring almost constantly, until the mixture has thickened to a jamlike consistency, 5 to 15 minutes. Place a spoonful of it on a plate and let it cool. Taste and stir in more salt if necessary and a few more drops of Tabasco if you like. Cook and stir for 1 minute longer after any addition you make.

**5.** Pour the chutney into the jars, leaving ¼ inch headspace. Cap and seal.

**6.** Process in a boiling-water bath for 10 minutes. Adjust for altitude, if necessary. (For altitudes of 1,001 to 6,000 feet, 15 minutes; above 6,000 feet, 20 minutes.)

**7.** Cool and test for a seal as on page 232. Store properly sealed jars in a closet or on shelves in a shady or dark place. If the seal is faulty, store the jars in the refrigerator and use within 2 weeks. If you plan to eat the chutney within 2 weeks, you need not can it; simply store it in the refrigerator.

CORIANDER

## THE SEED SAVERS EXCHANGE

In 1975, Kent and Diane Whealy founded Seed Savers Exchange (SSE), a nonprofit genetic preservation organization dedicated to conserving and promoting heirloom vegetables and fruits. Each January SSE publishes an extensive yearbook that lists all of the seeds being offered by SSE members. Listed members offer thousands of rare varieties through the yearbook, which is sent to gardeners across the United States and Canada, and to other countries.

The SSE Heritage Farm is a unique educational facility that maintains 18,000 heirloom vegetables, 700 varieties of nineteenth-century apples, 200 hardy grapes, and herds of endangered White Park cattle. Each summer the seeds of as many as 2,000 varieties are multiplied in Heritage Farm's organic Preservation Gardens. The farm site also includes offices, seed storage facilities, conference facilities, a greenhouse, and a root cellar.

SSE pioneered the modern seed-saving movement in the United States. Its members have sent to other members more than a million samples of seeds that were usually not in commercial catalogs and were often on the verge of extinction.

 # Tomato and Lemon Jam

MAKES 6 HALF-PINTS

**M**iss Eliza Leslie of Philadelphia was the best and one of the most popular food writers of the nineteenth century. Her fine palate and clear presentation of recipes makes her books *Directions for Cookery in Its Various Branches* (1829) and *Seventy-Five Receipts for Pastry, Cakes, and Sweetmeats* (1828) useful even today. This recipe is taken from the latter book. Miss Leslie notes, "Without lemons, tomatas makes one of the most unpalatable of sweetmeats, with lemons one of the very best. . . . This preserve should always be eaten with sponge cake or biscuit. It is very fine with a little cream poured into each saucer." A sweetmeat, for those not current with nineteenth-century food writing, is any small piece of sweet candy or pastry, particularly candied fruit. Sweetmeat or not, I think the jam is terrific on toast and wonderful on pound cake, just as Miss Leslie instructs.

6 large lemons

6 pounds red tomatoes, preferably plum tomatoes, peeled and seeded

about 6 cups brown sugar

**1.** Using a zester, scrape the zest from the lemons. Warm the lemons in a 250°F oven for 5 minutes or microwave them for 1 minute, and then halve them and squeeze the juice. (Heating the lemons makes them juicier, but it also makes them more likely to spurt when you cut them in half, so take care.)

**2.** Coarsely chop the tomatoes and place the pieces in a sieve set over a bowl to catch the juice. Combine the tomatoes, lemon zest, lemon juice, and ½ cup of the tomato juice in a large saucepan. Bring to a boil and cook until the tomatoes are soft, 5 to 10 minutes, depending on their ripeness. (If they are very juicy, raise the heat to evaporate some of the liquid during the boiling.)

**3.** Let the tomato mixture cool enough so that you can easily measure it. For each cup of tomatoes and their liquid, allow a cup of brown sugar. Stir it into the tomato mixture. When the sugar has dissolved, raise the heat to high and boil as rapidly as possible until the jam has set, 5 to 15 minutes.

**4.** While the jam cooks, wash half-pint canning jars and the lids as instructed on page 232. Prepare the canner by filling it half full of water and placing it over moderate heat to warm to 180°F.

**5.** Pour the jam into the jars, leaving ¼ inch headspace. Cap and seal.

**6.** Process in a boiling-water bath for 10 minutes. Adjust for altitude, if necessary. (For altitudes of 1,001 to 6,000 feet, 10 minutes; above 6,000 feet, 15 minutes.)

**7.** Cool and test for a seal as on page 232. Store properly sealed jars in a closet or on shelves in a shady or dark place. If the seal is faulty, store the jars in the refrigerator and use within 2 weeks. If you plan to eat the jam within 2 weeks, you need not can it; simply store it in the refrigerator.

## CANNED TOMATOES

Tomatoes were canned in jars beginning in the 1820s and '30s. In 1847, in New Jersey, Harrison Cosby developed a method for canning tomatoes in tin pails, boiling them, and then sealing them with a tin lid. Factories sprang up in New Jersey at several locations, and soon canning factories were located in New York as well. Other methods of canning were developed, particularly the glass Mason jar in 1858, which created the mass production of canning. Canned tomatoes, along with peas and corn, became relatively common at the close of the 1860s. By 1885, almost 50 million cans of tomatoes were produced annually, and that number nearly tripled three years later.

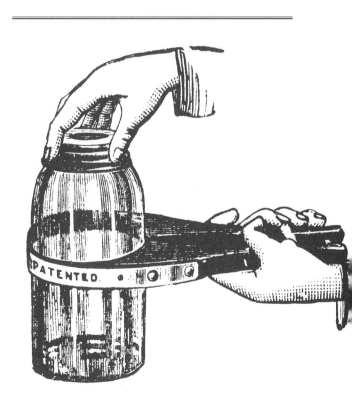

# Yellow Tomato and Pineapple Jam

## MAKES 4–5 HALF-PINTS

In her book *Canning and Preserving* (1887), Mrs. Sarah Rorer notes that "yellow Tomatoes with an equal quantity of grated pineapple . . . make a most delightful preserve." How right she was! Exact amounts of tomatoes and cooking times depend on the size and juiciness of the tomatoes. The recipe was tested with ultraripe Limmony tomatoes — very juicy but nonetheless firm-fleshed. Livingston's Golden Queen, Yellow Plum, Yellow Pear, Garden Peach, or Azoychka would all work well.

2 pounds (about 6 cups) peeled, chopped, and seeded yellow tomatoes

1 (20-ounce) can crushed pineapple in its juice

4 cups sugar

2 tablespoons lemon juice

**1.** Cook the tomatoes in a large covered pan over moderate heat until very juicy, 3 to 5 minutes. Uncover and simmer until the tomato is soft.

**2.** Add the pineapple and its juice, and then stir in the sugar. When the sugar has completely dissolved, stir in the lemon juice, and then raise the heat and boil rapidly until the jam is thick and glossy, 5 to 15 minutes, stirring with a wooden spoon to prevent sticking.

**3.** Meanwhile, sterilize half-pint canning jars and the lids as instructed on page 232. Prepare the canner by filling it half full of water and placing it over moderate heat to warm to 180°F. Put a plate into the freezer to chill.

**4.** When the jam is thick and glossy, test for setting by dropping a spoonful onto the cold plate. Return it to the freezer for 1 minute, and then check the jam. If it wrinkles when you tilt the plate or push the jam with your finger, it is set. Alternatively, test with a candy thermometer: Jams and jellies set at 220°F.

**5.** Pour the jam into the prepared jars, leaving ¼ inch headspace. Cap and seal.

**6.** Process in a boiling-water bath for 15 minutes. Adjust for altitude, if necessary. (For altitudes of 1,001 to 6,000 feet, 20 minutes; above 6,000 feet, 25 minutes.)

**7.** Cool and test for a seal as on page 232. Store properly sealed jars in a closet or on shelves in a dark place. If the seal is faulty, store the jars in the refrigerator and use within 2 weeks. If you plan to eat the chutney within 2 weeks, you need not can it; simply store it in the refrigerator.

# Tomato and Citrus Marmalade

### MAKES ABOUT 8 HALF-PINTS

A casual eater of this Italian-style marmalade might think it the standard citrus marmalade, but tomatoes give it a fruitiness and succulence that make it unusually delicious. Serve it with toast or muffins, and use it to make the Tomato Jam Tart on page 218. Both the marmalade and the tart come from owner-chef Roberto Donna of Galileo in Washington, DC.

4 oranges, scrubbed

1 lemon, scrubbed

4½ pounds ripe but firm red tomatoes, peeled and seeded

1 cup water

8 cups sugar

1. Slice the oranges and lemon as thinly as possible. Discard any seeds. Put them into a large pan and add enough water to cover them by an inch. Cover the pan; bring to a simmer and cook for 45 minutes. Strain and discard the liquid.

2. Coarsely chop the tomatoes and place them in the pan along with the strained oranges and lemon and the water. Bring to a simmer over low heat and cook until the peels and the tomatoes are soft and juicy, about 20 minutes.

3. Meanwhile, sterilize half-pint canning jars and the lids as instructed on page 232. Prepare the canner by filling it half full of water and placing it over moderate heat to warm to 180°F. Put a plate into the freezer to chill.

4. When the tomatoes are soft and juicy, stir in the sugar. Stir constantly until the sugar has dissolved. (Test by tapping the bottom of the pan with a wooden spoon; you should not hear or feel any crunch.) Raise the heat and boil rapidly, stirring frequently, until the jam looks thick, about 10 minutes.

5. Test by dropping a spoonful of the jam onto the chilled plate. Leave it for 1 minute. If it wrinkles when pushed with your finger, it is set.

6. Pour the jam into the prepared jars, leaving ¼ inch headspace. Cap and seal.

7. Process in a boiling-water bath for 10 minutes. Adjust for altitude, if necessary. (For altitudes of 1,001 to 6,000 feet, 15 minutes; above 6,000 feet, 20 minutes.)

8. Cool and test for a seal as on page 232. Store properly sealed jars in a closet or on shelves in a shady or dark place. If the seal is faulty, store the jars in the refrigerator and use within 1 month.

# Higdom

Recipes for higdom — a relish made of end-of-season crops — appear in many community cookbooks. Where the name comes from is anybody's guess. The ingredients vary greatly, because they are designed to use up whatever is still in the garden at summer's end, but green (unripe) tomatoes, cabbage, and peppers are invariably included. Precise amounts of each vegetable are not crucial, so don't worry if you have a little more or less of a particular vegetable, as long as you have a mixture. Cabbage combines with the green tomatoes to give this relish a flavor reminiscent of sauerkraut. Like sauerkraut, it is a fine accompaniment to pork and sausage dishes.

### Spiced Vinegar

- 4 cups cider vinegar
- 1½ cups sugar
- 1 teaspoon whole allspice
- 1 teaspoon peppercorns
- ½ teaspoon whole cloves
- ½ teaspoon hot pepper flakes

### Vegetables

- 4–5 pounds green cabbage, coarsely chopped (10–12 cups)
- 4–5 pounds green (unripe) tomatoes, peeled, seeded, and chopped (10–12 cups)
- 2 large onions, chopped
- 2 celery stalks, chopped
- 1 large green bell pepper, cut into 1-inch pieces
- 1 large red bell pepper, cut into 1-inch pieces
- ¾ cup kosher or pickling salt

**1.** Prepare the vinegar and the vegetables the day before you want to make the relish. Combine the vinegar, sugar, allspice, peppercorns, cloves, and pepper flakes in a medium saucepan. Bring to a boil, lower the heat, and simmer for 10 minutes. Let cool overnight.

**2.** Put the cabbage, tomatoes, onions, celery, and green and red peppers into a large shallow dish or tray and sprinkle with salt. Leave overnight.

**3.** When you are ready to make the relish, drain the vegetables through a colander and rinse by running cold water over them for 1 minute. Squeeze with your hands to remove excess water. Taste a piece of a vegetable. It should be salty but not excessively so; if it is unpalatably salty, rinse and squeeze a second time.

**4.** Put the vegetables into a large pan and strain the prepared vinegar onto them. Bring to a simmer and cook, stirring frequently, until the vegetables are tender, about 20 minutes.

**5.** Meanwhile, prepare half-pint canning jars and the lids as instructed on page 232. Prepare the canner by filling it half full of water and placing it over moderate heat to warm to 180°F.

**6.** When the vegetables are tender, raise the heat and cook until the mixture is thick, about 10 minutes, depending on the juiciness of the vegetables.

**7.** Ladle the relish into the prepared jars, leaving ½ inch headspace. Cap and seal.

**8.** Process in a boiling-water bath for 15 minutes. Adjust for altitude, if necessary. (For altitudes of 1,001 to 6,000 feet, 20 minutes; above 6,000 feet, 25 minutes.)

**9.** Cool and test for a seal as on page 232. Store properly sealed jars in a closet or on shelves in a shady or dark place. If the seal is faulty, store the jars in the refrigerator and use within 1 month.

LARGE RED DRUMHEAD

COPYRIGHTED 1890 BY W. ATLEE BURPEE & CO.

 # Green Tomato Mincemeat

Mincemeat arrived in America with the English colonists, who were accustomed to mixing spices and fruit with meat to make holiday dishes. Over the years meat was dropped from most recipes and now mincemeat is a spiced and sweetened confection of fruits. While apples are often the base, green tomatoes that don't ripen before the summer's end are a gardener's favorite on both sides of the Atlantic. One pint is enough to make one 9-inch pie.

2 pounds (about 8 medium) green (unripe) tomatoes, peeled and roughly chopped

1 pound (about 3 large) apples, grated and peeled

1 (15-ounce) package golden raisins

1 (15-ounce) package dark raisins

zest of 1 lemon

2 tablespoons lemon juice or white vinegar

2 teaspoons allspice

1 teaspoon cinnamon

1 teaspoon nutmeg

3 cups brown sugar

½ cup (1 stick) butter

½ cup sherry or Madeira

1. Combine the tomatoes with the apples, the golden and dark raisins, lemon zest, lemon juice, allspice, cinnamon, and nutmeg in a large pan. Cover and place over low heat. Cook gently for 10 minutes, until juicy, stirring often.

2. Stir in the sugar and butter. Boil until much of the liquid has evaporated and the mixture is thick, 15 to 20 minutes; stir often.

3. Wash pint jars and lids as instructed on page 232. Prepare the canner by filling it half full of water and warming it over moderate heat to 180°F.

4. When the mincemeat is as thick as jam or chutney, stir in the sherry and boil 1 minute longer. Ladle the mincemeat into the prepared jars, leaving ½ inch headspace. Cap and seal.

5. Process in a boiling-water bath for 25 minutes. Adjust for altitude, if necessary. (For altitudes of 1,001 to 6,000 feet, 20 minutes; above 6,000 feet, 25 minutes.)

6. Cool and test for a seal as on page 232. Store properly sealed jars in a closet or on shelves in a shady or dark place. If the seal is faulty, store the jars in the refrigerator and use within 1 month.

# Dilled Green Cherries

### MAKES 6 QUARTS

Pickled green (unripe) cherry tomatoes are a delicious, pop-in-your-mouth treat — a startling contrast to sweet ripe cherry tomatoes. If you like, you can omit the dill. Then these pickles (skinned) make the perfect trompe l'oeil garnish for the Tomato Consommé Martini on page 88. This recipe is adapted from *Garden Way's Red and Green Tomato Cookbook*, by Janet Ballantyne.

6 quarts green cherry tomatoes

2 quarts water

2 cups white vinegar

¾ cup pickling salt

4 tablespoons mixed pickling spices in a muslin bag

12 grape leaves

6 garlic cloves

24 peppercorns

6 heads of dill

**1.** Wash quart canning jars and the lids as instructed on page 232. Prepare the canner by filling it half full of water and placing it over moderate heat to warm to 180°F.

**2.** Wash and stem the tomatoes. Heat the water, vinegar, salt, and pickling spices to a boil. Lower the heat and simmer for 15 minutes.

**3.** In the bottom of each hot clear jar, place 2 grape leaves, 1 clove of garlic, 4 peppercorns, and 1 head of dill. Fill with tomatoes. Ladle the hot brine over the tomatoes, leaving ½-inch headspace. Cap and seal.

**4.** Process in a boiling-water bath for 10 minutes. Adjust for altitude, if necessary. (For altitudes of 1,001 to 6,000 feet, 15 minutes; above 6,000 feet, 20 minutes.)

**5.** Cool and test for a seal as on page 232. Store properly sealed jars in a closet or on shelves in a shady or dark place. If the seal is faulty, store the jars in the refrigerator. Allow the jars to sit for 6 weeks before serving.

 # Oven-Dried Tomatoes in Herbed Olive Oil

MAKES 3–4½ PINTS

I f you enjoy imported sun-dried tomatoes, you may have wondered if you could dry them yourself. The answer is yes — if you live in a place that has low humidity and temperatures in the high 90s to 100°F is perfect. If you live in cooler, damper regions, sun-drying is out of the question, as the air must be hot and dry enough to remove 90 percent of the water in the tomatoes, thus stopping the growth of the bacteria, molds, and yeasts that spoil fruits and vegetables. But don't despair: You can dry tomatoes in a dehydrator designed for this purpose or in your regular oven. This recipe has instructions for drying, then storing your tomatoes in an herbed olive oil, which makes them especially delicious. Any paste-type tomato will dry well. Black Plum, Purple Pear, King Humbert, Plum Lemon, and Opalka are among the many that yield particularly good results. You can also purchase sun-dried tomatoes, which will be dry and flimsy, and pack them in the herbed olive oil to restore them to lusciousness.

6 pounds ripe firm soft plum tomatoes without any blemishes

3–4 (3-inch) sprigs fresh rosemary

6–8 sprigs fresh thyme

3–4 bay leaves

9–12 peppercorns

1 tablespoon fresh lavender flowers (optional)

3 cups (or more as needed) fruity extra-virgin olive oil

1. Preheat the oven to 150°F.

2. Wash and dry the tomatoes. Cut them in half and scoop out the seeds and cores. Pat the interiors dry with paper towels.

3. If there are wide gaps between the bars of your oven racks that might allow the tomatoes to fall through, cover the racks with clean sheeting or thin tea towels. Arrange the tomatoes on them so they are not touching. Do not attempt to dry more than two racks of tomatoes at a time, as that will vastly increase the drying time. Place

the racks in the oven. Close the door and bake for 30 minutes.

**4.** Open the oven door to let out the moisture. Leave it propped with a wooden spoon or something similar that will allow it to rest about 1 inch ajar. Bake for 6 to 8 hours longer, until the tomatoes are pliable and slightly leathery.

**5.** Condition the tomatoes by placing them in a dry ceramic or glass (not aluminum) container and leaving it uncovered in a dry and airy place for 10 days. Stir the tomatoes at least once a day.

**6.** Pasteurize the tomatoes by preheating the oven to 175°F. Place the dried tomatoes on the racks in a single layer and put them into the oven for 10 minutes. If you do not want oil-packed tomatoes, you can stop at this point. Store the tomatoes in sterilized and tightly capped jars in a dark place. See page 232 for sterilizing instructions.

**7.** For oil-packed tomatoes, choose 3 or 4 jars of roughly half-pint capacity with screw-on lids. Loosely fill each jar with dried tomatoes, tuck into each one a rosemary sprig, a couple of thyme sprigs, a bay leaf, 3 peppercorns, and a couple of lavender blossoms if desired. Fill the jars with olive oil. Screw on the lids. Store in the refrigerator for 2 weeks before using. When you remove the tomatoes, press the remainder under the oil and return the jar to the refrigerator. The tomatoes will keep for at least 2 months.

# Confit Tomatoes

**MAKES ABOUT 1½ PINTS**

The deep flavor of these semidried tomatoes captures the vibrant tastes of summer. They do not keep very long — 1 month is about the limit.

> 1 dozen large ripe but firm plum tomatoes, peeled and halved
>
> sea salt
>
> 2 bay leaves or 3 stems thyme
>
> 3 tablespoons olive oil

**1.** Preheat the oven to 200°F.

**2.** With a small knife or teaspoon, remove the seeds and gel from the tomatoes; you want empty halves. Place the tomato halves on a baking sheet or shallow pan, open side up. Season with salt to taste. If you are using bay leaves, tear them into small pieces and scatter on top. Alternatively, strip the leaves from the thyme and sprinkle them over the tomatoes. Drizzle with oil.

**3.** Bake for 3 to 4 hours, until the tomatoes have shrunk and darkened somewhat, but do not let them get completely dry.

**4.** Cool. Pack in a jar and cover with a little olive oil. Stored in the refrigerator, they will keep for at least 1 month.

# Cooked Tomato Salsa

### MAKES 4 HALF-PINTS

**M**aggie Oster has a way with herbs. She is the author of 12 books, including *Herbal Vinegar,* from which this recipe was adapted. She uses cilantro- or garlic-flavored red wine vinegar. It can be made with plain red wine vinegar, if that is what you have on hand.

4 cups peeled, seeded, and chopped tomatoes

1 cup chopped onion

⅓ cup seeded and minced jalapeño

2 garlic cloves, minced

½ cup minced fresh cilantro

¼ cup cilantro or garlic red wine vinegar

1 teaspoon salt

1. Wash the canning jars and the lids as instructed on page 232.

2. Prepare the canner by filling it half full of water and placing it over moderate heat to warm to 180°F.

3. Combine all the ingredients in a large, heavy, nonreactive saucepan. Place over medium heat and bring to a boil. Lower the heat and simmer for 20 minutes.

4. Fill each jar with the hot salsa, leaving ½ inch headspace. Cap and seal.

5. Process in a boiling-water bath for 15 minutes. Adjust for altitude, if necessary. (For altitudes of 1,001 to 6,000 feet, 20 minutes; above 6,000 feet, 25 minutes.)

6. Cool and test for a seal as on page 232. Store properly sealed jars in a closet or on shelves in a dark place for up to 6 months. If the seal is faulty, store the jars in the refrigerator and use within 1 week.

# APPENDIX 1
# A Glossary of Heirloom Tomatoes

Heirloom tomatoes come in practically every size and shape imaginable. Most fall into a definable shape/size category or color. Sizes range from a dime-size round currant tomato to an oblate several-pound Brandywine. Colors vary from the green of Aunt Ruby's German Green to the classic red of Paragon, from the bright yellow of Limmony to the purplish red-green of Black Krim to the mixed hues of red and yellow in the bicolors such as Regina's Yellow.

Tomatoes can be classified according to size, shape, color, ripening, leaf type, indeterminate versus determinate, among other factors. For simplicity's sake I will categorize by basic shape and color. And then, of course, there's taste.

## Red Slicing Tomatoes

The larger slicing tomatoes come in varying degrees of roundness and typically range from about 4 to 16 ounces or more in weight. There are many historical varieties in this category that have great old-time flavor and are too little used. In red tomatoes, Livingston varieties are among my favorites for their flavor and relative uniformity, as well as for their history (for more about the history, see the box Reynoldsburg Tomato Festival, Reynoldsburg, Ohio, on page 53). These varieties include Livingston's Favorite, Paragon, and Stone. Other varieties of good to very good quality include Abe Lincoln, Burbank, Cardinal, Cuostralee, Druzba, Early Large Red, Earliana, Mikado, Red Ponderosa, Matchless, Maule's Success, Trophy, and the early-bearing Stupice and Cosmonaut Volkov.

## Pink to Purple Slicing Tomatoes

The pink to purple group includes tomatoes of varying shades of delicate rosy pink, while the purples tend to be very light, not deeply saturated. They include Livingston's Beauty, Livingston's Magnus, Livingston's Main Crop Pink, Pink Brandywine, Eva Purple Ball, June Pink, Lambert's General Grant (Dr. Neal), Mikado, Mortgage Lifter, Olena Ukrainian, Oli Rose de St. Dominique, Pink Ponderosa, Purple Perfect, Pruden's Purple, Purple Brandy, Redfield Beauty, Rose de Berne, Trucker's Favorite, Winsall (Wins All), and many others.

Brandywine, Lambert's, Purple Brandy, Pruden's, and Winsall are all meaty beefsteaks, having a rich tomato taste that is satisfying. Brandywine has been considered by many to be the best-tasting tomato, and there is no debate that it is excellent.

However, the rest of the above listed have a more complex composition of flavors and sweet-acid balance that, to me, makes them more interesting in taste, and more compelling, especially in "vintage" tomato years. In fact, you could practically use wine terminology to describe their taste. All of the above-mentioned pink Livingston varieties are to me classic tomatoes, tangy and sweet. They start off with sweet, fruity forward notes and end with a long-lasting tangy acid finish tempered with a hint of tropical fruit, which makes your lips pucker ever so slightly. Rose de Berne, Eva Purple Ball, Trucker's Favorite, and Redfield Beauty are all distinguished by their relative uniformity, tidy size, and balance of sweet and acid flavors.

## Yellow to Orange Slicing Tomatoes

I think the best-tasting orange tomato by far is Indian Moon. Earl of Edgecombe is close behind, Kellogg's Breakfast is tasty and meaty, while Jubilee and Valencia are both good. My favorite yellow tomato is Livingston's Golden Queen, mostly for historical reasons. It is a rare nineteenth–century tomato that was introduced by Alexander Livingston, who got the seeds from "someone" at a fair. The tomato is light yellow with a red blush on the blossom end, with good old-time acid-sweetness balance. Manyel and Limmony are both excellent, with very good taste and texture, relatively uniform. Azoycha, a Russsian heirloom, is more variable in shape. Lillian's Yellow Heirloom and Dr. Wyche's Yellow are quite good. Dr. Wyche's turns a golden color, as does Yellow Brandywine, which is mild–flavored and meaty. Garden Peach is considerably smaller than the preceding group, two to three ounces. I like it for its novelty and historical value, as it was introduced by the Gregory Seed Company of Marblehead, Massachusetts. The skin is lightly hairy like a peach, the fruit is mild and fairly seedy, and the plant yields prolifically.

## Black Slicing Tomatoes

The black tomato group ranges from reddish black to deep purple to brownish green in color, sometimes with bits of pink or any combination of the preceding colors. The color deepens under certain conditions, such as extended hot periods. Their taste is unique in tomatoes — variously described as rich, salty, and/or smoky. Black from Tula is one of the best, along with Black Krim, Cherokee Purple, and Black Aisberg and the smaller Black Prince. Sara Black and Black Early are two other tasty types. Most of these varieties are associated with Russia. While quite seedy and odd looking, Purple Calabash, an old land-race, is one of my favorites.

## Green Slicing Tomatoes

For green tomatoes, Aunt Ruby's German Green is the best and, frankly, everything else pales in comparison. The fruits are large, with an excellent spicy taste. Green Zebra, a recent introduction, is also very good, with similar spiciness, smaller size, and stripes. Other large green tomatoes, such as Dorothy's Green, Evergreen, Green Velvet, and Moldovan Green, are pleasant, often sweet and juicy, but just don't compare to Aunt Ruby's.

## Bicolor Slicing Tomatoes

Bicolor tomatoes are distinctive in appearance, but with the exception of Regina's Yellow (Regina's

Bicolor), I find them to be somewhat mealy, and often they have a dull taste, depending on the weather. On the other hand, in a good year, bicolor tomatoes can be pleasantly fruity and very attractive in appearance, especially when sliced. Some of the varieties are particularly prone to cracking. Striped German (Old German) is perhaps a little better than some of the others. Big Rainbow, Georgia Streak, Marizol Gold, and Pineapple are all similar. Fruits of all these types can be large, exceeding a pound.

## White Slicing Tomatoes

White-skinned tomatoes tend to be more typically creamy or very pale yellow in color, especially when ripe. The flavor is very mild. White Queen is the best large white tomato and the plant is quite productive. White Beauty has a pleasant flavor described by some as almost lemony and has half-pound fruit, while Great White is larger. Shah, a sport from Mikado, yields medium-size sweet fruit.

## Cherry Tomatoes

I always thought cherry tomatoes were about the size of cherries or smaller — some people have expanded the definition to include anything round under three ounces or so. Since these tomatoes cannot be called slicers, I, too, have lumped some of these larger types in with the cherries.

Currant tomatoes (*Lycopersicon pimpinellifolium*) are very small tomatoes that grow in clusters. These plants are usually rampant growers and resistant to diseases. Currant tomatoes are almost always very good, with intense flavor. The yellow and red currant varieties are the most common, but the white currant variety is excellent. Some varieties of currant tomatoes have tough skins; they are seedy and often have a tendency to split. Ciudad Victoria is an old heirloom variety of red currant tomatoes, but it is not as sweet as some other types.

Yellow cherries include Blondkopfchen and the larger Esther Hess Yellow Cherry, Sara Goldstar, Green Gage, Hartmann's Yellow Gooseberry, Livingston's Gold Ball, and Galina. All are good, but none of them have outstanding flavor. Red cherry tomatoes include Reisentraube, Peacevine Cherry, Hawaiian, and Matt's Wild Cherry.

Petit Pomme Blanche is a tasty and rare small cream-white cherry, vaguely apple shaped, but it is not entirely stable (meaning the seeds you grow may not be true to type). Snow White isn't snow white but ivory, developed by Joe Bratka with nice mild taste. Dr. Carolyn, named for Carolyn Male, is a cream to yellow one-inch cherry, derived from Galina cherry.

Several pink types exist, including the large Pink Ping Pong and Amish Salad, both with nice flavor. A bicolor cherry, Isis Candy, has outstanding sweet taste. Green Grape is prolific, producing fairly small yellow-green fruits with very good tangy flavor. It is of recent origination.

## Plum, Pear-Shaped, and Paste Tomatoes

Plum, pear, and paste is a category with a wide range of shapes and sizes, and the distinctions between one type and another are sometimes unclear. What is common to all of them is that they have a lower moisture content and higher solid content than the slicing tomatoes, and typically they are better cooked, though a few varieties have outstanding fresh taste.

The classic pear or fig tomato is small, teardrop-shaped, and either yellow or red. Yellow and Red Pear (Pear Shaped Red) have excellent yields. Larger red pears include King Humbert, Napoli, and Hungarian Oval — the later is prolific, but its fruits are not as tasty. Black Pear is excellent and Purple Pear, a dusky rose color, is also tasty. Both yield well.

Yellow Plum and Yellow Plum Formed have small oval plum-shaped fruits, while Roughwood Yellow Plum, a recently developed open-pollinated variety, and Peace Yellow Paste are much larger. While not strictly falling into this category, Plum Lemon, an interesting variety from a Russian market, looks vaguely like a lemon. Orange Banana is excellent and prolific.

Long red types include Amish Paste, Howard German, Tom Patti's Italian Paste, and Opalka, all with very good fresh taste, not typically found in paste types. Opalka is representative of a large group of long tapering heirlooms termed "carrot type" by author William Woys Weaver. Debarao is heavy bearing, producing tomatoes with a plum shape. Black Plum from Russia yields huge amounts of small oval brownish red-purple plum tomatoes that are excellent cooked.

Yellow Stuffer and Red Stuffer are two hollow, bell pepper–shaped fruits. The yellow form especially has excellent yields, and the tomatoes can fool the uninitiated into believing they are peppers.

## Hybrid Tomatoes

Hybrid tomatoes are essentially the combination (or crossbreeding) of two types of tomatoes. The resulting offspring is a hybrid. Typically, however, it must be understood that hybrids may actually involve several parents over more than one generation — a complex hybrid.

The advantage of hybrids is that they incorporate genes from varieties or species that may have resistance to certain common tomato diseases or may be tolerant of adverse environmental conditions such as salinity or aridity. They may possess genes for higher yields, earlier fruiting, or other characteristics useful for the home gardener and commercial grower.

The chief criticism that can be leveled at the hybrid varieties is that they have often been bred with fairly little consideration for flavor, one of the key reasons for eating a tomato in the first place. There are varieties that are clearly exceptions to this. Recently more attention has been paid to taste by breeders, and some of the larger varieties bred for the home gardener are better. Uniformity, high yield, and some disease resistance are the end results of many hybridization efforts. Another disadvantage to hybrids is that you cannot save seeds yourself. Some varieties are quite expensive because of the work involved in developing them.

While hybrids sometimes incorporate specialized genes for disease resistance in less-than-ideal field conditions, they may be only marginally better than similar unimproved varieties. When grown in proximity to susceptible varieties, they usually also get infected. The breeding programs try to get results that are applicable over very wide geographic areas — they are not breeding for the specialized soil and climate niches that exist almost everywhere. While much less advantageous to the seed company, a longer process of breeding could incorporate the same genes into an open-pollinated form from which you could save seed.

Hybrids do not begin to offer the variations in size, color, shape, and taste seen in the heirloom types. The focus with hybrids is on red round uniform fruit plus the occasional color variation. Similar breeding efforts apply to cherry and processing tomatoes. While hybrids are typically bred for higher yields, some farm studies have found there is not an appreciable difference in yields between hybrids and heirlooms.

## Hybrid Varieties

There are hundreds of varieties of hybrid tomatoes. Perhaps one of the best-known is still Burpee's Big Boy, introduced in 1949. Burpee's Big Girl and Better Boy are also good. Big Beef is a classic beefsteak tomato, with flavorful 10- to 12-ounce fruit, and very productive vines. Burpee's Supersteak Hybrid has good flavor, with large to very large fruits. Another tasty variety yielding big 1- to 2-pound fruits is Beefmaster.

Celebrity is a 6- to 8-ounce midseason determinate variety that produces very uniform, good-tasting tomatoes. Another determinate variety favored by Northeastern commercial growers is Johnny's 361, an early variety bearing 6- to 8-ounce tomatoes that arc fairly meaty and tasty but with somewhat tough skin. Buffalo, a Dutch-bred greenhouse tomato, performs well outside, yielding moderately tasty 8-ounce fruit. Florida 47 is a semi–bush type that yields a good-tasting 10-ounce flattened tomato.

One of the best-tasting early-yielding hybrids is Early Cascade, which produces 4-ounce fruit. The ultra series has several varieties with good sweetness, particularly Ultra Sweet and Ultrasonic. Both are relatively early semi–bush types, which yield 10- to 12-ounce fruits. Ultra Pink is similar with pink fruits.

Two orange varieties, Golden Boy and Golden Girl, are uniform and pleasant to look at and have little flavor. Lemon Boy is a yellow equivalent. Stick with the heirlooms here.

Sun Gold cherry is one of the best hybrid cherry tomatoes — it is a prolific plant that yields orange cherries with great complex flavor, though the skins are somewhat prone to splitting. Sun Sugar is also orange and reputed to be productive and tasty. Sweet 100 cherry is a very good all-around fairly sweet red cherry, though now it is sometimes replaced by an improved form, Sweet Million, which also has an orange form, Sweet Gold. Similar is Sun Cherry with somewhat sweeter fruits. Super Sweet 100 is another Sweet 100 type. Juliet is one of the better-tasting small tomatoes: red, sweet, with oval one-ounce fruit. Sweet Olive is a pleasant-tasting "grape" tomato, which seems to be an industry name for small cherries.

In paste tomatoes, San Marzano is one of the most recognized names, actually representing several types, which include open-pollinated forms. These tomatoes are typically three or four inches long, weighing four to six ounces, with a point at the end of the fruit. Viva Italia is an improved Roma, with a higher sugar content and more disease resistance. Italian Gold is a bright orange plum with good yields and appears to be a candidate for dehybridizing, as it seems to breed true in first- and second-generation grow-outs.

# APPENDIX 2
# Tomato Seed Saving

Seeds cannot be saved from every variety. Hybrid varieties usually have a complex parentage and will not breed true. Sometimes the parentage is not very complex and saving seeds from these varieties can produce good results — but more often than not the offspring are not stable. Some varieties may be plant protected or patented in some manner, making their unlicensed reproduction illegal.

You can reliably save seeds only from open-pollinated varieties; that is, nonhybrid seeds whose offspring will be the same as the parent, provided no cross-pollination with a different variety has taken place. All heirloom varieties are open-pollinated, though many open-pollinated varieties are not heirloom. The varieties most in need of preservation are the true heirlooms, though you cannot always be sure how old your variety is.

The most important varieties you can preserve are those that come from your family, friends, or community. These are varieties that may not be preserved anywhere else. Seeds that come from a seed-saving organization or from a small seed catalog are likely to be rarer than those coming from a larger commercial source. It is also important to save seeds from bigger companies. Many of the varieties that were featured in catalogs 30 years ago are no longer commercially available. Do not assume that because a variety is common now, it will always be so.

## Separation of Varieties

Saving tomato seeds is really pretty easy and fun. Tomatoes are largely self-pollinating or inbreeding, which means that relatively little cross-pollination will occur. You don't have to worry too much about your seeds' getting mixed up or hybridized with another variety.

For each flower, the pollen from the anthers, the male structure, falls onto the stigma, the female part of the same flower, which is below the anthers. The sperm travels from the pollen down the pollen tube and fertilizes the ovaries.

Most domesticated types of tomatoes will not cross readily. Generally only wild tomatoes or semidomesticated types will cross easily with each other. It is rare for most gardeners to be growing these. Sometimes pollen from the flowers of the plant of another variety is moved around by various insect pollinators, especially sweat bees, and that pollen reaches the ovaries first, thereby creating cross-pollination. The fruit may look the same as all the other fruit and you won't notice any difference until the following year. Or cross-pollination can take place by a variety (or some of its flowers) having exposed (exerted) stigmas that cannot receive pollen from its own anthers but only from another flower. According to some people, cross-pollination occurs particularly in the double-flowered and potato-leaved varieties, some of which have greater instances of exerted stigmas. I cannot say that I have noticed more crossing based on these characteristics.

Some crossing can take place routinely, depending on the floral structure of a particular variety, and occasionally by forced pollination. This is usually in the range of 1 to 2 percent to as much as 5 percent, but greater cross-pollination is sometimes possible. Aunt Ruby's German Green is more prone to crossing than most varieties if grown adjacent to other cultivars, and I have seen crossing as high as 30 percent.

To be totally safe, it is better to separate plants by at least 20 to 30 feet. Most larger gardens can safely accommodate two to five varieties. However, some growers, including the USDA, plant each variety within a few feet of any others. If you absolutely must plant varieties next to each other, try to separate them with greater distance in another year. I have done it both ways and generally seen more crossing when planted near each other but have also had crossing when varieties were well separated.

## Gathering Seed

You first need to gather your tomatoes. Ripe ones are best, but they can be a little overripe as well. Underripe fruit should be avoided.

The first part of the process is to select the tomatoes from which you are saving seed. Look carefully at your tomato plants and make sure that each plant is the same type. If you have five plants of the same type and a good description from a

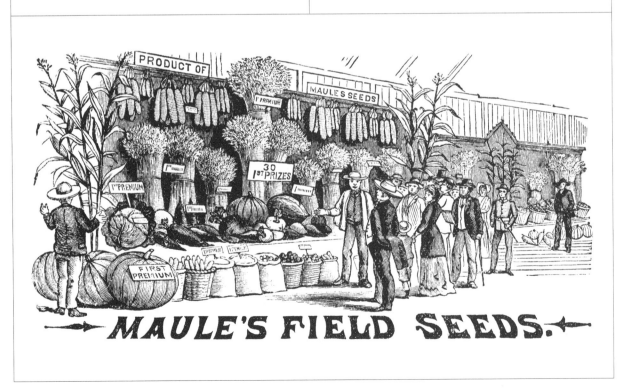

catalog or book on heirloom plants, you should have a pretty good idea of what the "correct" fruit should look like. If you have even more plants, you can more easily spot any fruits that are different. If you plant only three of one variety and one is incorrect, it may be hard to know which is the correct type.

Now that you know your plants are consistent, look at your fruit type. Are all the fruits on each plant similar? Usually they are, but not always. If they are not, you may want to select for just one type, especially if you know beforehand what the fruit is supposed to look like. As you look carefully at your tomatoes, you may notice that some fruits are rounder, longer, flatter, or more pointed or have skin color variation, different-shaped shoulders, and so on. If there is a lot of variety, it is possible that there has been cross-pollination and the fruits may not be representative of the original type or may have drifted away from the original type through lack of consistent selection. Some varieties are more "plastic" than others and after a period of time can revert to some predecessor type without proper selection. Or perhaps the original type was always variable.

Most of the time you can tell fairly easily what you are looking for, in which case you don't have to be so choosy as to which fruit you select. But you may encounter a variety that is more of an enigma, with much variation. If you are not sure what the "original" type is supposed to be, find the fruit type that is most consistent or select for all fruit types. Another means of selecting is to take fruit only from plants that are consistent — in other words, select by the plant first, not by the fruit type.

Aside from looking at fruit shape and color, there are many characteristics to select for. Typically, most people will select more obvious "macro" characteristics, those that are readily apparent. These might include taste, maturity, tendency to split, tendency to rot, green shoulders, susceptibility of the plant and fruit to various diseases, or obvious resistance to them. One example of a common tomato disease is late blight, which most varieties seem to get sooner or later in the Northeast. Some varieties are somewhat more resistant than others, especially currant tomatoes, which are a different species.

Other characteristics might include the amount of solids, thickness of skin, thickness of walls, and seediness. In selecting fruit you also must be careful not to select for only a single characteristic that may leave behind another desirable trait. For instance, if you selected only for early ripening and took only your first fruits, while you may get earlier ripening, it is possible you are selecting away from the correct fruit type.

Don't become intimidated by all the characteristics for which you can select. What is most important is to make sure you are selecting fruits that seem to be representative of the variety, and not those that are distinctly different. Most of you will want to keep this simple and make it fun!

If you want to select for earlier ripening or taste or size in particular, you can specially select outstanding fruit and process those seeds separately without affecting your entire seed stock.

Then if future grow-outs are not satisfactory, you have not lost the original type.

It is best to pick fruit at least several times throughout the growing season so you are not unconsciously selecting for early, middle, or late ripening.

## Processing Seeds

Now what you will do is create a tomato seed and juice mixture and ferment the seeds.

There are a variety of strategies for removing seeds, but essentially you want to cut your tomatoes in half crosswise and scoop or squeeze out the seeds into a container. Or rub the tomatoes across a hard wire screen, allowing the seeds and some of the pulp but not the skin to fall into a bucket. Plastic delicatessen or yogurt containers of various sizes work well for this purpose unless you are processing a much larger quantity. You are trying to get juice and seeds into the container with a minimum of pulp and no skin. Use an appropriate container for the volume of liquid and seeds you have; fill it up as much as possible. If you have a really tiny amount of liquid with your seeds, you may add a small amount of water, but it is better not to dilute the seed/juice mixture. Make sure you label the base of the container with the variety name and date.

Another method used for small cherry-size tomatoes is to mash the tomatoes together, skins and all, until every tomato is macerated and no seeds are left in them. A five-gallon bucket works very well for this. Strain off some of the juice and put it aside. Then fill the bucket partway with water and let the seeds fall to the bottom. As they do so, pour off as much of the skins and pulp as possible, without pouring out any of the seeds. Keep pouring off the skins and solids until none are left, usually three or four times. Then add back the juice and place the mixture in an appropriate container.

Cover the container, label it, and let the mixture ferment naturally at room temperature for two to four days. If any water is present in your mixture, fermentation typically should be on the shorter end. The warmer it is, the faster the mixture will ferment, so if it is 90°F outside, two days may be sufficient. You do not want to leave the seeds for such a long time that they sprout. Seeds from some varieties may sprout after two days, especially if the fruit was overripe, so keep your eyes on them.

This fermentation process kills many seed-borne diseases. After a couple of days, there will probably be a thick layer of fermented solids on top. Remove this layer entirely and discard it. The seed mixture may be somewhat frothy and will have a distinctive foul-smelling, rotten-tomato odor. Take the liquid and seeds and pour them into a mesh strainer. Most home-style cooking strainers work quite well for this. Make sure the mesh of the screen is tight enough so the seeds do not fall through.

Then you need to wash the seed and pulp mixture under gently running water or by dipping the strainer into a bucket. At the same time, stir and rub the seeds gently against the screen with your fingers or a wooden spoon to remove the remaining solids. After a few minutes, all the pulp should be gone and only the clean seeds remain. Alternatively, you can add water to the container and keep pouring off the solids and any seeds that float.

Put the seeds onto an absorbent surface or a very fine wire screen and spread them as thinly as possible. Thick uncoated paper plates work well. Avoid paper towels, because the seeds will stick to the paper. Make sure you write the variety name on the plate.

Ideally, you should let the seeds dry in an airy, warm place, not in a hot attic. A room with a dehumidifier and/or a fan is helpful. You do not want to dry the seeds at temperatures above 95°F. I initially let them dry in the sunlight to get rid of the major wetness. This is not a generally recommended seed-saving practice, but by September in Zone 5, it is rarely much above 80°F. We often have a preponderance of cool humid or rainy days, which slow natural drying down and can cause molding. So some initial drying is usually necessary. I have not noticed any loss of germination with seeds exposed to the sun while drying, but caution should be exercised. In climates with low humidity, mold is not a concern. Be careful wherever you dry the seeds to make sure they are protected from rodents. Mice particularly favor tomato seeds.

After the seeds are thoroughly dry, they may be placed in plastic or glass jars. Drying usually takes a few days under dry conditions, sometimes longer in humid climates. If you are unsure if the seeds are thoroughly dry, you can temporarily put them into seed or coin envelopes or paper bags and place them in permanent containers during a period of low humidity or once the indoor heating season has begun. In arid climates, such as the Southwest, the seeds will dry rapidly.

Tomato seeds will last for three to five years under average storage conditions, with some germination often persisting longer. Freezing or refrigerating seeds will further prolong their viability.

# APPENDIX 3 Recommended Reading

## Gardening

Coleman, Eliot. *The New Organic Grower: A Master's Manual of Tools and Techniques for the Home and Market Gardener.* White River Junction, Vermont: Chelsea Green Publishing Company, 1995.

Jeavons, John. *How to Grow More Vegetables: And Fruits, Nuts, Berries, Grains, and Other Crops Than You Ever Thought Possible on Less Than You Can Imagine.* Berkeley, California: Ten Speed Press, 2002.

Smith, Edward C. *The Vegetable Gardener's Bible.* North Adams, Massachusetts: Storey Publishing, 2000.

## Tomato Varieties

Burr, Fearing. *Field and Garden Vegetables of America.* Second edition 1865. Chillicothe, Illinois: American Botanist, Booksellers, 1990.

Henderson, Peter. *Gardening for Profit: A Guide to the Successful Cultivation of the Market and Family Garden.* New York: Orange Judd Company, 1887.

Livingston, A. W. *Livingston and the Tomato.* 1893. Foreword and appendix by Andrew F. Smith. Columbus, Ohio: Ohio State University Press, 1998.

Male, Carolyn J. *100 Heirloom Tomatoes for the American Garden.* New York: Workman Publishing, 1999.

Weaver, William Woys. *Heirloom Vegetable Gardening: A Master Gardener's Guide to Planting, Growing, Seed Saving, and Cultural History.* New York: Henry Holt and Company, 1997.

## Seed Saving and Breeding

Ashworth, Suzanne. *Seed to Seed.* Decorah, Iowa: Seed Savers Exchange, 2002.

Deppe, Carol. *Breed Your Own Vegetable Varieties: Popbeans, Purple Peas, and Other Innovations from the Backyard Garden.* Boston: Little, Brown and Company, 1993.

## History

If you are really interested in the history of tomatoes in America, Andy Smith's books are definitive.

Long, Janet in *The Cambridge History of Food,* ed. Kenneth F. Kiple and Kriemhild Coneè Ornelas. Volume 1, pp. 351–58. Cambridge, England: Cambridge University Press, 2000.

Smith, Andrew F. *Pure Ketchup: A History of America's National Condiment, with Recipes.* Washington, DC: Smithsonian Institution Press, 2001.

*Souper Tomatoes: The Story of America's Favorite Food.* New Brunswick, New Jersey; Rutgers University Press, 2000.

*The Tomato in America: Early History, Culture, and Cookery.* Columbia, South Carolina: University of South Carolina Press, 1994.

# APPENDIX 4 Sources

## Seed Suppliers

If you are interested in growing your own tomatoes from heirloom seeds, explore the varieties these vendors have to offer. This resource list is divided into two sections: companies that sell primarily open-pollinated and heirloom seeds and companies that sell primarily hybrid seeds or mixtures of types.

### Heirloom and Open-Pollinated Seed Sources

**Abundant Life Seeds**
541-767-9606
*www.abundantlifeseeds.com*

**Appalachian Seeds**
828-243-0222
*www.appalachianseeds.com*

**Baker Creek Heirloom Seeds**
417-924-8917
*www.rareseeds.com*

**Bountiful Gardens**
707-459-6410
*www.bountifulgardens.org*

**The Cook's Garden**
800-457-9703
*www.cooksgarden.com*

**Eden Organic Nursery Services**
954-382-8281
*www.eonseed.com*

**Fedco Seeds**
207-873-7333
*www.fedcoseeds.com*

**Garden State Heirloom Seed Society**
908-475-2730
*www.historyyoucaneat.org*

**Good Seed Company**
*moonmt@televar.com*
*www.goodseedco.net*

**Greta's Organic Gardens**
613-521-8648
*www.seeds-organic.com*

**Heirloom Seeds**
724-663-5356
*www.heirloomseeds.com*

**Heirloom Tomatoes**
*info@heirloomtomatoes.net*
*www.heirloomtomatoes.net*

**High Mowing Organic Seeds**
802-472-6174
*www.highmowingseeds.com*

**J. L. Hudson, Seedsman**
*inquiry@jlhudsonseeds.net*
*www.jlhudsonseeds.net*

**Landis Valley Museum**
717-569-0401
*www.landisvalleymuseum.org*

**Marianna's Heirloom Seeds**
615-446-9191
*www.mariseeds.com*

**Native Seeds/SEARCH**
520-622-5561
*www.nativeseeds.org*

**Nichols Garden Nursery**
800-422-3985
*www.nicholsgardennursery.com*

**The Pepper Gal**
954-537-5540
*www.peppergal.com*

**Prairie Garden Seeds**
306-682-1475
*www.prseeds.ca*

**R. H. Shumway's**
800-342-9461
*www.rhshumway.com*

**Redwood City Seed**
650-325-7333
*www.ecoseeds.com*

**Salt Spring Seeds**
250-537-5269
*www.saltspringseeds.com*

**Sand Hill Preservation Center**
563-246-2299
*www.sandhillpreservation.com*

**Seed Savers Exchange**
563-382-5990
*www.seedsavers.org*

**Seeds of Change**
888-762-7333
*www.seedsofchange.com*

**Southern Exposure Seed Exchange**
540-894-9480
*www.southernexposure.com*

**Swallowtail Garden Seeds**
707-538-3585
*www.swallowtailgardenseeds.com*

**Tanager Song Farm**
*cynthia_faverty@yahoo.com*
*www.tanagersongfarm.com*

**Terra Edibles**
613-961-0654
*www.terraedibles.ca*

**Underwood Gardens**
Terroir Seeds LLC
888-878-5247
*www.underwoodgardens.com*

**Upper Canada Seeds**
416-447-5321
*www.uppercanadaseeds.ca*

**Victory Seed Company**
503-829-3126
*info@victoryseeds.com*
*www.victoryseeds.com*

## Hybrid Sellers Plus Heirlooms and Open-Pollinated

**Artistic Gardens/Le Jardin du Gourmet**
802-748-1446
*www.artisticgardens.com*

**Berlin Seeds**
330-893-2091

**The Chef's Garden**
800-289-4644
*www.chefsgarden.com*

**Comstock, Ferre & Co.**
800-733-3773
*www.comstockferre.com*

**Crosman's Seeds**
800-446-7333
*www.crosmanseed.com*

**D. Landreth Seed Co.**
800-654-2407
*www.landrethseeds.com*

**D.V. Burrell Seed Growers Co.**
719-254-3318
*www.burrellseeds.us*

**Earl May Seed & Nursery**
712-246-1020
*www.earlmay.com*

**Ferry-Morse Seed Company**
800-626-3392
*www.ferry-morse.com*

**Germania Seed**
800-380-4721
*www.germaniaseed.com*

**Gurney's Seed & Nursery Co.**
513-354-1492
*www.gurneys.com*

**Halifax Seed Co. Inc.**
902-454-7456
*www.halifaxseed.com*

**Harris Seeds**
800-544-7938
*www.harrisseeds.com*

**Johnny's Selected Seeds**
877-564-6697
*www.johnnyseeds.com*

**Jung Quality Garden Seeds**
800-297-3123
*www.jungseed.com*

**Olds Garden Seed**
800-949-5017
*www.oldsgardenseed.com*

**Pinetree Garden Seeds**
207-926-3400
*www.superseeds.com*

**Rohrer Seeds**
717-299-2571
*www.rohrerseeds.com*

**Stokes Seeds**
800-396-9238
*www.stokeseeds.com*

**The Tasteful Garden**
866-855-6344
*www.tastefulgarden.com*

**Territorial Seed Company**
800-626-0866
*www.territorialseed.com*

**Thompson & Morgan Seeds**
800-274-7333
*www.tmseeds.com*

**Tomato Growers Supply Company**
888-478-7333
*www.tomatogrowers.com*

**Totally Tomatoes**
800-345-5977
*www.totallytomato.com*

**Vermont Bean Seed Company**
800-349-1071
*www.vermontbean.com*

**Vesey's**
800-363-7333
*www.veseys.com*

**Virtual Seeds**
888-249-2943
*www.virtualseeds.com*

**W. Atlee Burpee & Co.**
800-333-5808
*www.burpee.com*

**White Flower Farm**
800-503-9624
*www.whiteflowerfarm.com*

**William Dam Seeds Ltd.**
905-628-6641
*www.damseeds.com*

# Organizations and Farms that appear in this book

**Chefs Collaborative**
89 South Street
Boston, MA 02111
617-236-5200
*www.chefscollaborative.org*

**Full Belly Farm**
P.O. Box 251
Guinda, CA 95637
530-796-2214
*www.fullbellyfarm.com*

**Grow Alabama**
Jerry Spencer
2301 Finley Blvd.
Birmingham, AL 35202
205-991-0042
*www.growalabama.com*

**Seeds of Diversity Canada**
P.O. Box 36, Station Q
Toronto, ON M4T 2L7
Canada
866-509-7333
*www.seeds.ca*

# Contributing Chefs

**Jody Adams**
Rialto
1 Bennett Street
Cambridge, MA 02138
617-661-5050
*www.rialto-restaurant.com*

**Rick Bayless**
Frontera Grill
445 North Clark Street
Chicago, IL 60654
312-661-1434
*www.rickbayless.com*

**John Besh**
August Restaurant
301 Tchoupitoulas Street
New Orleans, LA 70130
504-299-9777
*www.chefjohnbesh.com*

**Blue Ginger**
583 Washington Street
Wellesley, MA 02482
781-283-5790
*www.ming.com/blueginger*

**Daniel Boulud**
Restaurant Daniel
60 East 65th Street
New York, NY 10065
212-288-0033
*www.danielnyc.com*

**Massimo Capra**
Mistura
265 Davenport Road
Toronto, ON M5R 1J9
Canada
416-515-0009
*www.mistura.ca*

**Floyd Cardoz**
Tabla
11 Madison Avenue
New York, NY 10010
212-889-0667
*www.tablany.com*

**Gary Danko**
Restaurant Gary Danko
800 North Point Street
San Francisco, CA 94109
415-749-2060
*www.garydanko.com*

**Roberto Donna**
Galileo
1110 21st Street, NW
Washington, DC 20036
202-293-7191
*www.robertodonna.com*

**Chris Douglass**
Ashmont Grill
555 Talbot Avenue
Dorchester, MA 02124
617-825-4300
*www.ashmontgrill.com*

**Shirl Gard**
The Old Inn On The Green
134 Hartsville New
Marlborough Road
New Marlborough, MA 01230
413-229-7924
*www.oldinn.com*

**Robert Gurvich**
Alison at the Maidstone Arms
207 Main Street
East Hampton, NY 11937
631-324-5440
*www.alisonrestaurant.com*

**Greg Higgins**
Higgins Restaurant and Bar
1239 SW Broadway
Portland, OR 97205
503-222-9070
*www.higgins.ypguides.net*

**Peter Hoffman**
Savoy
70 Prince Street
New York, NY 10012
212-219-8570
*www.savoynyc.com*

**Melissa Kelly**
Primo
2 South Main Street
Rockland, ME 04841
207-596-0770
*www.primorestaurant.com*

**Bob Kinkead**
Kinkead's
2000 Pennsylvania Avenue, NW
Washington, DC 20006
202-296-7700
*www.kinkead.com*

**Josie Le Balch**
Josie Restaurant
2424 Pico Boulevard
Santa Monica, CA 90405
310-581-9888
*www.josierestaurant.com*

**Mary O'Brien**
Chaiwalla
1 Main Street
Salisbury, CT 06068
860-435-9758

**Walter Pisano**
Tulio Ristorante
1100 Fifth Avenue
Seattle, WA 98101
206-624-5500
*www.tulio.com*

**Peter Platt**
The Old Inn on the Green
134 Hartsville New
Marlborough Road
New Marlborough, MA 01230
413-229-7924
*www.oldinn.com*

**Nora Pouillon**
Restaurant Nora
2132 Florida Avenue NW
Washington, DC 20008
202-462-5143
*www.noras.com*

**Chris Prosperi**
Metro Bis
928 Hopmeadow Street
Simsbury, CT 06070
860-651-1908
*www.metrobis.com*

**Kevin Schmitz**
Marketplace Kitchen
18 Elm Court
Sheffield, MA 01257
413-248-5040
*www.marketplacekitchen.com*

**Dan Smith**
John Andrews Restaurant
224 Hillsdale Road
South Egremont, MA 01258
413-528-3469
*www.jarestaurant.com*

**Susan Spicer**
Bayona
430 Dauphine Street
New Orleans, LA 70112
504-525-4455
*www.bayona.com*

**Stage Left Restaurant**
5 Livingston Ave
New Brunswick, NJ 08901
732-828-4444
*www.stageleft.com*

**Sarah Stegner**
Prairie Grass Café
601 Skokie Boulevard
Northbrook, IL 60062
847-205-4433
*www.prairiegrasscafe.com*

**Alice Waters**
Chez Panisse
1517 Shattuck Avenue
Berkeley, CA 94709
510-548-5525
*www.chezpanisse.com*

## Tomato Festivals in the United States

**Bradley County Pink Tomato Festival**
Warren, Arkansas
Second week in June
870-226-5225
*www.bradleypinktomato.com*

**Fairfield Tomato Festival**
Fairfield, California
Third weekend in August
707-422-0103
*www.fairfielddowntown.com*

**Grainger County Tomato Festival**
Rutledge, Tennessee
Last full weekend in July
865-828-4222
*www.graingercountytomatofestival.com*

**Harvest Farm-to-Table**
Carmel, California
Late September
831-622-7770
*www.harvestcarmel.com*

**Kendall-Jackson Heirloom Tomato Festival**
Kendall-Jackson Wine Center
Fulton, California
Mid-September
800-769-3649
*www.kj.com*

**Pittston Tomato Festival**
Pittston, Pennsylvania
Mid-August
570-655-1424
*www.pittstontomatofestival.com*

**Reynoldsburg Tomato Festival**
Reynoldsburg, Ohio
Mid-August
614-866-4888
*www.reynoldsburgtomatofestival.org*

**Ruskin Tomato Festival**
Ruskin, Florida
First weekend in May
813-645-6028
*www.ruskintomatofestival.org*

# Index

Page references in *italics* indicate photos or illustrations.

# C

cabbage
  Deconstructed Cabbage
    Rolls with Tomato
    Sauce, 186–87
  Higdom, 246–47
Cake, Green Tomato Choco-
  late, 226
Candied-Tomato Tart with
  Five-Spiced Hazelnut
  Crust, 220–21
*Canning and Preserving*
  (Rorer), 244
canning tomatoes/tomato
  preserves, 231–52
  boiling water bath for,
    231–32
  Canned Tomatoes, 233
  Canned Tomato Purée, 234
  Cooked Tomato Salsa, 252
  Dilled Green Cherries, 249
  equipment for, 231
  Green Tomato Chutney,
    238–39
  Green Tomato Mincemeat,
    248
  Higdom, 246–47
  Tomato, Orange, and Gin-
    ger Chutney, 240–41
  Tomato and Citrus Marma-
    lade, 245
  Tomato and Lemon Jam,
    242–43
  Tomato Juice, 235
  Tomato Ketchup, 236–37
  Yellow Tomato and Pine-
    apple Jam, 244
Caponata, 54–55
Capra, Massimo, 16, 28–29,
  181, 268
Cardinal tomato, 9, *151, 211,*
  219, 253
  in recipes, 111
Cardoz, Floyd, 100, 268
Caribbean Red Fish Sauce
  with Red Snapper, 170
Carmel TomatoFest, 126
"carrot type" tomatoes, 233,
  256
Catalan Tomato Toasts, 50
Celebrity tomato, 257
Chaiwalla Savory Tomato
  Pie, 114
Chaiwalla teashop, 114, 268

Chalk's Early Jewel tomato,
  151
cheese. *See also* mozzarella;
  parmesan
  Chaiwalla Savory Tomato
    Pie, 114
  Heirloom Tomato and Goat
    Cheese Salad, 96–97
  Heirloom Tomato and
    Toasted Garlic Gratin,
    204
  Heirloom Tomatoes with
    New Potatoes, Herbs,
    and Melted Taleggio
    Cheese, 104–5
  Herbed Goat Cheese
    Broiled in Tomato Sauce,
    56–57
  Pasta with Tomatoes,
    Garden Vegetables, and
    Crumbled Blue Cheese,
    *129,* 137
  Polenta Concia with
    Gorgonzola and Fresh
    Herbs, 181
  Red and Yellow Tomato
    Salad with Lentils, Basil,
    and Goat Cheese, 94–95
  Tomato, Watermelon, and
    Ricotta Salata Salad,
    *59,* 91
  Tomato and Potato Casse-
    role, 209
  Tomato Basil Quiche, 111
  Tomato-Rice Casserole
    with Poblanos, Beef, and
    Melted Cheese, 188–89
  Trio of Stuffed Tomatoes,
    *164,* 196–97
  Village Farm Greenhouse
    Tomato, Feta Cheese,
    and Basil Salad, 92
Chefs Collaborative, 14, 58,
  267
cherry tomatoes, 12
  Blondkopfchen, 13, 255
  Esther Hess Yellow Cherry,
    255
  Green Grape, 13, 256
  Hawaiian, 13, 255
  hybrid varieties, 258
  Matt's Wild Cherry, 13,
    138, 255
  Peacevine Cherry, 13, 138,
    173, 255

  Pink Ping Pong, 13, 136,
    256
  Reisentraube, 13, 255
  Sara Goldstar, 13, 136, 255
  Sun Gold, 13
  Sweet 100, 13
cherry tomatoes, recipes for
  Dilled Green Cherries, 249
  Tomato and Potato Casse-
    role, *165,* 209
Chez Panisse Restaurant and
  Café, 76, 269
chicken
  Chicken Niçoise, 176–77
  Easy Curried Chicken, 179
  Sautéed Chicken Breasts
    with Tomatoes and Sum-
    mer Vegetables, 178
  Trio of Stuffed Tomatoes,
    *164,* 196–97
  West African Stew, 180
chickpeas
  Spiced Tomato and Chick-
    pea Dip, 63
  Winter Bean Stew, 150
chiles. *See* chipotle chiles;
  green chiles; poblano chiles
chilled soups
  Chilled Soup of Creole
    Tomatoes with Tap-
    enade, 79
  Chilled Sun-Gold Tomato
    Soup, *26,* 78
chipotle chiles
  Rick Bayless's Essential
    Quick-Cooked Tomato-
    Chipotle Sauce, 31
chocolate
  Green Tomato Chocolate
    Cake, *166,* 226
Chowder, Manhattan Clam,
  82–83
chutneys
  Green Tomato Chutney,
    238–39
  Tomato, Orange, and Gin-
    ger Chutney, 240–41
Ciudad Victoria tomato, 13
clams
  Manhattan Clam Chowder,
    82–83
cocktails
  Bloody Bull, 65
  Bloody Mary, 149
  Spicy Tomato Cocktail, 66

  Tomato Consommé Mar-
    tini, 88
  Tomato-Orange Cocktail,
    55
cod
  Rosemary-Roasted Cod
    with Confit Tomatoes
    and Green Beans, *163,*
    168
  Salt Cod Ceviche with
    Tomatoes and Arugula,
    68–69
cold storage of green tomatoes, 231
collecting seed. *See* seed
  saving
community supported agri-
  culture (CSA), 4, 134
condiments. *See* chutneys;
  ketchup; sauces
Confit Tomatoes, 251
consumption of tomatoes,
  2, 69
container-grown tomatoes, 7
Cooked Tomato Salsa, 252
*Cooking at the Kasbah:*
  *Recipes from My Moroccan*
  *Kitchen* (Morse), 51
corn
  Corn Maque Chou, 212
  Roast Lobster with Tomato,
    Corn, and Fines Herbes,
    160–61
  Tomato and Corn Salsa, 38
  Trio of Stuffed Tomatoes,
    *164,* 196–97
Cosby, Harrison, 243
Cosmonaut Volkov tomato,
  211, 253
Costenbader, Carol W., 206
couscous
  Tomato Couscous Salad,
    103
Cream of Tomato Soup, 80
cross-pollination, 259–60
Crostini with Tomatoes,
  Avocado, and Preserved
  Lemons, *24,* 51
*Cuisines of Mexico, The* (Ken-
  nedy), 101, 213
Cuostralee tomato, 253
currant tomatoes, 11, 13, 255
Curry, Shahi Kofta, 191

jam *(continued)*
  Yellow Tomato and Pine-
    apple Jam, 244
Jeffrey's Restaurant and Bar,
  92, 198
John Andrews Restaurant,
  182, 184, 269
Johnny's 361 tomato, 257
Johnson, Robert Gibbon, 109
*Journal of the National
  Cancer Institute*, 208
Jubilee tomato, 254
Juliet tomato, 258
June Pink tomato, 136, 253

# K

kalamata olives. *See* olives
Kapuler, Alan, 43, 173
Kellogg, Mrs. E. E., 86
Kellogg's Breakfast tomato,
  55, 254
Kelly, Melissa, 120, 268
Kennedy, Diana, 101, 213
ketchup
  history of, 74
  Tomato Ketchup, 236–37
King Humbert tomato, 13,
  256
  for canning, 233
  for drying, 229
  in recipes, 17, 250
Kinkead, Robert, 94, 268
Kinkead's restaurant, 94, 268
Kitchiner, William, 239

# L

lamb
  Lamb Provençal, 190
  Lamb-Stuffed Green Chiles
    with Fresh Tomato
    Purée, 192–93
  Pizza Middle Eastern Style,
    116–17
  Shahi Kofta Curry, 191
  Trio of Stuffed Tomatoes,
    *164*, 196–97
Lambert's General Grant (Dr.
  Neal) tomato, 9, 79, 219,
  253
*Lancaster Journal*, 225
Large Rose Peach tomato, 153
Latini, Antonio, 18, 105

Lawn, CR, 211
*L. cheesmanii*, 77
Le Balch, Josie, 56, 108, 110,
  268
Lee, N. K. M., 223
Lemon Boy tomato, 257
lemons
  Angel-Hair Pasta with Sun-
    Dried Tomatoes, Lemon,
    and Shrimp, 162
  Crostini with Tomatoes,
    Avocado, and Preserved
    Lemons, 50
  Prawns with Garlic, Heir-
    loom Tomatoes, and
    Lemon, *130*, 156
  Tomato and Citrus Marma-
    lade, 245
  Tomato and Lemon Jam,
    242–43
lentils
  Red and Yellow Tomato
    Salad with Lentils, Basil,
    and Goat Cheese, 94–95
  Tomato, Lentil, and
    Almond Soup, 86–87
L'Ermitage restaurant, 110
*L. esculentum* (edible tomato
  group), 77
Leslie, Eliza, 223, 242
lettuce. *See also* arugula
  Bacon, Lettuce, and
    Tomato Sandwiches, 131
Lillian's Yellow Heirloom
  tomato, 10, 211, 254
Limmony tomato, 9, 37, 81,
  136, 240, 253, 254
Livingston, Alexander W.,
  53, 254
  as "father of the modern
    tomato," 99
  Reynoldsburg, Ohio and,
    153
  tomato varieties by, 9
Livingston, Robert, 99
*Livingston and the Tomato*
  (Livingston), 153
Livingston tomato varieties,
  37, 153
  Globe, 99, 101
  Gold Ball, 153, 255
  Golden Queen, 2, 10, 124,
    153, 244, 254
  Livingston's Beauty, 12, 67,
    99, 153, 219, 253

Livingston's Favorite, 67,
  253
Livingston's Main Crop
  Pink, 253
Magnus, 9, 92, 99, 219, 253
Paragon, 9, 53, 67, 99, 111,
  124, 131, 153, 170, 224,
  233, 253
lobster
  Roast Lobster with Tomato,
    Corn, and Fines Herbes,
    160–61
*Local Flavors: Cooking and
  Eating from America's
  Farmers' Markets* (Madi-
  son), 78
*Lo Scalco alla Moderna*
  (Latini), 18, 105
"Love Apple or Tomato
  Catchup" (Mease), 74
*L. peruvianum*, 77
lycopene, 208

# M

Madison, Deborah, 78
Magnus tomato, 9, 92, 99,
  219, 253
Male, Carolyn, 255
Ma Maison restaurant, 110
Manhattan Clam Chowder,
  82–83
Manyel tomato, 9, 254
Marinara Sauce, 19
Marizol Gold tomato, 168,
  255
Marketplace Kitchen, 20, 269
Mark Twain tomato, 211
marmalade
  Tomato and Citrus Marma-
    lade, 245
  Tomato Marmalade, 44
Martini, Tomato Consommé,
  88
Marvel Striped tomatoes, 204
mascarpone
  Panini of Heirloom Toma-
    toes, Pancetta, and Basil
    Mascarpone, 125, *128*
Matchless tomato, 253
Matthiolus, 199, 215
Matt's Wild Cherry tomato,
  13, 138, 255
Maule's New Imperial tomato,
  *1*, 109

Maule's Success tomato, 253
Mease, James, 74, 225
meatier tomatoes, 9
Metro Bis restaurant, 45, 103,
  106, 269
Metro Bis Tomato Salad
  Dressing, 45
Mikado tomato, *119*, 253, 255
Miller, Philip, 239
Mincemeat, Green Tomato,
  248
minestra of eggplant, 105
Minestrone, Summer, 85
Minkey, Bill, 63
Mistura restaurant, 16,
  28–29, 181, 268
M'Nahon, Bernard, 225
Morse, Kitty, 51, 185
Mortgage Lifter tomato, 2,
  131, 174, 253
mozzarella
  Eggplant Parmigiana, 145
  Insalata Caprese Verdura
    Style, 98
  Pizza Margherita, 118–19
  Tomato and Buffalo Moz-
    zarella Salad, 93
  Veal Parmigiana, 194
*Murrey's Salads and Sauces*,
  101
mushrooms
  Risotto of Heirloom Confit
    Tomatoes and Roasted
    Mushrooms, 140–41
mussels
  Mussels with Tomato-
    Saffron Sauce, 167
  Stuffed Mussels with
    Tomatoes and Almonds,
    67
  Yellow Tomato and Mussel
    Soup, 81

# N

Napoli tomato, 256
Nell Newman's Organic
  Tomatoes and Basil with
  Fusilli, 136
*New Art of Cookery, The*
  (Briggs), 223
New Dwarf Aristocrat tomato,
  153
Newman, Nell, 136
New Stone tomato, 153